HELP YOUR NEXT GENERATION
DISCOVER
THE MAJESTY OF THE GREAT LAKES

Sault Ste Marie
PURE MICHIGAN℠

◆ **Saultstemarie.com** ◆

1-800-MISAULT ◆ **(800)-647-2858**

Contents

54th Edition

Editor/Publisher: Roger LeLievre

Researchers: Matt Miner, Wade P. Streeter, John Vournakis, George Wharton

Crew: Kathryn O'Gould, Nancy Kuharevicz, Audrey LeLievre, Neil Schultheiss, William Soleau

Founder: Tom Manse (1915-1994)

ISBN: 978-1-891849-16-9 © **2013**

Marine Publishing Co. Inc.
P.O. Box 68, Sault Ste. Marie, MI 49783
855-KYS-SHIP   roger@knowyourships.com

KnowYourShips.com

FRONT: Hon. James L. Oberstar (Roger LeLievre)
BACK: Baie St. Paul loads her first cargo on Dec. 22, 2012, at Superior, Wis. (Nick Stenstrup)
THIS PAGE: Edwin H. Gott (Roger LeLievre)

GREAT LAKES MARITIME ACADEMY

Chart your course as a Merchant Marine Officer aboard the ships of the world. The Academy offers an exciting Bachelor's degree program which includes three semesters at sea and 100% job placement.

www.nmc.edu/maritime | **877.824.SHIP**
Great Lakes Maritime Academy, Traverse City, MI

4

Passages

Algobay was renamed Radcliffe R. Latimer in ceremonies last October. Chief Engineer Kaz Mankiewicz and Captain Clarence Vautier are at right. *(Algoma Central Marine)*

New names, even some new boats to watch

Boat News

Canada Steamship Lines' new, 740-foot Trillium-class vessel *Baie St. Paul* arrived from its Chinese builders in late 2012, in time to make one trip before the season closed. Next to come this year will be *Thunder Bay, Whitefish Bay* and *Baie Comeau.* ... Algoma Central Corp.'s first two new Equinox-class vessels under construction in China will be named *Algoma Equinox* and *Algoma Harvester.* They are expected to be in service on the lakes/seaway this year. ... The tug *Ken Boothe Sr.* and barge *Lakes Contender* entered service in May 2012, fresh from the Donjon shipyard in Erie, Pa. American Steamship Co. is leasing the vessel from a partnership formed by Donjon Marine and Seacor Holdings Inc. ... The tug *Defiance* and its self-unloading barge *Ashtabula* entered service for Lower Lakes Towing Co. last fall after a refit at Bay Shipbuilding Co. They had previously served on saltwater as *Beverly Anderson* and *Mary Turner.*

Continued on Page 6

Phoenix Star in the Welland Canal. *(Ron Walsh)*

... Algoma Central Corp. rechristened its self-unloader *Algobay* to honor *Radcliffe R. Latimer*, former company chairman, last October 4. ... Groupe Desgagnés purchased the cargo vessel *Elsborg* from Danish owner Nordana last summer and renamed her *Claude A. Desgagnés*. ... Vanguard Shipping Ltd. and Vanship Ltd.'s two grain-trade vessels were sold last summer to the T.F. Warren Group Inc. The *J.W. Shelley* and *VSL Centurion* were registered to Phoenix Star Shipping and Phoenix Sun Shipping as *Phoenix Star* and *Phoenix Sun*, however at press time there was doubt these ships would sail in 2013.

Museums

Two tugs eased the 105-year-old steamer *Keewatin* out of the muck at Douglas, Mich., on May 31, 2012, on the first leg of a journey that saw the historic vessel – a marine museum at Douglas since 1968 – move

Continued on Page 8

Lower Lakes Towing's *Tecumseh* on the Maumee River. *(Jim Hoffman)*

Preparing to launch *Algoma Equinox* in China. *(Algoma Central Corp.)*

New barge Lakes Contender upbound in the St. Marys River. Inset: Capt. Dean Hobbs. (Roger LeLievre)

to Port McNicoll, Ont., where she will continue in her role as a museum as part of a waterfront redevelopment project. ... Tugs towed the Toledo, Ohio, museum ship *Col. James M. Schoonmaker* down the Maumee River in late October 2012, en route to a new dock where she will become part of the Great Lakes Historical Society's new National Museum of the Great Lakes. ... The 418-foot destroyer *USS Edson* arrived at Bay City, Mich., in 2012, where she is expected to become a marine museum.

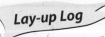

Lay-up Log The U.S.-flagged *American Valor* and *American Fortitude* (both at Toledo, Ohio), *American Victory* and *Edward L. Ryerson* (both at Superior, Wis.) continue in long-term lay-up. *Adam E. Cornelius* spent 2012 idle at Toledo. *John Sherwin* is still laid up at DeTour, Mich. *Algoma Transfer* was idle in 2012 at Goderich, Ont.

American Valor and American Fortitude in long-term lay-up. *(George Haynes)*

Lower Lakes Towing's new barge Ashtabula at Toledo. (Jim Hoffman)

Baie St. Paul downbound in the Seaway with her first cargo, December 2012. (Kent Malo)

Tugs Carol Ann and Matt Allen tow the historic museum ship Keewatin out of Saugatuck, Mich., on June 4, 2012. (Roger LeLievre)

(Roger LeLievre)

Scrapyard

Algoma Central Marine bulk carriers *Algocape* (above, *St. Marys River*) and *Gordon C. Leitch* (lower right, *Welland Canal*) were towed to Aliaga, Turkey, for scrapping in mid-2012. ... As 2913 began, Marine Recycling Corp. in Port Colborne, Ont., finished cutting up *James Norris*, and started on *Maumee*. Waiting its turn was the retired tanker *Provmar Terminal II* (below, *shown departing Hamilton under tow*) ... Purvis Marine in Sault Ste. Marie, Ont., was the final resting place of the Algoma bulker *Algonorth* (in service, upper right).

(Ted Wilush)

TERMINAL
HAMILTON

(Roger LeLievre)

Vessel Index

Kaye E. Barker unloading coal at Essar Steel Algoma in Sault Ste. Marie, Ont. (Peter Groh)

Vessel Name	Fleet #	Vessel Name	Fleet #

A

A-390	A-8	Amazoneborg	IW-2
A-397	A-8	Amber Mae	R-4
A-410	A-8	Americaborg	IW-2
Abegweit	C-19	American Century	A-5
Acacia	MU-22	American Courage	A-5
Acquamarina	IF-3	American Fortitude	A-5
Adanac III	P-10	American Girl	S-14
Adriaticborg	IW-2	American Integrity	A-5
Africaborg	IW-2	American Mariner	A-5
Agassiz	M-17	American Spirit	A-5
Aggersborg	IN-6	American Valor	A-5
AGS-359	M-12	American Victory	A-5
Aird, John B.	A-2	Amstelborg	IW-2
Aivik	T-14	Amundsen	C-3
Alamosborg	IW-2	Amur Star	IR-6
Alder	U-3	Anchor Bay	G-16, O-3
Aldo H.	M-12	Andean	IN-1
Alert	IC-2	Anderson, Arthur M.	G-14
Alessandro DP	ID-3	Andre H.	L-8
Alexandria Belle	U-1	Andrea Marie I	D-1
Alexia	II-1	Andrie, Barbara	A-8
Algocanada	A-3	Andrie, Karen	A-8
Algoeast	A-3	Anglian Lady	P-10
Algolake	A-2	Angus, D.J.	G-10
Algoma Dartmouth	A-3	Anke	IC-9
Algoma Discovery	A-2	Ann Marie	L-11
Algoma Enterprise	A-2	Anna May	S-19
Algoma Equinox	A-2	Annalisa	II-1
Algoma Guardian	A-2	Apalachee	Z-1
Algoma Harvester	A-2	Apollogracht	IS-11
Algoma Mariner	A-2	Apollon	IS-5
Algoma Montrealais	A-2	Appledore IV	B-5
Algoma Navigator	A-2	Appledore V	B-5
Algoma Olympic	A-2	Aragonborg	IW-2
Algoma Progress	A-2	Arca	P-1
Algoma Provider	A-2	Arctic	IF-2
Algoma Quebecois	A-2	Ardmore Calypso	IA-4
Algoma Spirit	A-2	Arizona	G-15
Algoma Transfer	A-2	Arkansas	G-15
Algoma Transport	A-2	Armand-Imbeau	S-9
Algomah	A-12	Arneborg	IW-2
Algomarine	A-2	Arubaborg	IW-2
Algonorth	P-10	Asher, Chas.	R-2
Algonova	A-3	Asher, John R.	R-2
Algorail	A-2	Asher, Stephan M.	R-2
Algosar	A-3	Ashland Bayfield	
Algoscotia	A-3	Express	A-9
Algosea	A-3	Ashtabula	L-10
Algosoo	A-2	Ashton, Meredith	A-8
Algosteel	A-2	ASI Clipper	A-13
Algoway	A-2	Asiaborg	IW-2
Algowood	A-2	Asphalt Carrier	IS-1
Alice E	A-4	Asphodel	IG-3
Alouette Spirit	M-12	Atantic Huron	C-2
Alpena	I-2	Atlantic Erie	C-2
Alphonse-Desjardins	S-9	Atlantic Steamer	IW-1
Alsterstern	IC-7	Atlantic Superior	C-2
Amalia	II-1	Atlanticborg	IW-2
		Atlas	A-14
		Audrie S.	C-1

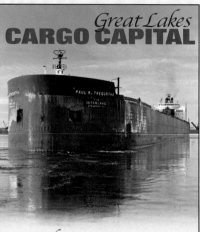

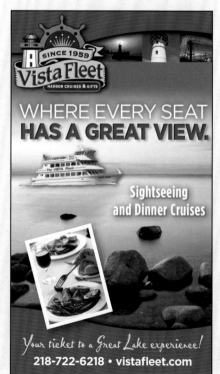

Vessel Name	Fleet #	Vessel Name	Fleet #
Aurora Borealis	T-7	Beaver State	M-1
Australiaborg	IW-2	Becotte Sr., Paul	T-5
Avantage	L-8	Bee Jay	G-4
Avataq	T-14	Bell I, Marilyn	T-12
Avenger IV	P-10	Ben	IL-4
		Bessie B	W-9
B		Betsiamites	L-7
		Bide-A-Wee	S-10
Badger	L-5	BIG 503	U-12
Bagotville	M-14	BIG 543	U-12
Baie Comeau	C-2	BIG 546	U-12
Baie St. Paul	C-2	BIG 548	U-12
Baird, Spencer F.	U-5	BIG 549	U-12
Baltic Carrier	IW-1	BIG 551	U-12
Barbro	IF-5	BIG 9708 B	U-12
Barker, James R.	I-5	BIG 9917 B	U-12
Barker, Kaye E.	I-5	Billmaier, D.L.	U-2
Barnacle	IN-1	Birchglen	C-2
Barry J	K-5	Biscayne Bay	U-3
Basse-Cote	L-7	Black, Martha L.	C-3
Batchawana	G-3	Blacky	IN-1
Bayfield	M-3	Blain M	M-12
Bayship	F-1	Block, Joseph L.	C-6
BBC Alaska	IW-1	Blough, Roger	G-14
BBC Amazon	IB-8	Blue Heron	U-9
BBC Arizona	IW-1	Blue Heron V	B-8
BBC Austria	IB-8	Bluebill	IN-1
BBC Balboa	IB-8	Bluewing	IO-1
BBC Campana	IW-1	BMI-192	B-3
BBC Carolina	IH-9	BMI-FDD-1	B-3
BBC Colorado	IW-1	BMT 3	B-15
BBC Delaware	IW-1	Boatman No. 3	M-12
BBC Elbe	IB-8	Boatman No. 6	M-12
BBC Ems	IB-8	Bogdan	IN-3
BBC England	IR-2	Boland, John J.	A-5
BBC Europe	IB-8	Bold World	IB-2
BBC Greenland	IB-8	Bonnie B III	M-12
BBC Hawaii	IR-3	Boothe Sr., Ken	A-5
BBC Houston	IB-8	Bowditch	A-1
BBC Jade	IB-8	Bowes, Bobby	D-2
BBC Louisiana	IW-1	Boyd, David	G-20
BBC Maine	IW-1	Bramble	MU-19
BBC Minnesota	IF-6	Brant	IN-1
BBC Mississippi	IB-8	Bras d'Or 400	MU-16
BBC Naples	IH-6	Breaker	N-4
BBC Ontario	IK-4	Bright Laker	ID-4
BBC Oregon	IW-1	Bristol Bay	U-3
BBC Plata	IW-1	Bro Alma	IB-9
BBC Rhine	IE-2	Brochu	A-10
BBC Steinhoeft	IE-2	Brown, Prentiss	S-1
BBC Sweden	IB-8	Brutus I	T-12
BBC Vermont	IW-1	Buckley	K-4
BBC Volga	IB-8	Buckthorn	U-3
BBC Washington	IF-6	Buffalo	A-5
BBC Wisconsin	IK-4	Bulk Sunset	IG-1
BBC Zarate	IW-1	Bunyan, Paul	U-2
Beaver	A-12	Burns Harbor	A-5
Beaver Delta II	M-14	Busch, Edwin C.	B-15
Beaver Gamma	M-14	Busch, Gregory J.	B-15
Beaver Islander	B-7	Busse, Fred A.	D-8
Beaver Kay	M-14	Buxton II	K-5

C

Vessel Name	Fleet #	Vessel Name	Fleet #	Vessel Name	Fleet #	Vessel Name	Fleet #
C.T.M.A. Vacancier	C-26	Cape Egmont	IC-8	Catherine-Legardeur	S-9	Chestnut	IN-1
C.T.M.A. Voyageur	C-26	Cape Hearne	C-3	Cavalier des Mers	C-23	Chi-Cheemaun	O-8
Cabot	IO-2	Cape Hurd	C-3	Cavalier Maxim	C-23	Chief Shingwauk	R-1
Cadillac	S-19	Cape Lambton	C-3	Cavalier Royal	C-23	Chippewa	A-12
California	G-15	Cape Mercy	C-3	Cedarglen	C-2	Chippewa III	S-13
Callaway, Cason J.	G-14	Cape Providence	C-3	Celebrezze, Anthony J.	C-16	Cinnamon	IO-1
Callie M.	M-8	Cape Rescue	C-3	Celine	IE-6	Citadel	IF-4
Calumet	L-10	Cape Storm	C-3	Cemba	C-5	City of Algonac	W-1
Cameron O.	S-3	Capt. Shepler	S-5	CGB-12001	U-3	City of Milwaukee	MU-22
Camille Marcoux	S-9	Captain George	W-3	CGB-12002	U-3	CL Hanse Gate	IS-13
Canadian	M-14	Captain Paul II	C-17	Challenge	G-18	Clarke, Philip R.	G-14
Canadian Argosy	M-14	Carey, Emmett J.	O-7	Champion	C-7, D-11	Cleveland Rocks	S-1
Canadian Empress	S-15	Cargo Carrier I	M-14	Channel Cat	M-16	Clinton	C-17
Canadian Jubilee	D-2	Cargo Master	M-14	Charlevoix	C-9	Clinton Friendship	C-17
Cantankerous	E-7	Caribou Isle	C-3	Charlotte Theresa	IH-10	Clipper Aki	IC-6
Cap Brulle	E-4	Carina	A-1	Chem Pegasus	IA-1	Clipper Anne	IC-6
Cap Streeter	S-8	Carl M.	M-14	Chemtrans Alster	IC-4	Clipper Gemini	IC-6
Cape Challion	C-3	Carlee Emily	K-2	Chemtrans Elbe	IC-4	Clipper Katja	IC-6
Cape Commodore	C-3	Carleton, George N.	G-11	Chemtrans Ems	IC-4	Clipper Klara	IC-6
Cape Crow	E-4	Carol Ann	K-5	Chemtrans Havel	IC-4	Clipper Lancer	IC-6
Cape Discovery	C-3	Carola	Il-1	Chemtrans Mabuhay	IC-4	Clipper Leander	IC-6
Cape Dundas	C-3	Carrick, John J.	M-11	Chemtrans Oste	IC-4	Clipper Legacy	IC-6
		Carrol C. 1	M-12	Chemtrans Weser	IC-4	Clipper Mari	IC-6
		Cassiopeia IV	M-24	Cheraw	U-2	Clipper Oceanica	IC-6

Cuyahoga on the Detroit River. *(Wade P. Streeter)*

19

Vessel Name	Fleet #	Vessel Name	Fleet #
Glen	IL-4	Havasu II	N-4
Glenada	T-5	Havelstern	IC-7
Glenora	M-24	Helen H.	H-4
Goodtime I	L-3	Hellespont Centurion	IH-7
Goodtime III	G-8	Hellespont Charger	IH-7
Gott, Edwin H.	G-14	Hellespont Chieftain	IH-7
Graham, Sandy	B-6	Heloise	IP-2
Grand Fleuve	C-23	Henry, Alexander	MU-14
Grand Island	P-3	HHL Amazon	IH-3
Grand Portal	P-3	HHL Amur	IH-3
Grande Baie	E-6	HHL Congo	IH-3
Grande Caribe	IB-6	HHL Nile	IH-3
Grande Mariner	IB-6	HHL Volga	IH-3
Grandon	O-2	Hiawatha	S-10
Grant, R.F.	L-8	Hoey, Carolyn	G-1
Grasse River	S-16	Hoey, Patricia	G-1
Grayfox	U-7	Hogan, Joseph J.	J-1
Grayling	G-19	Holden, John	M-14
Great Blue Heron	B-8	Holiday	S-10, T-17
Great Lakes	U-8	Hollyhock	U-3
Great Lakes Trader	V-1	Hornell VC, David	T-12
Great Republic	G-14	Houghton	K-1
Green, Seth	N-5	Howe Islander	C-22
Greenstone	B-3	HR Resolution	IH-2
Greenstone II	U-6	Huron	A-12, MU-18
Greenwing	IN-1	Huron Belle	L-6
Greta V	M-14	Huron Explorer	G-13
Gretchen B	L-11	Huron Explorer I	O-5
Greu-des-Iles	S-9	Huron Lady II	H-8
Griffon	C-3	Huron Maid	L-6
Gull Isle	C-3	Huron Service	H-5
		Huron Spirit	M-12

H

Vessel Name	Fleet #
Haida	MU-10
Hamilton Energy	P-8
Hamilton Harbour Queen	H-1
Hammond Bay	U-2
Hamp Thomas	H-7
Han Xin	IS-7
Handy Andy	M-14
Hanlan II, Ned	C-13
Hannah, Mary E.	C-1
Hannah, Mary Page	S-3
Happy River	IB-5
Happy Rover	IB-5
Harbor Seagull	M-22
Harbour Clear	IN-7
Harbour Cloud	IN-7
Harbour Fashion	IN-7
Harbour Feature	IN-7
Harbour First	IN-7
Harbour Kira	IN-7
Harbour Leader	IN-7
Harbour Legend	IN-7
Harbour Loyalty	IN-7
Harbour Progress	IN-7
Harbour Star	M-27
Harvey	U-2

I

Vessel Name	Fleet #
Ian Mac	M-2
Ida M.	R-1
Ida M. II	R-1
Ida Theresa	IH-10
Idaho	G-15
Idus Atwell	M-14
Iglehart, J.A.W.	I-2
Illinois	G-15
Ina	IP-4
Ina Theresa	IH-10
Indian Maiden	B-6
Indiana	G-15
Indiana Harbor	A-5
Infinity	I-1
Inglis, William	C-13
Inland Seas	I-3
Innisfree	C-12
Innovation	L-2
Integrity	L-2
Intrepid Canada	II-3
Intrepid III	N-1
Invincible	L-10
Iowa	G-15
Irene Theresa	IH-10
Irma	IP-4

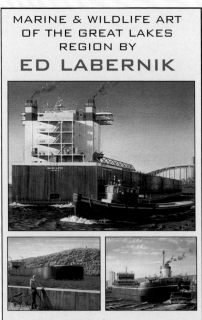

Vessel Name	Fleet #	Vessel Name	Fleet #	Vessel Name	Fleet #	Vessel Name	Fleet #
Lady Kate	P-7	Little Rock	MU-1	Maine	G-15	Mather, William G.	MU-8
Lady Kim I	C-21	Loireborg	IW-2	Maineborg	IW-2	Matt Allen	K-5
Lady Michigan	A-6	Lomer-Gouin	S-9	Mainland	IB-4	Maumee	M-7
Laguna D	ID-3	Louis S.	R-2	Maisonneuve	M-25	Maxima	II-1
Lake Char	M-16	Louisiana	G-15	Malden	P-10	McAsphalt 401	M-11
Lake Explorer II	U-4	LS Christine	IL-1	Mamry	IP-4	McBride, Sam	C-13
Lake Express	L-4	LS Jacoba	IL-1	Manatra	U-7	McCarthy Jr., Walter J.	A-5
Lake Guardian	U-4	LST-393	MU-28	Mandarin	IN-1	McCauley	U-2
Lake Ontario	IS-13	LT-5	MU-9	Manistee	L-10	McKee Sons	L-10
Lakes Contender	A-5	Lubie	IP-4	Manitoba	L-9	McKee, Bradshaw	S-1
Lambert Spirit	M-12	Lucien L.	S-9	Manitou	M-4, T-15	McKeil, Evans	M-12
Lapointe, Ernest	MU-16	Ludington	MU-2	Manitou Isle	M-6	McKeil, Jarrett	M-12
LaPrairie	L-7	Luebbert	II-1	Manitowoc	L-10, U-2, V-4	McKenzie, Wm. Lyon	T-10
Latimer, Radcliffe R.	A-2	Luedtke, Alan K.	L-11	Maple City	T-12	McLane	MU-7
Laud, Sam	A-5	Luedtke, Chris E.	L-11	Maple Grove	O-1	McLeod, Norman	M-11
Laurentian	G-13	Luedtke, Erich R.	L-11	Mapleglen	C-2	McQueen, F.R.	M-14
Le Cageux	Q-1	Luedtke, Karl E.	L-11	Mareike B.	IW-1	MCT Alioth	IM-6
Le Phil D.	L-7	Luedtke, Kurt R.	L-11	Margot	N-6	MCT Almak	IM-6
Le Voyageur	S-10	Lyulin	IN-3	Marida Melissa	IM-2	MCT Altair	IM-6
Leandra	II-1			Marida Mimosa	IM-2	MCT Arcturus	IM-6
Lehmann, Edgar	IL-2			Marida Mulberry	IM-2	MCT Monte Rosa	IM-6
Lehmann, Hans	IL-2	**M**		Marietje Deborah	ID-2	MCT Stockhorn	IM-6
Leitch, John D.	A-2	Macassa Bay	W-8	Marietje Marsilla	ID-2	Medemborg	IW-2
Leona B.	M-19	Maccoa	IN-1	Marlyn	S-8	Mehmet A	IC-3
Leonard M.	M-12	MacKay, Tony	M-12	Mariposa Belle	M-9	Mellum Trader	IH-9
Liamare	IL-3	Mackinac Express	A-12	Markborg	IW-2	Mellum Trader	IH-9
Lime Island	B-2	Mackinac Islander	A-12	Market, Wm.	M-20	Menasha	M-15
Limnos	C-3	Mackinaw	U-3, MU-11	Marquette	C-12, S-19	Menier Consol	T-9
Linda Jean	N-8	Madeline	M-3	Martin, Rt. Hon. Paul J.	C-2	Merweborg	IW-2
Linnea	W-6	Maemi	IK-3	Marysville	G-1	Mesabi Miner	I-5
Linnhurst	G-2	Maersk Illinois	IM-1	Massachusetts	G-15	Meteor	MU-24
						Metis	E-9

CSL Tadoussac unloading salt at Hallet 8 dock in Duluth, Minn. (Anders Gilbertson)

Vessel Name	Fleet #	Vessel Name	Fleet #	Vessel Name	Fleet #	Vessel Name	Fleet #
Metsaborg	IW-2	MM Newfoundland	M-5	Neeskay	U-10	North Channel	C-7
Michigan	U-8	Mobile Bay	U-3	Nels J.	H-4	North Contender	IE-1
Michipicoten	L-9	Moby Dick	G-7	Nelson, Gaylord	W-10	North Dakota	G-15
Middle Channel	C-7	Moezelborg	IW-2	Neptune III	D-2	North Fighter	IE-1
Miedwie	IP-4	Mohawk	M-1	New Beginnings	T-13	North Star	C-8
Mighty Jake	G-7	Molly M. 1	N-1	New Jersey	G-15	Northern Lighter	A-14
Mighty Jessie	G-7	Montana	G-15	New York	G-15	Northern Spirit I	M-9
Mighty Jimmy	G-7	Moor	IL-4	Niagara	MU-5	Northwestern	G-16
Mighty John III	G-7	Moore, Olive L.	L-10	Niagara Prince	IB-6	Noyes, Hack	W-10
Milwaukee	G-15	Morgan	K-4	Niagara Queen II	O-6		
Milwaukee Clipper	MU-25	Morholmen	IN-2	Niagara Spirit	M-12		
Miners Castle	P-3	Morraborg	IW-2	Nichevo II	M-3	**O**	
Minnesota	G-15	Morro Bay	U-3	Nickelena	B-3	Oakglen	C-2
Miramis	IE-3	Mottler	IN-1	Nicolet	U-2	Oberstar,	
Miro D	ID-3	Mrs. C.	C-21	Niki S	C-1	Hon. James L.	I-5
Miseford	T-5	MSM Douro	IM-5	Nipigon Osprey	O-5	Obsession III	C-25
Mishe Mokwa	M-6	Munson, John G.	G-14	Nirint Neerlandia	IE-6	Océan A. Simard	L-7
Misner, H.H.	G-17	Muntgracht	IS-11	No. 55	M-1	Océan Abys	L-7
Miss Buffalo II	B-13	Muskie	G-19	No. 56	M-1	Océan Bertrand	
Miss Edna	K-5	Mystic Blue	M-30	Noble, Robert	W-5	Jeansonne	L-7
Miss Laura	M-8			Nogat	IP-4	Océan Bravo	L-7
Miss Libby	D-10	**N**		Nokomis	S-10	Océan Charlie	L-8
Miss Midland	M-18			Nordic Copenhagen	IN-7	Océan Delta	L-7
Miss Munising	M-26	Nancy Anne	D-11	Nordic Oslo	IN-7	Océan Echo II	L-8
Miss Superior	P-3	Nassauborg	IW-2	Nordic Stockholm	IN-7	Océan Express	L-7
Mississagi	L-9	Nathan S	C-1	Nordik Express	G-21	Océan Foxtrot	L-8
Mississippi	G-15	Nautica Queen	N-2	Nordisle	IR-5	Océan Georgie Bain	L-7
Mississippiborg	IW-2	Navcomar No. 1	L-7	Nordport	IR-5	Océan Golf	L-7
Missouri	G-15	Neah Bay	U-3	Norgoma	MU-26	Océan Henry Bain	L-7
Missouriborg	IW-2	Nebraska	G-15	Norisle	MU-6	Océan Hercule	L-7
Mister Joe	M-14	Neebish Islander II	E-1	North Carolina	G-15	Océan Intrepide	L-7

Vessel Name	Fleet #	Vessel Name	Fleet #	Vessel Name	Fleet #	Vessel Name	Fleet #
Redhead	IP-2	Schulte, Ruth	IB-3	Sichem Hong Kong	IE-1	Spuds	R-2
Reiss	C-15	Schwartz, H.J.	U-2	Sichem Manila	IE-1	St. Clair	A-5
Reliance	P-10	SCL Bern	IE-6	Sichem Melbourne	IE-1	St. John, J.S.	E-8
Rennie, Thomas	C-13	SE Potentia	IS-4	Sichem Montreal	IE-1	St. Lawrence II	B-10
Resko	IP-4	Sea Bear	S-2	Sichem Mumbai	IE-1	St. Marys Cement	S-18
Rest, William	T-12	Sea Eagle II	S-18	Sichem New York	IE-1	St. Marys Cement II	S-18
Rhode Island	G-15	Sea Force	IP-3	Sichem Onomichi	IE-1	St. Marys Challenger	S-1
Richelieu	C-2	Sea Fox II	T-4	Sichem Paris	IE-1	St. Marys Conquest	S-1
Richter, Arni J.	W-5	Sea Hunter III	G-9	Silversides	MU-7	Stacey Dawn	C-21
Ridgway, Benjamin	H-7	Sea Prince II	R-1	Simano	IM-4	Star of Chicago	S-8
Risley, Samuel	C-3	Sea Service	H-5	Simcoe Islander	C-22	State of Michigan	G-16
Robert John	G-11	Seahound	N-1	Simonsen	U-2	STC 2004	B-15
Robert W.	T-5	Segwun	M-28	Simpson, Miss Kim	T-13	Ste. Claire	M-10
Robin Lynn	S-4	Selvick, Bonnie G.	C-1	Sioux	M-1	Ste. Claire V (The)	A-7
Robinson Bay	S-16	Selvick, Carla	C-1	Sir Henry	IH-8	Steelhead	M-16
Rochelle Kaye	R-4	Selvick, Carla Anne	S-3	Sjard	IB-8	Stefania I	IF-5
Rocket	P-10	Selvick, John M.	C-1	Sloman Dispatcher	IS-10	Stella Borealis	C-18
Roman, Stephen B.	E-9	Selvick, Kimberly	C-1	Sloman Hera	IS-10	Stella Polaris	IT-1
Rosalee D.	T-5	Selvick, Sharon M.	S-3	Smith Jr., L.L.	U-11	Stellanova	IJ-2
Rosemary	M-9	Selvick, Steven	C-1	Smith, Dean R.	M-8	Stella Polaris	IJ-2
Rouble, J.R.	D-10	Selvick, William C.	S-3	Smith, F.C.G.	C-3	Stellaprima	IJ-2
Roxane D	L-7	Seneca	IA-3	Snohomish	V-4	Sten Aurora	IR-1
Royal Pescadores	IS-8	Serena	II-1	Sofia	II-1	Sten Suomi	IR-1
Ruby-T	IT-3	Service Boat No. 1	L-8	Soley-1	IN-2	Sterling Energy	P-8
Ruddy	IN-1	Service Boat No. 2	L-7	Soley-2	IN-2	Stolt Kite	IS-12
Ryerson, Edward L.	C-6	Service Boat No. 4	L-8	Solina	IP-4	Stormont	N-1
		Seymour, Wilf	M-12	Songa Diamond	IB-7	Straits Express	A-12
		Shamrock	J-3	Songa Eagle	IB-7	Straits of Mackinac II	A-12
S		Shamrock Jupiter	IS-6	Songa Emerald	IB-7	Strandja	IN-3
		Shannon	G-1	Songa Falcon	IL-5	Sturgeon	G-19
S/VM 86	M-12	Shannon Star	IR-6	Songa Jade	IB-7	Sugar Islander II	E-1
Sabina	IE-6	Sheila P.	P-10	Songa Opal	IB-7	Sullivan, Denis	D-7
Sabrina	II-1	Shenehon	G-13	Songa Pearl	IB-7	Sullivans (The)	MU-1
Sacre Bleu	S-5	Sherwin, John	I-5	Songa Ruby	IB-7	Sundew	J-2
Saginaw	L-9	Shipsands	T-13	Songa Sapphire	IB-7	Sunflower E	IE-4
Saguenay	C-2	Shirley Ann	C-8	Songa Topaz	IB-7	Sunliner	W-6
Sakarya	IC-3	Shirley Irene	K-2	Soulanges	E-4	Superior	G-15
Salarium	C-2	Shoreline (The)	S-6	South Bass	M-20	Susan L.	S-3
Salvage Monarch	T-9	Shoreline II	S-8	South Carolina	G-15	Susan Michelle	D-1
Salvor	M-12	Shoveler	IN-1	South Channel	C-7	Susana S.	IU-1
Sandpiper	H-3	Showboat		Spartan	A-8, L-5	Sweezy, R.O.	H-9
Sandra Mary	M-14	Royal Grace	M-9	Spartan II	A-8	Sykes, Wilfred	C-6
Sapphire	IF-3	Sichem Beijing	IE-1	Speer, Edgar B.	G-14		
Sarah B.	G-12	Sichem Challenge	IE-1	Spence, John	M-12		
Sarah No. 1	D-10	Sichem Contestor	IE-1	Spencer, Sarah	T-3	**T**	
Schlaeger, Victor L.	C-11	Sichem Defiance	IE-1	Spirit of Buffalo	B-14		
Schoening, Hermann	II-1	Sichem Dubai	IE-1	Spirit of Chicago	S-12	Tandem	C-23
Schoonmaker,		Sichem Edinburgh	IE-1	Spring	IN-5	Tanker II	J-3
Col. James M.	MU-17	Sichem Hiroshima	IE-1	Spruceglen	C-2	Tatjana	II-1
Schulte, Elisalex	IB-3					Team Spirit	IT-2
						Tecumseh	L-9

25

Vessel Name	Fleet #	Vessel Name	Fleet #	Vessel Name	Fleet #	Vessel Name	Fleet #
Tecumseh II	P-10	Tregurtha, Paul R.	I-5	Victorian Princess	V-3	Wenonah	N-7
Tenacious	R-4	Trillium	C-13	Victorious	M-11	Wenonah II	M-28
Tennessee	G-15	Tromso	IP-1	Victory	L-10	Westcott II, J.W.	J-1
Ternen	IS-2	Tufty	IN-1	Vigilant I	N-1	Wheatley,	
Texas	G-15	Tundra	IN-1	Viking I	V-4	Christopher	C-11
The Hope	S-5	Tuscarora	IA-3	Vikingbank	IP-5	Whistler	IP-2
Thekla	II-1	Twolan, W.N.	B-11	Virginia	G-15	Whitby	M-14
Thompson, Joseph H.	U-13			Virginiaborg	IW-2	White, H. Lee	A-5
Thompson Jr.,				Vista King	M-21	Whitefish Bay	C-2, U-2
Joseph H	U-13	**U**		Vista Queen	V-5	Wicko	IP-4
Thompson, Maxine	F-3			Vista Star	V-5	Wigeon	IP-2
Thorco Arctic	IM-3	Umiak I	IF-2	Vitosha	IN-3	Willmac	M-14
Thousand Islander	G-5	Umiavut	T-14	Vlieborg	IW-2	Windmill Point	T-12
Thousand Islander II	G-5	Uncle Sam 7	U-1	Vlistborg	IW-2	Windy	T-1
Thousand Islander III	G-5	Undaunted	P-2	VM/S Hercules	S-17	Winnebago	J-5
Thousand Islander IV	G-5			VM/S Maisonneuve	S-17	Winona	II-1
Thousand Islander V	G-5			VM/S St. Lambert	S-17	Winter	IN-5
Three Rivers	IF-6	**V**		Voorneborg	IW-2	Wisconsin	G-11, G-15
Thunder Bay	C-2			Voyageur	M-21, S-8	Wolfe Islander III	M-24
Thunder Cape	C-3	Vaasaborg	IW-2	Voyageur II	G-9	Wolf River	G-11
Timberland	G-7	Vac	N-1			Wyandot	S-5
Timesaver II	D-10	Vachon	A-10			Wyatt M.	M-12
Timmy A.	R-2	Vale	IL-4	**W**		Wyoming	G-15
Titan	E-10	Valerie B.	D-11				
Toni D.	V-2	Valley Camp	MU-13	Walpole Islander	W-1		
Torrent	IN-1	Vancouverborg	IW-2	Wanda III	M-28	**X-Y-Z**	
Townsend, Paul H.	I-2	VanEnkevort,		Warner Provider	W-4		
Tracer	IB-5	Joyce L.	V-1	Warner, Coloma L.	W-4	Xenia	II-1
Tracy	C-3	Varnebank	IP-5	Warner, William L.	W-4	Yankcanuck	P-10
Tradewind Service	H-5	Vechtborg	IW-2	Washington	G-15, W-5	Yankee Clipper	V-6
Tramper	IB-5	Veler	U-2	Wayward Princess	N-3	YM Saturn	IY-2
Transit	C-23	Vermont	G-15	Welland	D-1	Yorktown	IT-4
Transporter	IB-5	Versluis, James J.	C-10	Wendella	W-6	Zeus	IF-4, M-29
Tregurtha, Lee A.	I-5	Viateur's Spirit	M-12	Wendella LTD	W-6	Zeynep A.	IC-3
		Victoria	II-1	Wendy Anne	S-14	Ziemia Lodzka	IP-4
		Victoriaborg	IW-2				

Saguenay comes off a wintry Lake Huron. (Fred Miller)

Lee A. Tregurtha follows the track made by other vessels in winter ice. (Brad Newland)

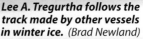

The information in this book, current as of March 1, 2013, was obtained from the U.S. Army Corps of Engineers, the U.S. Coast Guard, the Lake Carriers' Association, Lloyd's Register of Shipping, Transport Canada, St. Lawrence Seaway Authority, Internet Ships Register, Shipfax, Tugfax, Tugboat Enthusiasts Society of the Americas, vessel owners/operators, BoatNerd.com and publications of the Toronto Marine Historical Society and the Marine Historical Society of Detroit.

Sam Laud, turning on the Fox River at Green Bay, Wis. The tug Texas assists. (Scott Best)

Nighttime unload for Kaye E. Barker at Marquette, Mich. (Chris Mazzella)

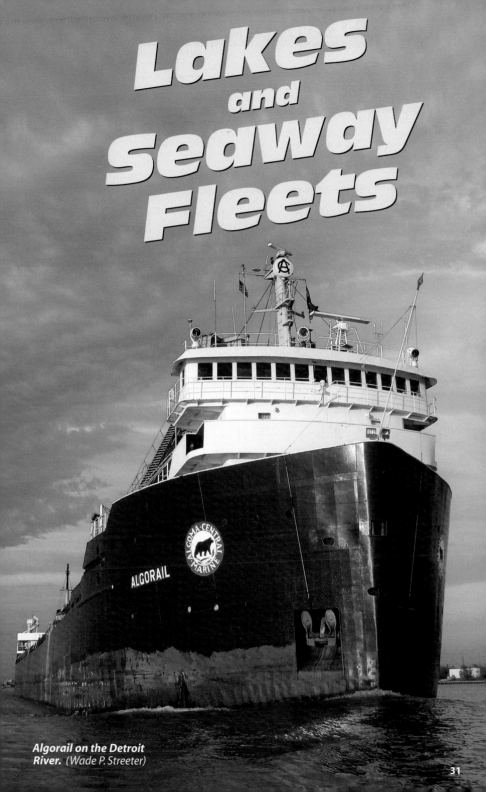

Lakes
and
Seaway
Fleets

Algorail on the Detroit River. (Wade P. Streeter)

LAKES / SEAWAY FLEETS

Listed after each vessel in order are: Type of Vessel, Year Built, Type of Engine, Maximum Cargo Capacity (at midsummer draft in long tons) or Gross Tonnage*, Overall Length, Breadth and Depth (from the top of the keel to the top of the upper deck beam) or Draft*. Only vessels over 30 feet long are included. The figures given are as accurate as possible and are given for informational purposes only. Vessels and owners are listed alphabetically as per American Bureau of Shipping and Lloyd's Register of Shipping format. Builder yard and location, as well as other pertinent information, are listed for major vessels; former names of vessels and years of operation under the former names appear in parentheses. A number in brackets following a vessel's name indicates how many vessels, including the one listed, have carried that name. Web addresses can change without notice.

KEY TO TYPE OF VESSEL

2B............................Brigantine	DS............................Spud Barge	PB............................Pilot Boat
2S..................2-Masted Schooner	DV............................Drilling Vessel	PF.......................Passenger Ferry
3S..................3-Masted Schooner	DW............................Scow	PK.....................Package Freighter
4S..................4-Masted Schooner	ES..........................Excursion Ship	RR......................Roll On/Roll Off
AC............................Auto Carrier	EV..........Environmental Response	RT.......................Refueling Tanker
AT............................Articulated Tug	FB............................Fireboat	RV..........................Research Vessel
ATB.............Articulated Tug/Barge	FD....................Floating Dry Dock	SB............................Supply Boat
BC............................Bulk Carrier	FT............................Fishing Tug	SC............................Sand Carrier
BK................Bulk Carrier/Tanker	GC....................General Cargo	SR................Search and Rescue
BT............................Buoy Tender	GL............................Gate Lifter	SU............................Self-Unloader
CA............................Catamaran	GU................Grain Self-Unloader	SV............................Survey Vessel
CC............................Cement Carrier	HL....................Heavy Lift Vessel	TB............................Tugboat
CF............................Car Ferry	IB............................Ice Breaker	TF............................Train Ferry
CO............................Container Vessel	IT............................Integrated Tug	TK............................Tanker
CS............................Crane Ship	ITB................Integrated Tug/Barge	TW............................Towboat
DB............................Deck Barge	MB............................Mailboat	TT................Tractor Tugboat
DH............................Hopper Barge	MU....................Museum Vessel	TV............................Training Vessel
DR............................Dredge	PA....................Passenger Vessel	

KEY TO PROPULSION

B............................Barge	R.................Steam – Triple Exp. Compound Engine	
D............................Diesel	S.................Steam – Skinner "Uniflow" Engine	
DE............................Diesel Electric	T.................Steam – Turbine Engine	
Q.................Steam – Quad Exp. Compound Engine	W.................Sailing Vessel (Wind)	

Fleet Name Vessel Name	IMO #	Vessel Type	Year Built	Engine Type	Cargo Cap. or Gross*	Overall Length	Breadth	Depth
A-1 **ABACO MARINE TOWING LLC, CLAYTON, NY**								
Bowditch		TB	1954	D	76*	65' 00"	22' 00"	8' 04"
Built: Missouri Valley Steel, Inc., Leavenworth, KS (Oriskany, Hot Dog)								
Carina		TB	1954	D	64*	61' 05"	17' 09"	8' 03"
Built: Higgins Inc., New Orleans, LA (Charles R. Higgins, Augusta Withington)								
A-2 **ALGOMA CENTRAL CORP., ST. CATHARINES, ON** *(algonet.com)*								
Algolake	7423093	SU	1977	D	32,807	730' 00"	75' 00"	46' 06"
Built: Collingwood Shipyards, Collingwood, ON								
Algoma Discovery	8505848	BC	1987	D	34,380	729' 00"	75' 09"	48' 05"
Built: 3 Maj Brodogradiliste d.d., Rijeka, Croatia (Malinska '87-'97, Daviken '97-'08)								
Algoma Enterprise	7726677	SU	1979	D	33,854	730' 00"	75' 11"	46' 07"
Built: Port Weller Dry Docks, Port Weller, ON (Canadian Enterprise '79-'11)								
Algoma Equinox	9613927	SU	2013	D	39,400	740' 00"	78' 00"	48' 03
Built: Nantong Mingde Heavy Industry Co., Ltd., Nantong City, China								
Algoma Guardian	8505850	BC	1987	D	34,380	729' 00"	75' 09"	48' 05"
Built: 3 Maj Brodogradiliste d.d., Rijeka, Croatia (Omisalj '87-'97, Goviken '97-'08)								
Algoma Harvester		BC	2013	D	39,400	740' 00"	78' 00"	48' 03
Built: Nantong Mingde Heavy Industry Co., Ltd., Nantong City, China								
Algoma Mariner	9587893	SU	2011	D	37,399	740' 00"	77' 11"	49' 03
Built: Chengxi Shipyard Co. Ltd., Jiangyin City, China (Laid down as Canadian Mariner {2})								
Algoma Montrealais	5241142	BC	1962	T	29,072	730' 00"	75' 00"	39' 02"
Built: Canadian Vickers, Montreal, QC (Launched as Montrealer, Montrealais '62-'12)								

Fleet Name / Vessel Name	IMO #	Vessel Type	Year Built	Engine Type	Cargo Cap. or Gross*	Overall Length	Breadth	Depth
Algoma Navigator	6707961	SU	1967	D	30,324	729' 00"	75' 10"	40' 06"

Built: J. Readhead & Sons, South Shields, England; converted from a saltwater bulk carrier in '80; converted to a self-unloader in '97; both conversions by Port Weller Dry Docks, St. Catharines, ON (Demeterton '67-'75, St. Lawrence Navigator '75-'80, Canadian Navigator '80-'81)

| **Algoma Olympic** | 7432783 | SU | 1976 | D | 33,859 | 730' 00" | 75' 00" | 46' 06" |

Built: Port Weller Dry Docks, Port Weller, ON (Canadian Olympic '76-'11)

| **Algoma Progress** | 6821999 | SU | 1968 | D | 31,637 | 730' 00" | 75' 00" | 46' 06" |

Built: Port Weller Dry Docks, Port Weller, ON (Canadian Progress '68-'11)

| **Algoma Provider** | 5407277 | BC | 1963 | T | 28,960 | 730' 00" | 75' 00" | 39' 02" |

Built: Collingwood Shipyards, Collingwood, ON (Murray Bay {3} '63-'94, Canadian Provider '94-'11)

| **Algoma Quebecois** | 5287847 | BC | 1963 | T | 28,716 | 730' 00" | 75' 00" | 39' 01" |

Built: Canadian Vickers, Montreal, QC (Quebecois '63-'12)

| **Algoma Spirit** | 8504882 | BC | 1986 | D | 34,380 | 729' 00" | 75' 09" | 48' 05" |

Built: 3 Maj Brodogradiliste d.d., Rijeka, Croatia (Petka '86-'00, Sandviken '00-'08)

| **Algoma Transfer** | 6514869 | SU | 1943/65 | D | 15,719 | 650' 00" | 60' 00" | 35' 00" |

Algoma Transfer was built by joining the stern section of Canadian Explorer (engine room, machinery) with the bow and mid-body of the World War II-era laker Hamilton Transfer in '98; all work by Port Weller Dry Docks, St. Catharines, ON; spent 2012 season laid up at Goderich, ON

(Fore Section) Built: Great Lakes Engineering Works, Ashtabula, OH (J. H. Hillman Jr. '43-'74, Crispin Oglebay {2} '74-'95, Hamilton Transfer '95-'98, Canadian Transfer '98-'11); converted to a self-unloader in '74
(Stern Section) Built: Davie Shipbuilding Co., Lauzon, QC, as Cabot {1} '65-'83, Canadian Explorer '83-'98)

| **Algoma Transport** {2} | 7711737 | SU | 1979 | D | 32,678 | 730' 00" | 75' 11" | 46' 07" |

Built: Port Weller Dry Docks, Port Weller, ON (Canadian Transport '79-'11)

| **Algomarine** | 6816607 | SU | 1968 | D | 26,755 | 730' 00" | 75' 00" | 39' 08" |

Built: Davie Shipbuilding Co., Lauzon, QC; converted to a self-unloader by Port Weller Dry Docks, St. Catharines, ON, in '89 (Lake Manitoba '68-'87)

| **Algorail** {2} | 6805531 | SU | 1968 | D | 23,810 | 640' 05" | 72' 00" | 40' 00" |

Built: Collingwood Shipyards, Collingwood, ON

| **Algosoo** {2} | 7343619 | SU | 1974 | D | 30,284 | 730' 00" | 75' 00" | 44' 06" |

Built: Collingwood Shipyards, Collingwood, ON; last Great Lakes vessel built with cabins at the bow

| **Algosteel** {2} | 6613299 | SU | 1966 | D | 26,949 | 730' 00" | 75' 00" | 39' 08" |

Built: Davie Shipbuilding Co., Lauzon, QC; converted to a self-unloader by Port Weller Dry Docks, St. Catharines, ON, in '89; entered long-term lay-up at Montreal, QC, on Dec. 27, 2010 (A. S. Glossbrenner '66-'87, Algogulf {1} '87-'90)

| **Algoway** {2} | 7221251 | SU | 1972 | D | 23,812 | 646' 06" | 72' 00" | 40' 00" |

Built: Collingwood Shipyards, Collingwood, ON

| **Algowood** | 7910216 | SU | 1981 | D | 32,253 | 740' 00" | 75' 11" | 46' 06" |

Built: Collingwood Shipyards, Collingwood, ON; lengthened 10' in '00 at Port Weller Dry Docks, St. Catharines, ON

| **Capt. Henry Jackman** | 8006323 | SU | 1981 | D | 30,590 | 730' 00" | 75' 11" | 42' 00" |

Built: Collingwood Shipyards, Collingwood, ON; converted to a self-unloader by Port Weller Dry Docks, St. Catharines, ON, in '96 (Lake Wabush '81-'87)

| **John B. Aird** | 8002432 | SU | 1983 | D | 31,000 | 730' 00" | 75' 10" | 46' 06" |

Built: Collingwood Shipyards, Collingwood, ON

| **John D. Leitch** | 6714586 | SU | 1967 | D | 34,127 | 730' 00" | 77' 11" | 45' 00" |

Built: Port Weller Dry Docks, Port Weller, ON; rebuilt with new mid-body, widened 3' by the builders in '02 (Canadian Century '67-'02)

| **Peter R. Cresswell** | 8016641 | SU | 1982 | D | 30,590 | 730' 00" | 75' 11" | 42' 00" |

Built: Collingwood Shipyards, Collingwood, ON; converted to a self-unloader by Port Weller Dry Docks, St. Catharines, ON, in '98 (Algowest '82-'01)

| **Radcliffe R. Latimer** | 7711725 | SU | 1978 | D | 36,668 | 740' 00" | 77' 11" | 49' 03" |

Built: Collingwood Shipyards, Collingwood, ON; rebuilt with a new forebody at Chengxi Shipyard Co. Ltd., Jiangyin City, China, in '09 (Algobay '78-'94, Atlantic Trader '94-'97, Algobay '97-'12)

| **Tim S. Dool** | 6800919 | BC | 1967 | D | 31,054 | 730' 00" | 77' 11" | 39' 08" |

Built: Saint John Shipbuilding & Drydock Co., Saint John, NB; widened by 3' at Port Weller Dry Docks, St. Catharines, ON, in '96 (Senneville '67-'94, Algoville '94-'08)

| **A-3** | | **ALGOMA TANKERS LTD., ST. CATHARINES, ON – DIVISION OF ALGOMA CENTRAL CORP.** | | | | | | |
| **Algocanada** | 9378591 | TK | 2008 | D | 11,453 | 426' 01" | 65' 00" | 32' 08" |

Built: Eregli Shipyard, Zonguldak, Turkey

| **Algoeast** | 7526924 | TK | 1977 | D | 10,350 | 431' 05" | 65' 07" | 35' 05" |

Built: Mitsubishi Heavy Industries Ltd., Shimonoseki, Japan; converted from single to double hull by Port Weller Dry Docks, St. Catharines, ON, in '00 (Texaco Brave {2} '77-'86, Le Brave '86-'97, Imperial St. Lawrence {2} '97-'97)

| **Algoma Dartmouth** | 9327516 | RT | 2007 | D | 3,512 | 296' 11" | 47' 11" | 24' 11" |

Built: Turkter Shipyard, Tuzla, Turkey; vessel is engaged in bunkering operations at Halifax, NS (Clipper Bardolino '07-'08, Samistal Due '08-'09)

Fleet Name / Vessel Name	IMO #	Vessel Type	Year Built	Engine Type	Cargo Cap. or Gross*	Overall Length	Breadth	Depth
Algonova {2}	9378589	TK	2008	D	11,453	426' 01"	65' 00"	32' 08"

Built: Eregli Shipyard, Zonguldak, Turkey (Eregli 04 '07-'08)

Algosar {2}	7634288	TK	1978	D	12,000	434' 06"	65' 00"	29' 04"

Built: Levingston Shipbuilding Co., Orange, TX (Gemini '78-'05)

Algoscotia	9273222	TK	2004	D	19,160	488' 03"	78' 00"	42' 00"

Built: Jiangnan Shipyard (Group) Co. Ltd., Shangahi, China

Algosea {2}	9127198	TK	1998	D	17,258	472' 07"	75' 04"	40'08"

Built: Alabama Shipyard Inc., Mobile, AL (Aggersborg '98-'05)

A-4 AMERICAN MARINE CONSTRUCTORS INC., BENTON HARBOR, MI *(americanmarineconstructors.com)*

Alice E		TB	1944	D	146*	86' 00"	25' 00"	9' 08"

Built: George Lawley & Son Corp., Neponset, MA

Defiance		TW	1966	D	39*	48' 00"	18' 00"	6' 03"

A-5 AMERICAN STEAMSHIP CO., WILLIAMSVILLE, NY *(americansteamship.com)*

Adam E. Cornelius {4}	7326245	SU	1973	D	29,200	680' 00"	78' 00"	42' 00"

Built: American Shipbuilding Co., Toledo, OH; spent 2012 season laid up at Toledo, OH (Roger M. Kyes '73-'89)

American Century	7923196	SU	1981	D	80,900	1,000' 00"	105' 00"	56' 00"

Built: Bay Shipbuilding Co., Sturgeon Bay, WI (Columbia Star '81-'06)

American Courage	7634226	SU	1979	D	24,300	636' 00"	68' 00"	40' 00"

Built: Bay Shipbuilding Co., Sturgeon Bay, WI (Fred R. White Jr. '79-'06)

American Fortitude	5105843	SU	1953	T	23,400	690' 00"	70' 00"	37' 00"

Built: American Shipbuilding Co., Lorain, OH; converted to a self-unloader by Bay Shipbuilding Co., Sturgeon Bay, WI, in '81; entered long-term lay-up Nov. 11, 2008, at Toledo, OH (Ernest T. Weir {2} '53-'78, Courtney Burton '78-'06)

American Integrity	7514696	SU	1978	D	80,900	1,000' 00"	105' 00"	56' 00"

Built: Bay Shipbuilding Co., Sturgeon Bay, WI (Lewis Wilson Foy '78-'91, Oglebay Norton '91-'06)

American Mariner	7812567	SU	1980	D	37,300	730' 00"	78' 00"	42' 00"

Built: Bay Shipbuilding Co., Sturgeon Bay, WI (Laid down as Chicago {3})

American Spirit	7423392	SU	1978	D	62,400	1,004' 00"	105' 00"	50' 00"

Built: American Shipbuilding Co., Lorain, OH (George A. Stinson '78-'04)

American Valor	5024738	SU	1953	T	26,200	767' 00"	70' 00"	36' 00"

Built: American Shipbuilding Co., Lorain, OH; lengthened 120' by Fraser Shipyard, Superior, WI, in '74, converted to a self-unloader in '82; entered long-term lay-up Nov. 13, 2008, at Toledo, OH (Armco '53-'06)

American Victory	5234395	SU	1942	T	26,700	730' 00"	75' 00"	39' 03"

Built: Bethlehem Shipbuilding and Drydock Co., Sparrows Point, MD; converted from saltwater tanker to a Great Lakes bulk carrier by Maryland Shipbuilding in '61; converted to a self-unloader by Bay Shipbuilding Co., Sturgeon Bay, WI, in '82; entered long-term lay-up Nov. 12, 2008, at Superior, WI
(Laid down as Marquette. USS Neshanic [AO-71] '42-'47, Gulfoil '47-'61, Pioneer Challenger '61-'62, Middletown '62-'06)

Buffalo {3}	7620653	SU	1978	D	24,300	634' 10"	68' 00"	40' 00"

Built: Bay Shipbuilding Co., Sturgeon Bay, WI

Burns Harbor {2}	7514713	SU	1980	D	80,900	1,000' 00"	105' 00"	56' 00"

Built: Bay Shipbuilding Co., Sturgeon Bay, WI

H. Lee White {2}	7366362	SU	1974	D	35,400	704' 00"	78' 00"	45' 00"

Built: Bay Shipbuilding Co., Sturgeon Bay, WI

Indiana Harbor	7514701	SU	1979	D	80,900	1,000' 00"	105' 00"	56' 00"

Built: Bay Shipbuilding Co., Sturgeon Bay, WI

John J. Boland {4}	7318901	SU	1973	D	34,000	680' 00"	78' 00"	45' 00"

Built: Bay Shipbuilding Co., Sturgeon Bay, WI (Charles E. Wilson '73-'00)

Sam Laud	7390210	SU	1975	D	24,300	634' 10"	68' 00"	40' 00"

Built: Bay Shipbuilding Co., Sturgeon Bay, WI

St. Clair {3}	7403990	SU	1976	D	44,800	770' 00"	92' 00"	52' 00"

Built: Bay Shipbuilding Co., Sturgeon Bay, WI

Walter J. McCarthy Jr.	7514684	SU	1977	D	80,500	1,000' 00"	105' 00"	56' 00"

Built: Bay Shipbuilding Co., Sturgeon Bay, WI (Belle River '77-'90)

OWNED BY SEAJON LLC, FORT LAUDERDALE, FL; OPERATED BY AMERICAN STEAMSHIP CO.

Ken Boothe Sr.		ATB	2011	D	1,179*	135' 04"	50' 00"	26' 00"

Built: Donjon Shipbuilding & Repair, Erie, PA; paired with the self-unloading barge Lakes Contender.

Lakes Contender		SU	2012	B	33,892	740' 04"	78' 00"	45' 00"

Built: Donjon Shipbuilding & Repair, Erie, PA

A-6 ALPENA SHIPWRECK TOURS, ALPENA, MI *(alpenashipwrecktours.com)*

Lady Michigan		ES	2010	D	90*	65' 00"	19' 00"	11' 00"

Stewart J. Cort passes John J. Boland above the Soo Locks. (Mike Sipper)

Fleet Name Vessel Name	IMO #	Vessel Type	Year Built	Engine Type	Cargo Cap. or Gross*	Overall Length	Breadth	Depth
A-7	**AMHERSTBURG FERRY CO. INC, AMHERSTBURG, ON**							
The Columbia V		PA/CF	1946	D	46*	65' 00"	28' 10"	8' 06"
Built: Champion Auto Ferries, Algonac, MI (Crystal O, St. Clair Flats)								
The Ste. Claire V		PA/CF	1997	D	82*	86' 06"	32' 00"	6' 00"
Built: Les Ateliers Maurice Bourbonnais Ltée, Gatineau, QC (Courtney O., M. Bourbonnais)								
A-8	**ANDRIE INC., MUSKEGON, MI** (andrie.com)							
A-390		TK	1982	B	2,346*	310' 00"	60' 00"	17' 00"
Built: St. Louis Shipbuilding & Steel Co., St. Louis, MO (Canonie 40 '82-'92)								
A-397		TK	1962	B	2,928*	270' 00"	60' 01"	22' 05"
Built: Dravo Corp., Pittsburgh, PA (Auntie Mame '62-'91, Iron Mike '91-'93)								
A-410		TK	1955	B	3,793*	335' 00"	54' 00"	17' 00"
Built: Ingalls Shipbuilding Corp., Birmingham, AL (Methane '55-'63, B-6400 '63-'71, Kelly '71-'86, Canonie 50 '86-'93)								
Barbara Andrie	5097187	TB	1940	D	298*	122'00"	29' 07"	16' 00"
Built: Pennsylvania Shipyards Inc., Beaumont, TX (Edmond J. Moran '40-'76)								
Endeavour		TK	2009	B	7,232*	360' 00"	60' 00"	24' 00"
Built: Jeffboat LLC, Jeffersonville, IN								
Karen Andrie {2}	6520454	TB	1965	D	516*	120' 00"	31' 06"	16' 00"
Built: Gulfport Shipbuilding, Port Arthur, TX (Sarah Hays '65-'93)								
Meredith Ashton	8951487	TB	1981	D	127*	68' 08"	26' 01"	9' 04"
Built: Service Marine Group Inc., Amelia, LA (The Rock, Specialist, Alpha)								
Rebecca Lynn	6511374	TB	1964	D	433*	112' 07"	31' 06"	16' 00"
Built: Gulfport Shipbuilding, Port Arthur, TX (Kathrine Clewis '64-'96)								
Robert W. Purcell		TB	1943	D	29*	45' 02"	12' 10"	7' 08"
Built: Sturgeon Bay Shipbuilding, Sturgeon Bay, WI								
	OPERATED BY ANDRIE INC. FOR OCCIDENTAL CHEMICAL CORP., DALLAS, TX							
Spartan	7047461	AT	1969	D	190*	121' 01"	32' 01"	10' 09"
Built: Burton Shipyard, Port Arthur, TX; Paired with barge Spartan II								
(Lead Horse '69-'73, Gulf Challenger '73-'80, Challenger {2} '80-'93, Mark Hannah '93-'10)								
Spartan II		TK	1980	B	8,050	407' 01"	60' 00"	21' 00"
Built: Sturgeon Bay Shipbuilding Co., Sturgeon Bay, WI (Hannah 6301 '80-'10)								
A-9	**APOSTLE ISLANDS CRUISES INC., BAYFIELD, WI** (apostleisland.com)							
Ashland Bayfield Express		PA	1995	D	13*	49' 00"	18' 05"	5' 00"
Island Princess {2}		ES	1973	D	63*	65' 07"	20' 05"	7' 03"
A-10	**ARCELORMITTAL MINES CANADA INC., MONTREAL, QC** (arcelormittal.com/minescanada)							
Brochu	7305899	TT	1973	D	390*	98' 11"	36' 00"	12' 04"
Built: Star Shipyards Ltd., New Westminster, BC								
Vachon	7305904	TT	1973	D	390*	98' 11"	36' 00"	12' 04"
Built: Star Shipyards Ltd., New Westminster, BC								
A-11	**ARGEE BOAT CRUISES LTD., PENETANGUISHENE, ON** (georgianbaycruises.com)							
Georgian Queen		ES	1918	D	249*	119' 00"	36' 00"	16' 06"
Built: Port Arthur Shipbuilding, Port Arthur, ON (Victoria '18-'18, Murray Stewart '18-'48, David Richard '48-'79)								
A-12	**ARNOLD TRANSIT CO., MACKINAC ISLAND, MI** (arnoldline.com)							
Algomah		PF/PK	1961	D	81*	93' 00"	29' 08"	5' 02"
Built: Paasch Marine Services Inc., Erie, PA								
Beaver		CF	1952	D	84*	64' 09"	30' 02"	6' 05"
Built: Lock City Machine/Marine, Sault Ste. Marie, MI								
Chippewa {6}		PF/PK	1962	D	81*	93' 00"	29' 08"	5' 02"
Built: Paasch Marine Services Inc., Erie, PA								
Corsair		CF	1955	D	98*	94' 06"	33' 01"	8' 01"
Built: Blount Marine Corp., Warren, RI								
Huron {5}		PF/PK	1955	D	99*	91' 06"	25' 00"	7' 00"
Built: Paasch Marine Services Inc., Erie, PA								
Island Express		PF/CA	1988	D	90*	82' 07"	28' 06"	8' 04"
Built: Gladding-Hearn Shipbuilding, Somerset, MA								
Mackinac Express		PF/CA	1987	D	90*	82' 07"	28' 04"	8' 04"
Built: Gladding-Hearn Shipbuilding, Somerset, MA								
Mackinac Islander		CF	1947	D	99*	84' 00"	30' 00"	8' 02"
Built: Sturgeon Bay Shipbuilding, Sturgeon Bay, WI (Drummond Islander '47-'02)								
Ottawa {2}		PF/PK	1959	D	81*	93' 00"	29' 08"	5' 02"
Built: Paasch Marine Services Inc., Erie, PA								

Fleet Name / Vessel Name	IMO #	Vessel Type	Year Built	Engine Type	Cargo Cap. or Gross*	Overall Length	Breadth	Depth
Straits Express		PF/CA	1995	D	99*	101' 00"	28' 08"	10' 00"
Built: Marinette Marine Corp., Marinette, WI								
Straits of Mackinac II		PF/PK	1969	D	89*	89' 11"	27' 00"	8' 08"
Built: Blount Marine Corp., Warren, RI								

A-13 ASI GROUP LTD., ST. CATHARINES, ON *(asi-group.com)*

ASI Clipper		SV	1939	D	64*	70' 00"	23' 00"	6' 06"
Built: Port Colborne Iron Works, Port Colborne, ON (Stanley Clipper '39-'94, Nadro Clipper '94-'08)								

A-14 ATLAS MARINE SERVICES LLC, FISH CREEK, WI

Atlas		PA	1992	D	12*	30' 04"	11' 05"	5' 04"
Northern Lighter		GC	1973	D	5*	36' 00"	9' 09"	1' 06"

B-1 B & L TUG SERVICE, THESSALON, ON

C. West Pete		TB	1958	D	29*	65' 00"	17' 05"	6' 00"
Built: Erieau Shipbuilding & Drydock Co. Ltd., Erieau, ON								

B-2 BABCOCK MARINE SERVICES, SARNIA, ON

Lime Island		TB	1953	D	24*	42' 08"	12' 00"	6' 00"

B-3 BASIC MARINE INC., ESCANABA, MI *(basicmarine.com)*

BMI-192		DB	2009	B	1219*	220' 02"	55' 00"	12' 00"
BMI-FDD-1		FD	1981		301*	160' 02"	65' 00"	8 08"
Danicia	8991774	TB	1943	DE	240*	110' 02"	26' 04"	14' 08"
Built: Ira S. Bushy and Sons Inc., Brooklyn, NY; inactive at Escanaba, MI (USCGC Chinook [WYT / WYTM-96] '44-'86, Tracie B '86-'98)								
Erika Kobasic		TB	1939	DE	226*	110' 00"	25' 01"	14' 03"
Built: Gulfport Shipbuilding, Port Arthur, TX (USCGC Arundel [WYT / WYTM-90] '39-'84, Karen Andrie {1} '84-'90)								
Escort		TB	1969	D	26*	50' 00"	14' 00"	6' 03"
Built: Jakobson Shipyard, Oyster Bay, NY								
Greenstone		TK	1977	B	114*	81' 00"	24' 00"	7' 09"
Krystal		TB	1954	D	23*	45' 02"	12' 08"	6' 00"
Built: Roamer Boat Co., Holland, MI (ST-2168 '54-'62, Thunder Bay '62-'02)								
Nickelena		TB	1973	D	240*	109' 00"	30' 07"	15' 08"
Built: Marinette Marine Corp., Marinette, WI (USS Chetek [YTB-827] '73-'96, Chetek '96-'00, Koziol '00-'08)								

B-4 BAY CITY BOAT LINES LLC, BAY CITY, MI *(baycityboatlines.com)*

Islander {1}		ES	1946	D	39*	53' 04"	19' 09"	5' 04"
Princess Wenonah		ES	1954	D	96*	64' 09"	31' 00"	7' 03"
Built: Sturgeon Bay Shipbuilding Co., Sturgeon Bay, WI (William M. Miller '54-'98)								

B-5 BAYSAIL, BAY CITY, MI *(baysailbaycity.org)*

Appledore IV		2S/ES	1989	W/D	48*	85' 00"	18' 08"	8' 08"
Built: Treworgy Yachts, Palm Coast, FL								
Appledore V		2S/ES	1992	W/D	34*	65' 00"	14' 00"	8' 06"
Built: Treworgy Yachts, Palm Coast, FL (Westwind, Appledore)								

B-6 BEAUSOLEIL FIRST NATION TRANSPORTATION, CHRISTIAN ISLAND, ON *(chimnissing.ca)*

Indian Maiden		PA/CF	1987	D	91.5*	73' 06"	23' 00"	8' 00"
Built: Duratug Shipyard & Fabricating Ltd., Port Dover, ON								
Sandy Graham		PA/CF	1957	D	212*	125' 07"	39' 09"	8' 00"
Built: Barbour Boat Works Inc., New Bern, NC								

B-7 BEAVER ISLAND BOAT CO., CHARLEVOIX, MI *(bibco.com)*

Beaver Islander		PF/CF	1963	D	95*	96' 03"	27' 02"	8' 03"
Built: Sturgeon Bay Shipbuilding, Sturgeon Bay, WI								
Emerald Isle {2}		PF/CF	1997	D	95*	130' 00"	38' 00"	12' 00"
Built: Washburn & Doughty Associates Inc., East Boothbay, ME								

B-8 BLUE HERON CO. LTD., TOBERMORY, ON *(blueheronco.com)*

Blue Heron V		ES	1983	D	24*	54' 06"	17' 05"	7' 02"
Flowerpot Express		ES	2011	D	59*	49' 07"	16' 05"	1' 25"
Great Blue Heron		ES	1994	D	112*	79' 00"	22' 00"	6' 05"

B-9 BLUEWATER FERRY CO., SOMBRA, ON *(bluewaterferry.com)*

Daldean		CF	1951	D	145*	75' 00"	35' 00"	7' 00"
Built: Erieau Shipbuilding & Drydock Co. Ltd., Erieau, ON								
Ontamich		CF	1939	D	55*	65' 00"	28' 10"	8' 06"
Built: Champion Auto Ferries, Harsens Island, MI (Harsens Island '39-'73)								

Fleet Name Vessel Name	IMO #	Vessel Type	Year Built	Engine Type	Cargo Cap. or Gross*	Overall Length	Breadth	Depth
B-10 **BRIGANTINE INC., KINGSTON, ONT.** (brigantine.ca)								
St. Lawrence II		TV	1954	W/D	34*	72' 00"	15' 00"	8' 06"
Built: Kingston Shipyards, Kingston, ON								
B-11 **BUCHANAN FOREST PRODUCTS LTD., THUNDER BAY, ON**								
Radium Yellowknife	5288956	TB	1948	D	235*	120' 00"	28' 00"	6' 06"
Built: Yarrow's Ltd., Esquimalt, BC; spent 2012 season laid up at Toronto, ON								
W. N. Twolan	5384360	TB	1962	D	299*	106' 00"	29' 05"	15' 00"
Built: George T. Davie & Sons, Lauzon, QC								
B-12 **BUFFALO DEPARTMENT OF PUBLIC WORKS, BUFFALO, NY**								
Edward M. Cotter		FB	1900	D	208*	118' 00"	24' 00"	11' 06"
Built: Crescent Shipbuilding, Elizabeth, NJ (W. S. Grattan 1900-'53, Firefighter '53-'54)								
B-13 **BUFFALO HARBOR CRUISES, BUFFALO, NY** (buffaloharborcruises.com)								
Miss Buffalo II		ES	1972	D	88*	81' 09"	24' 00"	6' 00"
B-14 **BUFFALO SAILING ADVENTURES INC., AMHERST, NY** (spiritofbuffalo.com)								
Spirit of Buffalo		2S/ES	1992	D/W	34*	73' 00"	15' 06"	7' 02"
Built: Rover Marine Lines, Norfolk, VA (Jolly Rover '92-'09)								
B-15 **BUSCH MARINE INC., CARROLLTON, MI** (buschmarine.com)								
BMT 3		DB	1965	B	280*	120' 01"	36' 01"	7' 06"
Built: Hillman Barge & Construction Co., Brownsville, PA (BC 12 '65-'09)								
Edwin C. Busch		TB	1935	D	18*	42' 06"	11' 11"	5' 00"
Built: Manitowoc Shipbuilding Co., Manitowoc, WI (Paul L. Luedtke '35-'02, Joanne '02-'09)								
Gregory J. Busch	5156725	TB	1919	D	299*	151' 00"	27' 06"	14' 07"
Built: Whitney Bros. Co., Superior, WI (Humaconna '19-'77)								
STC 2004		TK	1963	B	1,230*	250' 00"	50' 00"	12' 00"
Built: St. Louis Shipbuilding & Steel Co., St. Louis, MO								

Melissa Desgagnés on the seaway, east of Montreal. (Delphis Duhamel)

Fleet Name Vessel Name	IMO #	Vessel Type	Year Built	Engine Type	Cargo Cap. or Gross*	Overall Length	Breadth	Depth

C

C-1 CALUMET RIVER FLEETING INC., CHICAGO, IL *(calumetriverfleeting.com)*

Audrie S.		TW	1956	D	268*	102' 00"	28' 00"	8' 00"

Built: Calumet Shipyard & Drydock Co., Chicago, IL (Cindy Jo '56-'66, Katherine L. '66-'93, Daryl C. Hannah '93-'12)

Bonnie G. Selvick		TB	1981	D	45*	57' 08"	17' 00"	6' 01"

(Captain Robbie '81-'90, Philip M. Pearse '90-'97, Chris Ann '97-'09)

Carla Selvick		TB	1954	D	76*	66' 00"	19' 00"	9' 00"

(Sanita '54-'77, Soo Chief '77-'81, Susan M. Selvick '81-'96, Nathan S. '96-'02, John M. Perry '02-'08, Zuccolo '08-'12)

John M. Selvick	8993370	TB	1898	D	256*	118' 00"	24' 03"	16' 00"

Built: Chicago Shipbuilding Co., Chicago, IL (Illinois {1} 1898-'41, John Roen III '41-'74)

Kimberly Selvick		TW	1975	D	93*	57' 07"	28' 00"	10' 00"

Built: Grafton Boat Co., Grafton, IL (Scout '75-'02)

Mary E. Hannah		TB	1945	D	612*	149' 00"	33' 00"	16' 00"

Built: Marietta Manufacturing, Marietta, GA (U. S. Army LT-821 '45-'47, Brooklyn '47-'66, Lee Reuben '66-'75)

Nathan S		TB	1951	D	144*	84' 01"	23' 06"	9'06"

Built: Ira S. Bushey & Sons Inc., Brooklyn, NY (Huntington '51-'05, Spartacus '05-'06, Huntington '06-'08)

Niki S		TW	1971	D	39*	42' 00"	18' 00"	6' 00"

Built: Scully Bros. Boat Builders, Morgan City, LA (Miss Josie '71-'79, Matador VI '79-'08)

Steven Selvick		TB	1954	D	120*	82' 00"	23' 06"	9' 09"

Built: Defoe Shipbuilding Co., Bay City, MI (John A. McGuire '54-'87, William Hoey {1} '87-'94, Margaret Ann '94-'08)

C-2 CANADA STEAMSHIP LINES INC., MONTREAL, QC – A DIVISION OF THE CSL GROUP INC. *(csl.ca)*

Atlantic Erie	8016639	SU	1985	D	37,411	736' 07"	75' 10"	50' 00"

Built: Collingwood Shipyards, Collingwood, ON (Hon. Paul Martin '85-'88)

Atlantic Huron {2}	8025680	SU	1984	D	34,860	736' 07"	77' 11"	46' 04"

*Built: Collingwood Shipyards, Collingwood, ON; converted to a self-unloader in '89 and widened 3' in '03 at Port
Weller Dry Docks, St. Catharines, ON (Prairie Harvest '84-'89, Atlantic Huron {2} '89-'94, Melvin H. Baker II {2} '94-'97)*

Atlantic Superior	7927805	SU	1982	D	36,219	730' 00"	75' 10"	50' 00"

Built: Collingwood Shipyards, Collingwood, ON (Atlantic Superior '82-'97, M. H. Baker III '97-'03)

Cement carrier Alpena has just cleared the EJ&E bridge at South Chicago. (Gary R. Clark)

| Fleet Name Vessel Name | IMO # | Vessel Type | Year Built | Engine Type | Cargo Cap. or Gross* | Overall Length | Breadth | Depth |

C

Fleet Name / Vessel Name	IMO #	Vessel Type	Year Built	Engine Type	Cargo Cap. or Gross*	Overall Length	Breadth	Depth
Baie Comeau {3}	9639892	SU	2013	D	37,690	739' 10"	77' 11"	48' 05"

Built: Chengxi Shipyard Co. Ltd., Jiangyin City, China

Baie St. Paul {2}	9601027	SU	2012	D	37,690	739' 10"	77' 11"	48' 05"

Built: Chengxi Shipyard Co. Ltd., Jiangyin City, China

Birchglen {2}	8119273	BC	1983	D	33,824	730' 01"	75' 09"	48' 00"

Built: Govan Shipyards, Glasgow, Scotland
(Canada Marquis '83–'91, Federal Richelieu '91-'91, Federal MacKenzie '91-'01, MacKenzie '01-'02)

Cedarglen {2}	5103974	BC	1959	D	29,518	730' 00"	75' 09"	40' 04"

Built: Schlieker-Werft, Hamburg, Germany; rebuilt, lengthened with a new forebody at Davie Shipbuilding
Co., Lauzon, QC, in '77 ([Stern Section] Ems Ore '59-'76, [Fore Section] Montcliffe Hall '76-'88, Cartierdoc '88-'02)

CSL Assiniboine	7413218	SU	1977	D	36,768	739' 10"	78' 00"	48' 05"

Built: Davie Shipbuilding Co., Lauzon, QC; rebuilt with a new forebody at Port Weller Dry Docks, St.
Catharines, ON, in '05 (Jean Parisien '77-'05)

CSL Laurentien	7423108	SU	1977	D	37,795	739' 10"	78' 00"	48' 05"

Built: Collingwood Shipyards, Collingwood, ON; rebuilt with new forebody in '01 at Port Weller Dry Docks,
St. Catharines, ON (Stern section: Louis R. Desmarais '77-'01)

CSL Niagara	7128423	SU	1972	D	37,694	739' 10"	78' 00"	48' 05"

Built: Collingwood Shipyards, Collingwood, ON; rebuilt with a new forebody in '99 at Port Weller Dry Docks,
St. Catharines, ON (Stern section: J. W. McGiffin '72-'99)

CSL Tadoussac	6918716	SU	1969	D	30,051	730' 00"	77' 11"	41' 11"

Built: Collingwood Shipyards, Collingwood, ON; rebuilt with new mid-body, widened 3' at Port Weller
Dry Docks, St. Catharines, ON, in '01 (Tadoussac {2} '69-'01)

Frontenac {5}	6804848	SU	1968	D	26,822	729' 07"	75' 00"	39' 08"

Built: Davie Shipbuilding Co., Lauzon, QC; converted to a self-unloader by Collingwood Shipyards, Collingwood, ON, in '73

Mapleglen {3}	7910163	BC	1981	D	35,067	729' 11"	75' 10"	47' 01"

Built: Cockerill Yards N.V., Hoboken, Belgium (Federal Maas {1} '81-'95, Lake Michigan '95-'09)

Oakglen {3}	7901148	BC	1980	D	35,067	729' 11"	75' 10"	47' 01"

Built: Boelwerf Vlaanderen Shipbuilding N.V., Temse, Belgium (Federal Danube '80-'95, Lake Ontario '95-'09)

Pineglen {2}	8409331	BC	1985	D	33,197	736' 07"	75' 11"	42' 00"

Built: Collingwood Shipyards, Collingwood, ON (Paterson '85-'02)

Richelieu {3}	7901150	BC	1980	D	35,067	729' 11"	75' 10"	47' 01"

Built: Boelwerf Vlaanderen Shipbuilding N.V., Temse, Belgium (Federal Ottawa '80-'95, Lake Erie '95-'09)

Rt. Hon. Paul J. Martin	7324405	SU	1973	D	37,694	739' 07"	77' 11"	48' 04"

Built: Collingwood Shipyards, Collingwood, ON; rebuilt with a new forebody in '00 at Port Weller Dry Docks,
St. Catharines, ON (Stern section: H. M. Griffith '73-'00)

Saguenay {4}	7910175	BC	1981	D	35,067	729' 11"	75' 10"	47' 01"

Built: Boelwerf Vlaanderen Shipbuilding N.V., Temse, Belgium (Federal Thames '81-'95, Lake Superior '95-'09)

Salarium	7902233	SU	1980	D	35,123	730' 00"	75' 11"	46' 06"

Built: Collingwood Shipyards, Collingwood, ON (Nanticoke '80-'09)

Spruceglen {2}	8119261	BC	1983	D	33,824	730' 01"	75' 09"	48' 00"

Built: Govan Shipyards, Glasgow, Scotland
(Selkirk Settler '83-'91, Federal St. Louis '91-'91, Federal Fraser {2} '91-01, Fraser '01-'02)

Thunder Bay {2}	9601039	SU	2013	D	37,690	739' 10"	77' 11"	48' 05"

Built: Chengxi Shipyard Co. Ltd., Jiangyin City, China

Whitefish Bay {2}	9639880	SU	2013	D	37,690	739' 10"	77' 11"	48' 05"

Built: Chengxi Shipyard Co. Ltd., Jiangyin City, China

C-3   CANADIAN COAST GUARD (FISHERIES AND OCEANS CANADA), OTTAWA, ON
(www.ccg-gcc.gc.ca) CENTRAL AND ARCTIC REGION, SARNIA, ON

Cape Chaillon, Cape Commodore, Cape Discovery, Cape Dundas, Cape Hearne,								
Cape Providence, Cape Rescue		SR	2004	D	34*	47' 09"	14' 00"	4' 05"
Cape Hurd		SR	1982	D	55*	70' 10"	18' 00"	8' 09"
Cape Lambton, Cape Mercy,								
Thunder Cape		SR	2000	D	34*	47' 09"	14' 00"	4' 05"
Cape Storm		SR	1999	D	34*	47' 09"	14' 00"	4' 05"
Caribou Isle		BT	1985	D	92*	75' 06"	19' 08"	7' 04"

Built: Breton Industrial & Marine Ltd., Port Hawkesbury, NS

Cove Isle		BT	1980	D	80*	65' 07"	19' 08"	7' 04"

Built: Canadian Dredge & Dock Co. Ltd., Kingston, ON

Griffon	7022887	IB	1970	D	2,212*	234' 00"	49' 00"	21' 06"

Built: Davie Shipbuilding Co., Lauzon, QC

Gull Isle		BT	1980	D	80*	65' 07"	19' 08"	7' 04"

Built: Canadian Dredge & Dock Co. Ltd., Kingston, ON

Fleet Name / Vessel Name	IMO #	Vessel Type	Year Built	Engine Type	Cargo Cap. or Gross*	Overall Length	Breadth	Depth
Isle Rouge		SR	1980	D	58*	70' 08"	18' 00"	5' 02"
Kelso		RV	2009	D	63*	57' 07"	17' 01"	4' 09"
Limnos	6804903	RV	1968	D	489*	147' 00"	32' 00"	12' 00"
Built: Port Weller Dry Docks, St. Catharines, ON								
Samuel Risley	8322442	IB	1985	D	1,988*	228' 09"	47' 01"	21' 09"
Built: Vito Steel Boat & Barge Construction Ltd., Delta, BC								
LAURENTIAN REGION, QUÉBEC, QC _(Vessels over 100' only have been listed)_								
Amundsen	7510846	IB	1978	D	5,910*	295' 09"	63' 09"	31' 04"
Built: Burrard Dry Dock Co., North Vancouver, BC (Sir John Franklin '78-'03)								
Des Groseilliers	8006385	IB	1983	D	5,910*	322' 07"	64' 00"	35' 06"
Built: Port Weller Dry Docks, St. Catharines, ON								
F. C. G. Smith	8322686	SV	1985	D	439*	114' 02"	45' 11"	11' 02"
Built: Georgetown Shipyard, Georgetown, PEI								
Martha L. Black	8320432	IB	1986	D	3,818*	272' 04"	53' 02"	25' 02"
Built: Versatile Pacific Shipyards, Victoria, BC								
Pierre Radisson	7510834	IB	1978	D	5,910*	322' 00"	62' 10"	35' 06"
Built: Burrard Dry Dock Co., North Vancouver, BC								
Tracy	6725432	BT	1968	D	837*	181' 01"	38' 00"	16' 00"
Built: Port Weller Dry Docks, St. Catharines, ON								

C-4 CAUSLEY MARINE CONTRACTING LLC, BAY CITY, MI

Jill Marie		TB	1891	D	24*	60' 00"	12' 06"	6' 00"
Built: Cleveland Shipbuilding Co., Cleveland, OH (Cisco 1891-1952, Capama-S '52-'07)								

C-5 CEMBA MOTOR SHIPS LTD., PELEE ISLAND, ON

Cemba		TK	1960	D	17*	50' 00"	15' 06"	7' 06"

Fleet Name / Vessel Name	IMO #	Vessel Type	Year Built	Engine Type	Cargo Cap. or Gross*	Overall Length	Breadth	Depth

C-6   **CENTRAL MARINE LOGISTICS INC., GRIFFITH, IN** *(centralmarinelogistics.com)*

Edward L. Ryerson	5097606	BC	1960	T	27,500	730' 00"	75' 00"	39' 00"

Built: Manitowoc Shipbuilding Co., Manitowoc, WI; in lay-up at Superior, WI, since May 2009

Joseph L. Block	7502320	SU	1976	D	37,200	728' 00"	78' 00"	45' 00"

Built: Bay Shipbuilding Co., Sturgeon Bay, WI

Wilfred Sykes	5389554	SU	1949	T	21,500	678' 00"	70' 00"	37' 00"

Built: American Shipbuilding Co., Lorain, OH; converted to a self-unloader by Fraser Shipyards, Superior, WI, in '75

C-7   **CHAMPION MARINE INC., ALGONAC, MI**

Champion		CF	1941	D	69*	65' 00"	25' 09"	5' 08"
Middle Channel		CF	1997	D	81*	79' 00"	30' 00"	6' 05"
North Channel		CF	1967	D	67*	75' 00"	30' 04"	6' 01"
South Channel		CF	1973	D	94*	79' 00"	30' 03"	6' 01"

C-8   **CHARITY ISLAND TRANSPORT INC., AU GRES, MI** *(charityisland.net)*

North Star		PA	1949	D	14*	50' 05"	14' 06"	3' 06"
Shirley Ann		PA	2007	D	11*	45' 00"	14' 00"	3' 05"

C-9   **CHARLEVOIX COUNTY TRANSPORTATION AUTHORITY, CHARLEVOIX, MI**

Charlevoix {1}		CF	1926	D	43*	47' 00"	30' 00"	3' 08"

C-10   **CHICAGO DEPARTMENT OF WATER MANAGEMENT, CHICAGO, IL**

James J. Versluis		TB	1957	D	126*	83' 00"	22' 00"	11' 02"

Built: Sturgeon Bay Shipbuilding Co., Sturgeon Bay, WI

C-11   **CHICAGO FIRE DEPARTMENT, CHICAGO, IL** *(chicagofireboat.com)*

Christopher Wheatley		FB	2011	D	300*	90' 00"	25' 00"	12' 02"
Victor L. Schlaeger		FB	1949	D	350*	92' 06"	24' 00"	11' 00"

Joseph L. Block unloading at Indiana Harbor, seen from the pilothouse of the Wilfred Sykes. (Roger LeLievre)

C-12 CHICAGO FROM THE LAKE INC., CHICAGO, IL (chicagoline.com)

Vessel	IMO #	Vessel Type	Year Built	Engine Type	Cargo Cap. or Gross*	Overall Length	Breadth	Depth
Ft. Dearborn		ES	1985	D	72*	64' 10"	22' 00"	7' 03"
Innisfree		ES	1980	D	35*	61' 09"	15' 06"	5' 07"
Marquette {6}		ES	1957	D	39*	50' 07"	15' 00"	5' 05"

C-13 CITY OF TORONTO, TORONTO, ON (toronto.ca/parks)

Vessel	IMO #	Vessel Type	Year Built	Engine Type	Cargo Cap. or Gross*	Overall Length	Breadth	Depth
Ned Hanlan II		TB	1966	D	22*	41' 06"	14' 01"	5' 05"
Built: Erieau Shipbuilding & Drydock Co. Ltd., Erieau, ON								
Ongiara	6410374	PA/CF	1963	D	180*	78' 00"	12' 04"	9' 09"
Built: Russel Brothers Ltd., Owen Sound, ON								
Sam McBride		PF	1939	D	387*	129' 00"	34' 11"	6' 00"
Built: Toronto Dry Dock Co. Ltd., Toronto, ON								
Thomas Rennie		PF	1951	D	387*	129' 00"	32' 11"	6' 00"
Built: Toronto Dry Dock Co. Ltd., Toronto, ON								
Trillium		PF	1910	R	564*	150' 00"	30' 00"	8' 04"
Built: Poulson Iron Works, Toronto, ON; last sidewheel-propelled vessel on the Great Lakes								
William Inglis		PF	1935	D	238*	99' 00"	24' 10"	6' 00"
Built: John Inglis Co. Ltd., Toronto, ON (Shamrock {2} '35-'37)								

C-14 CJC CRUISES INC., GRAND LEDGE, MI (detroitprincess.com)

Vessel	IMO #	Vessel Type	Year Built	Engine Type	Cargo Cap. or Gross*	Overall Length	Breadth	Depth
Detroit Princess		PA	1993	D	1,430*	222' 00"	62' 00"	11' 01"
Built: Leevac Shipyards Inc., Jennings, LA (Players Riverboat Casino II '93-'04)								

C-15 CLEARWATER MARINE LLC, HOLLAND, MI (clearwatermarinellc.com)

Vessel	IMO #	Vessel Type	Year Built	Engine Type	Cargo Cap. or Gross*	Overall Length	Breadth	Depth
G.W. Falcon		TB	1936	D	22*	49' 07"	13' 08"	6' 02"
Built: Fred E. Alford, South Haven, MI (J.W. Walsh, Anna Marie)								
Reiss		TB	1913	R	99*	71' 00"	20' 00"	12' 06"
Built: Great Lakes Towing Co., Cleveland, OH; former Reiss Steamship Co. tug last operated in 1969; scheduled to undergo historic preservation at Holland, MI (Q. A. Gillmore '13-'32)								

C-16 CLEVELAND FIRE DEPARTMENT, CLEVELAND, OH

Vessel	IMO #	Vessel Type	Year Built	Engine Type	Cargo Cap. or Gross*	Overall Length	Breadth	Depth
Anthony J. Celebrezze		FB	1961	D	42*	66' 00"	17' 00"	5' 00"
Built: Paasch Marine Services Inc., Erie, PA								

C-17 CLINTON RIVER CRUISE CO., MOUNT CLEMENS, MI (clintonrivercruisecompany.com)

Vessel	IMO #	Vessel Type	Year Built	Engine Type	Cargo Cap. or Gross*	Overall Length	Breadth	Depth
Captain Paul II		PA	1960	D	14*	44' 07"	11' 00"	4' 00"
Clinton		PA	1949	D	10*	63' 07"	15' 03"	4' 08"
Clinton Friendship		PA	1984	D	43*	64' 08"	22' 00"	4' 05"

C-18 CLUB CANAMAC CRUISES, TORONTO, ON (canamac.com)

Vessel	IMO #	Vessel Type	Year Built	Engine Type	Cargo Cap. or Gross*	Overall Length	Breadth	Depth
Stella Borealis		ES	1989	D	356*	118' 00"	26' 00"	7' 00"
Built: Duratug Shipyard & Fabricating Ltd., Port Dover, ON								

C-19 COLUMBIA YACHT CLUB, CHICAGO, IL (columbiayachtclub.com)

Vessel	IMO #	Vessel Type	Year Built	Engine Type	Cargo Cap. or Gross*	Overall Length	Breadth	Depth
Abegweit		CF	1947	D	6,694*	372' 06"	61' 00"	24' 09"
Built: Marine Industries Ltd., Sorel, QC; former CN Marine Inc. vessel last operated in 1981; in use as a private, floating clubhouse in Chicago, IL (Abegweit '47- 81, Abby '81-'97)								

C-20 CONSTRUCTION POLARIS INC., L'ANCIENNE-LORETTE, QC (constructionpolaris.com)

Vessel	IMO #	Vessel Type	Year Built	Engine Type	Cargo Cap. or Gross*	Overall Length	Breadth	Depth
Point Viking	5118840	TB	1962	D	207*	98' 05"	27' 10"	13' 05"
Built: Davie Shipbuilding Co., Lauzon, QC (Foundation Viking '62-'75)								

C-21 COOPER MARINE LTD., SELKIRK, ON

Vessel	IMO #	Vessel Type	Year Built	Engine Type	Cargo Cap. or Gross*	Overall Length	Breadth	Depth
J. W. Cooper		PB	1984	D	25*	48' 00"	14' 07"	5' 00"
Juleen I		PB	1972	D	23*	46' 00"	14' 01"	4' 05"
Lady Kim I		PB	1974	D	20*	44' 00"	13' 00"	4' 00"
Mrs. C.		PB	1991	D	26*	50' 00"	14' 05"	4' 05"
Stacey Dawn		TB	1993	D	14*	35' 09"	17' 04"	3' 05"
Wilson T. Cooper		DB	2009	D	58*	56' 08"	23' 06"	5' 08"

C-22 CORPORATION OF THE TOWNSHIP OF FRONTENAC ISLANDS, WOLFE ISLAND, ON

Vessel	IMO #	Vessel Type	Year Built	Engine Type	Cargo Cap. or Gross*	Overall Length	Breadth	Depth
Howe Islander		CF	1946	D	13*	53' 00"	12' 00"	3' 00"
Built: Canadian Dredge & Dock Co. Ltd., Kingston, ON								
Simcoe Islander		PF	1964	D	24*	47' 09"	18' 00"	3' 06"
Built: Canadian Dredge & Dock Co. Ltd., Kingston, ON								

C-23 CROISIÈRES AML INC., QUÉBEC, QC (croisieresaml.com)

Vessel	IMO #	Vessel Type	Year Built	Engine Type	Cargo Cap. or Gross*	Overall Length	Breadth	Depth
Cavalier des Mers	7431430	ES	1974	D	161*	91' 08"	21' 03"	8' 05"
Built: Camcraft Inc., Crown Point, LA (Marine Sprinter '74-'84)								

Fleet Name / Vessel Name	IMO #	Vessel Type	Year Built	Engine Type	Cargo Cap. or Gross*	Overall Length	Breadth	Depth
Cavalier Maxim	5265904	ES	1962	D	752*	191' 02"	42' 00"	11' 07"
Built: John I. Thornycroft & Co., Wollston, Southampton, England (Osborne Castle '62-'78, Le Gobelet D' Argent '78-'88, Gobelet D' Argent '88-'89, Le Maxim '89-'93)								
Cavalier Royal		ES	1971	D	283*	125' 00"	24' 00"	5' 00"
Built: Beaux's Bay Craft, Loreauville, LA (Bob Cat)								
Grand Fleuve		ES	1987	D	499*	145' 00"	30' 00"	5' 06"
Built: Kanter Yacht Co., St. Thomas, ON								
Louis Jolliet	5212749	ES	1938	R	2,436*	170' 01"	70' 00"	17' 00"
Built: Davie Shipbuilding Co., Lauzon, QC								
Tandem		ES	1991	D	112*	76' 00"	22' 00"	4' 06"
Transit		ES	1992	D	102*	66' 00"	22' 00"	2' 08"

C-24 CROISIÈRES M/S JACQUES-CARTIER, TROIS-RIVIÈRES, QC (croisieres.qc.ca)

Jacques-Cartier		ES	1924	D	457*	135' 00"	35' 00"	10' 00"
Built: Davie Shipbuilding Co., Lauzon, QC								

C-25 CRUISE TORONTO INC., TORONTO ON (cruisetoronto.com)

Obsession III		ES	1967	D	160*	66' 00"	25' 00"	6' 01"
Built: Halter Marine Services, New Orleans, LA (Mystique)								

C-26 CTMA GROUP, CAP-AUX-MEULES, QC (ctma.ca)

C.T.M.A. Vacancier	7310260	PA/RR	1973	D	11,481*	388' 04"	70' 02"	43' 06"
Built: J.J. Sietas KG Schiffswerft, Hamburg, Germany (Aurella '80-'82, Saint Patrick II '82-'98, Egnatia II '98-'00, Ville de Sete '00-'01, City of Cork '01-'02)								
C.T.M.A. Voyageur	7222229	PA/RR	1972	D	4,526*	327' 09"	52' 06"	31' 07"
Built: Trosvik Versted A/S, Brevik, Norway (Anderida)								

D-1 DAN MINOR & SONS INC., PORT COLBORNE, ON

Andrea Marie I		TB	1986	D	87*	75' 02"	24' 07"	7' 03"
Built: Ralph Hurley, Port Burwell, ON								
Jeanette M.		TB	1981	D	31*	70' 00"	20 01"	6' 00"
Built: Hike Metal Products, Wheatley, ON								
Susan Michelle		TB	1995	D	89*	79' 10"	20' 11"	6' 02"
Built: Vic Powell Welding Ltd., Dunnville, ON								
Welland		TB	1954	D	94*	86' 00"	20' 00"	8' 00"
Built: Russel-Hipwell Engines, Owen Sound, ON								

D-2 DEAN CONSTRUCTION CO. LTD., BELLE RIVER, ON (deanconstructioncompany.com)

Americo Dean		TB		D	15*	45' 00"	15' 00"	5' 00"
Annie M. Dean		TB	1981	D	58*	50' 00"	19' 00"	5' 00"
Bobby Bowes		TB	1944	D	11*	37' 04"	10' 02"	3' 06"
Canadian Jubilee		DR	1978	B	896*	149' 09"	56' 01"	11' 01"
Neptune III		TB	1939	D	23*	53' 10"	15' 06"	5' 00"

D-3 DEAN MARINE & EXCAVATING INC., MOUNT CLEMENS, MI (deanmarineandexcavating.com)

Kimberly Anne		**TB**	**1965**	**D**	**65***	55' 02"	18' 08"	8' 00"
Built: Main Iron Works, Houma, LA (Lady Lisa, Lucy, Mrs. Alma)								

D-4 DETROIT CITY FIRE DEPARTMENT, DETROIT, MI

Curtis Randolph		FB	1979	D	85*	77' 10"	21' 06"	9' 03"
Built: Peterson Builders Inc., Sturgeon Bay, WI								

D-5 DEWEY LEASING LLC, ROCHESTER, NY

Ronald J. Dahlke		TB	1903	D	58*	63' 04"	17' 06"	9' 00"
Built: Johnston Bros., Ferrysburg, MI (Bonita '03-'14, Chicago Harbor No. 4 '14-'60, Eddie B. '60-'69, Seneca Queen '69-'70, Ludington '70-'96, Seneca Queen '96-'04)								

D-6 DIAMOND JACK'S RIVER TOURS, DETROIT, MI (diamondjack.com)

Diamond Belle		ES	1958	D	93*	93' 06"	25' 00"	7' 00"
Built: Hans Hansen Welding Co., Toledo, OH (Mackinac Islander {2} '58-'90, Sir Richard '90-'91)								
Diamond Jack		ES	1955	D	82*	72' 00"	25' 00"	7' 03"
Built: Christy Corp., Sturgeon Bay, WI (Emerald Isle {1} '55-'91)								
Diamond Queen		ES	1956	D	94*	92' 00"	25' 00"	7' 02"
Built: Marinette Marine Corp., Marinette, WI (Mohawk '56-'96)								

D-7 DISCOVERY WORLD AT PIER WISCONSIN, MILWAUKEE, WI (voyage.pierwisconsin.org)

Denis Sullivan		TV/ES	2000	W/D	99*	138' 00"	22' 08"	10' 06"
Built: Wisconsin Lake Schooner, Milwaukee, WI								

Fleet Name / Vessel Name	IMO #	Vessel Type	Year Built	Engine Type	Cargo Cap. or Gross*	Overall Length	Breadth	Depth

D-8 DOOR COUNTY CRUISES LLC, STURGEON BAY, WI (doorcountyfireboatcruises.com)

Fred A. Busse		ES	1937	D	99*	92' 00"	22' 04"	9' 06"

Built: Defoe Boat & Motor Works, Bay City, MI; former Chicago fireboat offers cruises at Sturgeon Bay, WI

D-9 DUC D' ORLEANS CRUISE BOAT, CORUNNA, ON (ducdorleans.com)

Duc d' Orleans II		ES	1987	D	120*	71' 03	23' 02"	7' 07"

Built: Blount Marine Corp., Warren, RI (Spirit of Newport '87-'06)

D-10 DUNDEE OIL AND GAS LTD., TORONTO, ON

Vessels are engaged in oil and gas exploration on Lake Erie

Dr. Bob		DV	1973	B	1,022*	160' 01"	54' 01"	11' 01"
Built: Cenac Shipyard Co. Inc., Houma, LA (Mr. Chris '73-'03)								
J.R. Rouble		DV	1958	D	562*	123' 06"	49' 08"	16' 00"
Built: American Marine Machinery Co., Nashville, TN (Mr. Neil)								
Miss Libby		DV	1972	B	924*	160' 01"	54' 01"	11' 01"
Built: Service Machine & Shipbuilding Corp., Morgan City, LA								
Sarah No. 1		TB	1969	D	43*	72' 01"	17' 03"	6' 08"
Built: Halter Boats Ltd., New Orleans, LA								
Timesaver II		DB	1964	B	510*	91' 08"	70' 08"	9' 01"
Built: Russel Bros. Ltd., Owen Sound, ON								

D-11 DUROCHER MARINE, DIV. OF KOKOSING CONSTRUCTION CO., CHEBOYGAN, MI (kokosing.biz)

Champion {3}		TB	1974	D	125*	75' 00"	23' 05"	9' 05"
Built: Service Machine & Shipbuilding Co., Amelia, LA								
General {2}		TB	1954	D	119*	71' 00"	19' 06"	10' 00"

Built: Missouri Valley Bridge & Iron Works, Leavenworth, KS (U. S. Army ST-1999 '54-'61, USCOE Au Sable '61-'84, Challenger {3} '84-'87)

Joe Van		TB	1955	D	32*	57' 09"	15' 00"	7' 00"
Built: W.J. Hingston, Buffalo, NY								
Nancy Anne		TB	1969	D	73*	60' 00"	20' 00"	8' 00"
Built: Houma Shipbuilding Co., Houma, LA								
Ray Durocher		TB	1943	D	20*	45' 06"	12' 05"	7' 06"
Valerie B.		TB	1981	D	101*	65' 00"	25' 06"	10' 00"
Built: Rayco Shipbuilders & Repairers, Bourg, LA (Mr. Joshua, Michael Van)								

E-1 EASTERN UPPER PENINSULA TRANSPORTATION AUTH., SAULT STE. MARIE, MI (www.eupta.net)

Drummond Islander III		CF	1989	D	96*	108' 00"	37' 00"	7' 02"
Built: Moss Point Marine Inc., Escatawpa, MS								
Drummond Islander IV		CF	2000	D	97*	148' 00"	40' 00"	12' 00"
Built: Basic Marine Inc., Escanaba, MI								
Neebish Islander II		CF	1946	D	90*	89' 00"	25' 09"	5' 08"
Built: Lock City Machine/Marine, Sault Ste. Marie, MI (Sugar Islander '46-'95)								
Sugar Islander II		CF	1995	D	90*	114' 00"	40' 00"	10' 00"
Built: Basic Marine Inc., Escanaba, MI								

E-2 EDWARD E. GILLEN MARINE LLC, MEQUON, WI (gillenmarine.com)

Edward E. Gillen III		TB	1988	D	97*	75' 00"	26' 00"	9' 06"
Built: Terrebonne Shipbuilders Inc., Houma, LA								

E-3 EMPRESS OF CANADA ENTERPRISES LTD., TORONTO, ON (empressofcanada.com)

Empress of Canada		ES	1980	D	399*	116' 00"	28' 00"	6' 06"
Built: Hike Metal Products, Wheatley, ON (Island Queen V {2} '80-'89)								

E-4 ENTERPRISE MARISSA INC., QUEBEC, QC

Cap Brulé		TB		D	12*	39' 09"	10' 00"	2' 00"
Cape Crow		TB	1951	D	14*	37' 08"	10' 05"	5' 00"
Soulanges		TB	1905	D	72*	77' 00"	17' 00"	8' 00"
Built: Cie Pontbriand Ltee., Sorel, QC (Dandy '05-'39)								

E-5 ERICSON MARINE FREIGHT INC., BAYFIELD, WI

Outer Island		PK	1942	D	173*	112' 00"	32' 00"	8' 06"
(LCT 203 '42-'46, Pluswood '46-'53)								

E-6 EQUIPMENTS VERREAULT INC., LES MÉCHINS, QC

Epinette II		TB	1965	D	75*	61' 03"	20' 01"	8' 05"
Built: Russel Brothers Ltd., Owen Sound, ON								
Grande Baie		TT	1972	D	194*	86' 06"	30' 00"	12' 00"
Built: Prince Edward Island Lending Authority, Charlottetown, PEI								

Fleet Name / Vessel Name	IMO #	Vessel Type	Year Built	Engine Type	Cargo Cap. or Gross*	Overall Length	Breadth	Depth
E-7 **ERIE ISLANDS PETROLEUM INC., PUT-IN-BAY, OH** *(putinbayfuels.com)*								
Cantankerus		TK	1955	D	43*	56' 00"	14' 00"	6' 06"
Built: Marinette Marine Corp., Marinette, WI								
E-8 **ERIE SAND AND GRAVEL CO., ERIE, PA** *(eriesandandgravel.com)*								
J. S. St. John	5202524	SC	1945	D	415*	174' 00"	31' 09"	15' 00"
Built: Smith Shipyards & Engineering Corp., Pensacola, FL (USS YO-178 '45-'51, Lake Edward '51-'67)								
E-9 **ESSROC CANADA INC., MISSISSAUGA, ON** *(essroc.com)*								
VESSELS MANAGED BY ALGOMA CENTRAL CORP.								
Metis	5233585	CC	1956	B	5,800	331' 00"	43' 09"	26' 00"
Built: Davie Shipbuilding Co., Lauzon, QC; lengthened 72', deepened 3'06" in '59 and converted to a self-unloading cement barge in '91 by Kingston Shipbuilding & Dry Dock Co., Kingston, ON								
Stephen B. Roman	6514900	CC	1965	D	7,600	488' 09"	56' 00"	35' 06"
Built: Davie Shipbuilding Co., Lauzon, QC; converted to a self-unloading cement carrier by Collingwood Shipyards, Collingwood, ON, in '83 (Fort William '65-'83)								
E-10 **EVERETTE J. GAYTON, OAK PARK, MI**								
Titan		TB	1940	D	31*	56' 03"	15' 08"	7' 00"
F-1 **FINCANTERI MARINE GROUP LLC., STURGEON BAY, WI** *(bayshipbuildingcompany.com)*								
Bayship		TB	1943	D	19*	45' 00"	12' 04"	5' 03"
Built: Sturgeon Bay Shipbuilding Co., Sturgeon Bay, WI (Sturshipco)								
F-2 **FOXY LADY CRUISES, GREEN BAY, WI** *(foxyladycruises.com)*								
Foxy Lady II		ES	2003	D	61*	73' 05"	20' 00"	5' 05"
(Marco Island Princess)								
F-3 **FRASER SHIPYARDS INC., SUPERIOR, WI** *(frasershipyards.com)*								
Maxine Thompson		TB	1959	D	30*	47' 04"	13' 00"	6' 06"
(Susan A. Fraser '59-'78)								
Wally Kendzora		TB	1956	D	24*	43' 00"	12' 00"	5' 06"
G-1 **GAELIC TUGBOAT CO., LINCOLN PARK, MI** *(gaelictugboat.com)*								
Carolyn Hoey	5029946	TB	1951	D	149*	88' 06"	25' 06"	11' 00"
Built: Alexander Shipyard Inc., New Orleans, LA (Atlas '51-'84, Susan Hoey {1} '84-'85, Atlas '85-'87)								
Marysville		TK	1973	B	1,136*	200' 00"	50' 00"	12' 06"
(N.M.S. No. 102 '73-'81)								
Patricia Hoey {2}		TB	1949	D	146*	88' 06"	25' 06"	11' 00"
Built: Alexander Shipyard Inc., New Orleans, LA (Propeller '49-'82, Bantry Bay '82-'91)								
Shannon	8971669	TB	1944	D	145*	101' 00"	25' 08"	13' 00"
Built: Consolidated Shipbuilding Corp., Morris Heights, NY (USS Connewango [YT / YTB / YTM-388] '44-'77)								
G-2 **GAFCO CORP., GROSSE POINTE FARMS, MI**								
Linnhurst		TB	1930	D	11*	37' 05"	10' 05"	4' 08"
Built: Great Lakes Engineering Works, Ecorse, MI (G.L.E. WKS, Toledoan, Grosse Ile)								
G-3 **GALCON MARINE LTD., TORONTO, ON** *(galconmarine.com)*								
Batchawana		TB	1912	D	40*	49' 00"	13' 00"	7' 08"
Built: Polson Iron Works Ltd., Toronto, ON								
Kenteau		TB	1937	D	15*	54' 07"	16' 04"	4' 02"
Built: George Gamble, Port Dover, ON								
Pitts Carillon		DB	1959	B	260*	91' 08"	39' 00"	8' 01"
Built: Walter Young Machinery & Equipment Ltd., Waubaushine, ON (Omar D.S. 34 '59-'80)								
Pitts No. 3		DB	1961	B	107*	78' 02"	32' 00"	5' 05"
Built: Thomas Storey Engineers Ltd., Stockport, England								
The Barney Drake		DB	1954	B	10*	31' 02"	9 05"	3' 04"
Built: Toronto Dry Dock Co Ltd., Toronto ON (T.T.&S. No. 9)								
G-4 **GALLAGHER MARINE CONSTRUCTION CO. INC., ESCANABA, MI**								
Bee Jay		TB	1939	D	19*	45' 00"	13' 00"	7' 00"
G-5 **GANANOQUE BOAT LINE LTD., GANANOQUE, ON** *(ganboatline.com)*								
Thousand Islander	7227346	ES	1972	D	200*	96' 11"	22' 01"	5' 05"
Thousand Islander II	7329936	ES	1973	D	200*	99' 00"	22' 01"	5' 00"
Thousand Islander III		ES	1975	D	376*	118' 00"	28' 00"	6' 00"
Thousand Islander IV	7947984	ES	1976	D	347*	110' 09"	28' 04"	10' 08"
Thousand Islander V		ES	1979	D	246*	88' 00"	24' 00"	5' 00"
(Concordia '79-'97)								

Manitowoc sporting a fresh coat of paint.   (Sam Lapinski)

Fleet Name Vessel Name	IMO #	Vessel Type	Year Built	Engine Type	Cargo Cap. or Gross*	Overall Length	Breadth	Depth
G-6 **GANNON UNIVERSITY, ERIE, PA** *(gannon.edu)*								
Environaut		RV	1950	D	18*	48' 00"	13' 00"	4' 05"
G-7 **GEO. GRADEL CO., TOLEDO, OH** *(geogradelco.com)*								
Crow		DB	1955	B	416*	110' 00"	42' 00"	9' 06"
John Francis		TB	1965	D	99*	75' 00"	22' 00"	9' 00"
Built: Bollinger Shipbuilding Inc., Lockport, LA (Dad '65-'98, Creole Eagle '98-'03)								
Mighty Jake		TB	1969	D	15*	36' 00"	12' 03"	7' 03"
Mighty Jessie		TB	1954	D	57*	61' 02"	18' 00"	7' 03"
Mighty Jimmy		TB	1945	D	34*	56' 00"	15' 10"	6' 05"
Mighty John III		TB	1962	D	24*	45' 00"	15' 00"	5' 10"
(Niagara Queen '62-'99)								
Moby Dick		DB	1952	B	835	121' 00"	33' 02"	10' 06"
Pioneerland		TB	1943	D	53*	58' 00"	16' 08"	8' 00"
Prairieland		TB	1955	D	35*	49' 02"	15' 02"	6' 00"
Timberland		TB	1946	D	20*	41' 03"	13' 01"	7' 00"
G-8 **GOODTIME CRUISE LINE INC., CLEVELAND, OH** *(goodtimeiii.com)*								
Goodtime III		ES	1990	D	95*	161' 00"	40' 00"	11' 00"
Built: Leevac Shipyards Inc., Jennings, LA								
G-9 **GRAND PORTAGE / ISLE ROYALE TRANSPORTATION LINE, WHITE BEAR LAKE, MN** *(isleroyaleboats.com)*								
Sea Hunter III		ES	1985	D	47*	65' 00"	16 00"	7' 05"
Voyageur II		ES	1970	D	40*	63' 00"	18' 00"	5' 00"
GRAND RIVER NAVIGATION CO. – SEE LOWER LAKES TRANSPORTATION CO. , Fleet L-10								
G-10 **GRAND VALLEY STATE UNIVERSITY, ANNIS WATER RESOURCES, MUSKEGON, MI** *(gvsu.edu/wri)*								
D. J. Angus		RV	1986	D	16*	45' 00"	14' 00"	4' 00"
W. G. Jackson		RV	1996	D	80*	64' 10"	20' 00"	5' 00"
G-11 **GRAVEL AND LAKE SERVICES LTD., THUNDER BAY, ON**								
Donald Mac		TB	1914	D	69*	71' 00"	17' 00"	10' 00"
Built: Thor Iron Works Ltd., Toronto, ON								
George N. Carleton		TB	1943	D	97*	82' 00"	21' 00"	11' 00"
Built: Russel Brothers, Owen Sound, ON (HMCS Glenlea [W-25] '43-'45, Bansaga '45-'64)								
Peninsula		TB	1944	D	261*	111' 00"	27' 00"	13' 00"
Built: Montreal Drydock Ltd., Montreal, QC (HMCS Norton [W-31] '44-'45, W.A.C. 1 '45-'46)								
Robert John		TB	1945	D	98*	82' 00"	20' 01"	11' 00"
Built: Canadian Dredge & Dock Co., Kingston, ON (HMCS Gleneagle [W-40] '45-'46, Bansturdy '46-'65)								
Wolf River		BC	1956	D	5,880	349' 02"	43' 07"	25' 04"
Built: Port Weller Dry Docks, Port Weller, ON; last operated in 1998; laid up at Thunder Bay, ON								
(Tecumseh {2} '56-'67, New York News {3} '67-'86, Stella Desgagnés '86-'93, Beam Beginner '93-'95)								
G-12 **GREAT LAKES DOCK & MATERIALS LLC, MUSKEGON, MI** *(greatlakesdock.com)*								
Duluth		TB	1954	D	87*	70' 01"	19' 05"	9' 08"
Built: Missouri Valley Bridge & Iron Works, Leavenworth, KS (U. S. Army ST-2015 '54-'62)								
Fischer Hayden		TB	1967	D	64*	54' 00"	22' 01"	7' 01"
Built: Main Iron Works Inc., Houma, LA (Gloria G. Cheramie, Joyce P. Crosby)								
Sarah B.		TB	1953	D	23*	45' 00"	13' 00"	7' 00"
Built: Nashville Bridge Co., Nashville, TN (ST-2161 '53-'63, Tawas Bay '63-'03)								
G-13 **GREAT LAKES ENVIRONMENTAL RESEARCH LABORATORY, ANN ARBOR, MI** *(glerl.noaa.gov)*								
Huron Explorer		RV	1979	D	15*	41' 00"	14'08"	4' 08"
Laurentian		RV	1974	D	129*	80' 00"	21' 06"	11' 00"
Shenehon		SV	1953	D	90*	65' 00"	17' 00"	6' 00"
G-14 **GREAT LAKES FLEET INC., DULUTH, MN (KEY LAKES INC., MANAGER)** *(greatlakesfleet.com)*								
Arthur M. Anderson	5025691	SU	1952	T	25,300	767' 00"	70' 00"	36' 00"
Built: American Shipbuilding Co., Lorain, OH; lengthened 120' in '75 and converted to a self-unloader in '82 at Fraser Shipyards, Superior, WI								
Cason J. Callaway	5065392	SU	1952	T	25,300	767' 00"	70' 00"	36' 00"
Built: Great Lakes Engineering Works, River Rouge, MI; lengthened 120' in '74 and converted to a self-unloader in '82 at Fraser Shipyards, Superior, WI								
Edgar B. Speer	7625952	SU	1980	D	73,700	1,004' 00"	105' 00"	56' 00"
Built: American Shipbuilding Co., Lorain, OH								

Fleet Name / Vessel Name	IMO #	Vessel Type	Year Built	Engine Type	Cargo Cap. or Gross*	Overall Length	Breadth	Depth
Edwin H. Gott	7606061	SU	1979	D	74,100	1,004' 00"	105' 00"	56' 00"

Built: Bay Shipbuilding Co., Sturgeon Bay, WI; converted from shuttle self-unloader to deck-mounted self-unloader at Bay Shipbuilding, Sturgeon Bay, WI, in '96

Great Republic	7914236	SU	1981	D	25,600	634' 10"	68' 00"	39' 07"

Built: Bay Shipbuilding Co., Sturgeon Bay, WI (American Republic '81-'11)

John G. Munson {2}	5173670	SU	1952	T	25,550	768' 03"	72' 00"	36' 00"

Built: Manitowoc Shipbuilding Co., Manitowoc, WI; lengthened 102' at Fraser Shipyards, Superior, WI, in '76

Philip R. Clarke	5277062	SU	1952	T	25,300	767' 00"	70' 00"	36' 00"

Built: American Shipbuilding Co., Lorain, OH; lengthened 120' in '74 and converted to a self-unloader in '82 at Fraser Shipyards, Superior, WI

Presque Isle {2}	7303877	IT	1973	D	1,578*	153' 03"	54' 00"	31' 03"

Built: Halter Marine Services, New Orleans, LA; paired with the self-unloading barge Presque Isle

Presque Isle {2}		SU	1973	B	57,500	974' 06"	104' 07"	46' 06"

Built: Erie Marine Inc., Erie, PA

[ITB Presque Isle OA dimensions together]						1,000' 00"	104' 07"	46' 06"
Roger Blough	7222138	SU	1972	D	43,900	858' 00"	105' 00"	41' 06"

Built: American Shipbuilding Co., Lorain, OH

G-15 THE GREAT LAKES GROUP, CLEVELAND, OH (thegreatlakesgroup.com)

THE GREAT LAKES TOWING CO., CLEVELAND, OH – DIVISION OF THE GREAT LAKES GROUP

Vessel Name	IMO #	Vessel Type	Year Built	Engine Type	Cargo Cap. or Gross*	Overall Length	Breadth	Depth
Arizona		TB	1931	D	98*	74' 08"	19' 09"	11' 06"
Arkansas {2}		TB	1909	D	97*	74' 08"	19' 09"	11' 06"
(Yale '09-'48)								
California		TB	1926	DE	97*	74' 08"	19' 09"	11' 06"
Colorado		TB	1928	D	98*	78' 08"	20' 00"	12' 04"
Delaware {4}		TB	1924	DE	97*	78' 08"	20' 00"	12' 05"
Favorite		FD	1983			90' 00"	50' 00"	5' 00"
Florida		TB	1926	D	99*	71' 00"	20' 02"	11' 02"
(Florida '26-'83, Pinellas '83-'84)								
Idaho		TB	1931	DE	98*	78' 08"	20' 00"	12' 04"
Illinois {2}		TB	1914	D	98*	71' 00"	20' 00"	12' 05"
Indiana		TB	1911	DE	97*	74' 08"	19' 09"	11' 06"
Iowa		TB	1915	D	97*	74' 08"	19' 09"	11' 06"
Kansas		TB	1927	D	97*	74' 08"	19' 09"	11' 06"
Kentucky {2}		TB	1929	D	98*	78' 08"	20' 00"	12' 04"
Louisiana		TB	1917	D	97*	74' 08"	19' 09"	11' 06"
Maine {1}		TB	1921	D	96*	71' 00"	20' 01"	11' 02"
(Maine {1} '21-'82, Saipan '82-'83, Hillsboro '83-'84)								
Massachusetts		TB	1928	D	98*	78' 08"	20' 00"	12' 04"
Milwaukee		DB	1924	B	1,095	172' 00"	40' 00"	11' 06"
Minnesota {1}		TB	1911	D	98*	78' 08"	20' 00"	12' 04"
Mississippi		TB	1916	DE	97*	74' 08"	19' 09"	11' 06"
Missouri {2}		TB	1927	D	149*	88' 04"	24' 06"	12' 03"
(Rogers City {1} '27-'56, Dolomite {1} '56-'81, Chippewa {7} '81-'90)								
Montana		TB	1929	DE	98*	78' 08"	20' 00"	12' 05"
Nebraska		TB	1929	D	98*	78' 08"	20' 00"	12' 05"
New Jersey		TB	1924	D	98*	78' 08"	20' 00"	12' 04"
(New Jersey '24-'52, Petco-21 '52-'53)								
New York		TB	1913	D	98*	78' 08"	20' 00"	12' 04"
North Carolina {2}		TB	1952	DE	145*	87' 09"	24' 01"	10' 07"
(Limestone '52-'83, Wicklow '83-'90)								
North Dakota		TB	1910	D	97*	74' 08"	19' 09"	11' 06"
(John M. Truby '10-'38)								
Ohio {3}	6507440	TB	1903	D	194*	101' 02"	26' 00"	13' 07"

Built: Great Lakes Towing Co., Chicago, IL (M.F.D. No. 15 '03-'52, Laurence C. Turner '52-'73)

Vessel Name	IMO #	Vessel Type	Year Built	Engine Type	Cargo Cap. or Gross*	Overall Length	Breadth	Depth
Oklahoma		TB	1913	DE	97*	74' 08"	19' 09"	11' 06"
(T. C. Lutz {2} '13-'34)								
Pennsylvania {3}		TB	1911	D	98*	78' 08"	20' 00"	12' 04"
Rhode Island		TB	1930	D	98*	78' 08"	20' 00"	12' 04"
South Carolina		TB	1925	D	102*	79' 06"	21' 01"	11' 03"
(Welcome {2} '25-'53, Joseph H. Callan '53-'72, South Carolina '72-'82, Tulagi '82-'83)								
Superior {3}		TB	1912	D	147*	82' 00"	22' 00"	10' 07"
(Richard Fitzgerald '12-'46)								

Fleet Name / Vessel Name	IMO #	Vessel Type	Year Built	Engine Type	Cargo Cap. or Gross*	Overall Length	Breadth	Depth
Tennessee		TB	1917	D	98*	81'00"	20'00"	12'06"
Texas		TB	1916	DE	97*	74'08"	19'09"	11'06"
Vermont		TB	1914	D	98*	71'00"	20'00"	12'05"
Virginia {2}		TB	1914	DE	97*	74'08"	19'09"	11'06"
Washington {1}		TB	1925	DE	97*	74'08"	19'09"	11'06"
Wisconsin {4}		TB	1897	D	105*	83'00"	21'02"	9'06"
(America {3}, Midway)								
Wyoming		TB	1929	D	104*	78'08"	20'00"	12'04"

G-16   GREAT LAKES MARITIME ACADEMY, TRAVERSE CITY, MI *(nmc.edu/maritime)*

Anchor Bay		TV	1953	D	23*	45'00"	13'00"	7'00"
Built: Roamer Boat Co., Holland, MI (ST-2158 '53-'62)								
Northwestern {2}		TV	1969	D	12*	55'00"	15'00"	6'06"
Built: Paasch Marine Services Inc., Erie, PA (USCOE North Central '69-'98)								
State of Michigan	8835451	TV	1985	D	1,914*	224'00"	43'00"	20'00"
Built: Tacoma Boatbuilding Co., Tacoma, WA (USNS Persistent '85-'98, USCG Persistent '98-'02)								

G-17   GREAT LAKES OFFSHORE SERVICES INC., PORT DOVER, ON

H. H. Misner		TB	1946	D	28*	66'09"	16'04"	4'05"
Built: George Gamble, Port Dover, ON								

G-18   GREAT LAKES SCHOONER CO., TORONTO, ON *(greatlakesschooner.com)*

Challenge		ES	1980	W/D	76*	96'00"	16'06"	8'00"
Built: Kanter Yachts Co., Port Stanley, ON								
Kajama		ES	1930	W/D	263*	128'09"	22'09"	11'08"
Built: Nobis Krug, Rensburg, Germany								

Capt. Henry Jackman arriving at Stoneport, Mich. *(Chanda McClain)*

H

| Fleet Name / Vessel Name | IMO # | Vessel Type | Year Built | Engine Type | Cargo Cap. or Gross* | Overall Length | Breadth | Depth |

G-19 GREAT LAKES SCIENCE CENTER, ANN ARBOR, MI *(glsc.usgs.gov)*

Grayling		RV	1977	D	198*	75′00″	22′00″	9′10″
Kaho		RV	2011	D	55*	70′02″	18′00″	
Kiyi		RV	1999	D	290*	107′00″	27′00″	12′02″
Muskie		RV	2011	D	55*	70′02″	18′00″	
Sturgeon		RV	1977	D	325*	100′00″	25′05″	10′00″

G-20 GREAT LAKES SHIPWRECK HISTORICAL SOCIETY, SAULT STE. MARIE, MI *(shipwreckmuseum.com)*

David Boyd		RV	1982	D	26*	47′00″	17′00″	3′00″*

G-21 GROUPE DESGAGNÉS INC., QUÉBEC CITY, QC *(groupedesgagnes.com)*

ALL VESSELS OPERATED BY SUBSIDIARY TRANSPORT DESGAGNÉS

Amelia Desgagnés	7411167	GC	1976	D	7,349	355′00″	49′00″	30′06″

Built: Collingwood Shipyards, Collingwood, ON (Soodoc {2} '76-'90)

Anna Desgagnés	8600507	RR	1986	D	17,850	569′03″	75′07″	44′11″

Built: Kvaerner Warnow Werft GmbH, Rostock, Germany; re-registered in the Bahamas in 2006 (Truskavets '86-'96, Anna Desgagnés '96-'98, PCC Panama '98-'99)

Camilla Desgagnés	8100595	GC	1982	D	6,889ww	436′04″	67′07″	46′03″

Built: Kroeger Werft GmbH & Co. KG, Rendsburg, Germany (Camilla 1 '82-'04)

Catherine Desgagnés	5133979	GC	1962	D	8,394	410′03″	55′06″	31′00″

Built: Hall, Russel and Co., Aberdeen, Scotland (Gosforth '62-'72, Thorold {4} '72-'85)

Claude A. Desgagnés	9488059	GC	2011	D	12,671	454′05″	69′11″	36′01″

Built: Sanfu Ship Engineering, Taizhou Jiangsu, China (Elsborg '11-'12)

Melissa Desgagnés	7356501	GC	1975	D	7,500	355′00″	49′00″	30′06″

Built: Collingwood Shipyards, Collingwood, ON (Ontadoc {2} '75-'90)

Rosaire A. Desgagnés	9363534	GC	2007	D	12,575	453′00″	68′11″	36′01″

Built: Quingshan/Jiangdong/Jiangzhou Shipyards, Jiangzhou, China (Beluga Fortification '07-'07)

Sedna Desgagnés	9402093	GC	2009	D	12,413	456′00″	68′11″	36′01″

Built: Quingshan/Jiangdong/Jiangzhou Shipyards, Jiangzhou, China (Beluga Festivity '09-'09)

Zelada Desgagnés	9402081	GC	2008	D	12,413	453′00″	68′11″	36′01″

Built: Quingshan/Jiangdong/Jiangzhou Shipyards, Jiangzhou, China (Beluga Freedom '09-'09)

THE FOLLOWING VESSELS CHARTERED TO PETRO-NAV INC., MONTREAL, QC, A SUBSIDIARY OF GROUPE DESGAGNÉS INC.

Dara Desgagnés	9040089	TK	1992	D	10,511	405′10″	58′01″	34′09″

Built: MTW Shipyard, Wismar, Germany (Elbestern '92-'93, Diamond Star, '93-'10)

Esta Desgagnés	9040077	TK	1992	D	10,511	405′10″	58′01″	34′09″

Built: MTW Shipyard, Wismar, Germany (Emsstern '92-'92, Emerald Star '92-'10)

Jana Desgagnés	9046564	TK	1993	D	10,511	405′10″	58′01″	34′09″

Built: MTW Shipyard, Wismar, Germany (Jadestern '93-'94, Jade Star '94-'10)

Maria Desgagnés	9163752	TK	1999	D	13,199	393′08″	68′11″	40′05″

Built: Qiuxin Shipyard, Shanghai, China (Kilchem Asia '99-'99)

Sarah Desgagnés	9352171	TK	2007	D	18,000	483′11″	73′06″	41′04″

Built: Gisan Shipyard, Tuzla, Turkey (Besiktas Greenland '07-'08)

Thalassa Desgagnés	7382988	TK	1976	D	9,748	441′05″	56′05″	32′10″

Built: Ankerlokken Verft Glommen, Fredrikstad, Norway (Joasla '76-'79, Orinoco '79-'82, Rio Orinoco '82-'93)

Véga Desgagnés	7927960	TK	1982	D	11,548	461′11″	69′07″	35′01″

Built: Kvaerner Masa-Yards, Helsinki, Finland (Shelltrans '82-'94, Acila '94-'99, Bacalan '99-'01)

THE FOLLOWING VESSELS CHARTERED TO RELAIS NORDIK INC., RIMOUSKI, QC A SUBSIDIARY OF GROUPE DESGAGNÉS INC.

Bella Desgagnés	9511519	PF/RR	2012	D	1,054	312′00″	63′06″	22′08″

Built: Kraljevica Brodogradil dd, Kraljevica, Croatia

Nordik Express	7391290	GC/CF	1974	D	1,697	219′11″	44′00″	16′01″

Built: Todd Pacific Shipyards Corp., Seattle, WA (Theriot Offshore IV '74-'77, Scotoil 4 '77-'79, Tartan Sea '79-'87)

H-1 HAMILTON HARBOUR QUEEN CRUISES, HAMILTON, ON *(hamiltonwaterfront.com)*

Hamilton Harbour Queen		ES	1956	D	252*	100′00″	22′00″	4′05″

Built: Russel-Hipwell Engines, Owen Sound, ON (Johnny B. '56-'89, Garden City '89-'00, Harbour Princess '00-'05)

H-2 HAMILTON PORT AUTHORITY, HAMILTON, ON *(hamiltonport.ca)*

Judge McCombs		TB	1948	D	10*	33′01″	10′03″	4′00″

Built: Northern Shipbuilding & Repair Co. Ltd., Bronte, ON (Bronte Sue '48-'50)

H-3 HARBOR LIGHT CRUISE LINES INC., TOLEDO, OH *(sandpiperboat.com)*

Sandpiper		ES	1984	D	37*	65′00″	16′00″	3′00″

H-4 HERITAGE MARINE, TWO HARBORS, MN

Edward H.		TB	1944	D	142*	86' 00"	23' 00"	10' 03"

Built: Equitable Equipment Co., Madisonville, LA (ST-707 '44-'60, Forney '60-'07)

Helen H.	8624670	TB	1967	D	138*	82' 03"	26 08"	10' 05"

Built: Bludworth Shipyard, Corpus Christi, TX (W. Douglas Masterson '67-'11)

Nels J.		TB	1958	D	194*	103' 00"	26 06"	12' 00"

Built: Gulfport Shipbuilding Co., Port Arthur, TX (Gatco Alabama, Ares)

H-5 HORNBECK OFFSHORE SERVICES, COVINGTON, LA *(hornbeckoffshore.com)*

Eagle Service	9117260	TB	1996	D	195*	124' 08"	37' 00"	18' 00"

Built: Bollinger Shipyard Inc., Lockport, LA (Grant Candies)

Freedom Service	8207599	TB	1983	B	169*	126' 00"	37' 00"	16' 04"

Built: McDermott Shipyards, Morgan City, LA (Mac Tide 62, Jaramac 62)

Huron Service	8973942	TB	1981	D	398*	105' 00"	34' 00"	17' 00"

Built: Halter Marine, New Orleans, LA (Eric Candies)

Sea Service	7643708	TB	1975	D	173*	109' 00"	31' 00"	16' 05"

Built: Halter Marine, New Orleans, LA (Sea Star)

Tradewind Service	7612307	TB	1975	D	183*	104' 07"	30' 00"	12' 08"

Built: Bollinger Shipyard Inc., Lockport, LA (New Jersey)

H-6 HORNE TRANSPORTATION LTD., WOLFE ISLAND, ON *(wolfeisland.com/ferry.php)*

William Darrell		CF	1952	D	66*	66' 00"	28' 00"	6' 00"

Built: Harry Gamble, Port Dover, ON

H-7 HUFFMAN EQUIPMENT RENTAL INC., EASTLAKE, OH

Benjamin Ridgway		TW	1969	D	51*	53' 00"	18' 05"	7' 00"
Hamp Thomas		TB	1968	D	22*	43' 00"	13' 00"	4' 00"
Paddy Miles		TB	1934	D	16*	45' 04"	12' 04"	4' 07"

H-8 HURON LADY II INC., PORT HURON, MI *(huronlady.com)*

Huron Lady II		ES	1993	D	82*	65' 00"	19' 00"	10' 00"

Built: Navigator Boat Works (Lady Lumina '93-'99)

H-9 HYDRO-QUEBEC, MONTREAL, QC

R.O. Sweezy		TB	1991	D	29*	41' 09"	14' 00"	5' 07"

Built: Jean Fournier, Quebec City, QC (Citadelle I '91-'92)

I-1 INFINITY AND OVATION YACHT CHARTERS LLC, ST. CLAIR SHORES, MI *(infinityandovation.com)*

Infinity		PA	2001	D	82*	117' 00"	22' 00"	6' 00"
Ovation		PA	2005	D	97*	138' 00"	27' 00"	7' 00"

I-2 INLAND LAKES MANAGEMENT INC., ALPENA, MI

Alpena {2}	5206362	CC	1942	T	13,900	519' 06"	67' 00"	35' 00"

Built: Great Lakes Engineering Works, River Rouge, MI; shortened by 120' and converted to a self-unloading cement carrier at Fraser Shipyards, Superior, WI, in '91 (Leon Fraser '42-'91)

J. A. W. Iglehart	5139179	CC	1936	T	12,500	501' 06"	68' 03"	37' 00"

Built: Sun Shipbuilding and Drydock Co., Chester, PA; converted from a saltwater tanker to a self-unloading cement carrier at American Shipbuilding Co., South Chicago, IL , in '65; last operated Oct. 29, 2006; in use as a cement storage/transfer vessel at Superior, WI (Pan Amoco '36-'55, Amoco '55-'60, H. R. Schemm '60-'65)

Paul H. Townsend	5272050	CC	1945	D	7,850	447' 00"	50' 00"	29' 00"

Built: Consolidated Steel Corp., Wilmington, DE; converted from a saltwater cargo vessel to a self-unloading cement carrier at Bethlehem Steel Co., Shipbuilding Div., Hoboken, NJ, & Calumet Shipyard, Chicago, IL, in '52-'53; lengthened at Great Lakes Engineering Works, Ashtabula, OH, in '58; last operated Dec. 5, 2005; in long-term lay-up at Muskegon, MI (USNS Hickory Coll '45-'46, USNS Coastal Delegate '46-'52)

S. T. Crapo	5304011	CC	1927	B	8,900	402' 06"	60' 03"	29' 00"

Built: Great Lakes Engineering Works, River Rouge, MI; last operated Sept. 4, 1996; in use as a cement storage and transfer vessel at Green Bay, WI

I-3 INLAND SEAS EDUCATION ASSOCIATION, SUTTONS BAY, MI *(schoolship.org)*

Inland Seas		RV	1994	W	41*	61' 06"	17' 00"	7' 00"

Built: Treworgy Yachts, Palm Coast, FL

I-4 INLAND TUG & BARGE LTD., BROCKVILLE, ON

Katanni		TB	1991	D	19*	34' 08"	14' 05"	5' 05"

I-5 INTERLAKE STEAMSHIP CO., MIDDLEBURG HEIGHTS, OH *(interlakesteamship.com)*

Dorothy Ann	8955732	AT/TT	1999	D	1,090*	124' 03"	44' 00"	24' 00"

Built: Bay Shipbuilding Co., Sturgeon Bay, WI; Paired with self-unloading barge Pathfinder

Fleet Name Vessel Name	IMO #	Vessel Type	Year Built	Engine Type	Cargo Cap. or Gross*	Overall Length	Breadth	Depth
Herbert C. Jackson	5148417	SU	1959	T	24,800	690' 00"	75' 00"	37' 06"

Built: Great Lakes Engineering Works, River Rouge, MI; converted to a self-unloader at Defoe Shipbuilding Co., Bay City, MI, in '75

Hon. James L. Oberstar	5322518	SU	1959	D	31,000	806' 00"	75' 00"	37' 06"

Built: American Shipbuilding Co., Lorain, OH; lengthened 96' in '72; converted to a self-unloader in '81 at Fraser Shipyards, Superior, WI (Shenango II '59-'67, Charles M. Beeghly '67-'11)

James R. Barker	7390260	SU	1976	D	63,300	1,004' 00"	105' 00"	50' 00"

Built: American Shipbuilding Co., Lorain, OH

Mesabi Miner	7390272	SU	1977	D	63,300	1,004' 00"	105' 00"	50' 00"

Built: American Shipbuilding Co., Lorain, OH

Pathfinder {3}	5166768	SU	1953	B	10,577	606' 00"	70' 03"	36' 03"

Built: Great Lakes Engineering Works, River Rouge, MI; converted from a powered vessel to a self-unloading barge at Bay Shipbuilding Co., Sturgeon Bay, WI, in '98 (J. L. Mauthe '53-'98)

Paul R. Tregurtha	7729057	SU	1981	D	68,000	1,013' 06"	105' 00"	56' 00"

Built: American Shipbuilding Co., Lorain, OH; this is the largest vessel on the Lakes. (William J. DeLancey '81-'90)

INTERLAKE LEASING III – A SUBSIDIARY OF INTERLAKE STEAMSHIP CO.

Stewart J. Cort	7105495	SU	1972	D	58,000	1,000' 00"	105' 00"	49' 00"

Built: Erie Marine Inc., Erie, PA; built for Bethlhem Steel Corp., this was the Great Lakes' first 1,000-footer

LAKES SHIPPING CO. INC. – A SUBSIDIARY OF INTERLAKE STEAMSHIP CO.

John Sherwin {2}	5174428	BC	1958	D	31,500	806' 00"	75' 00"	37' 06"

Built: American Steamship Co., Lorain, OH; lengthened 96' at Fraser Shipyards, Superior, WI, in '73; last operated Nov. 16, 1981; repowering and conversion to a self-unloader was begun at Bay Shipbuilding Co., Sturgeon Bay, WI, in 2008 but was canceled pending an improvement in the economy; moved to DeTour, MI, Oct. 17, 2009, for continued lay-up

Kaye E. Barker	5097450	SU	1952	D	25,900	767' 00"	70' 00"	36' 00"

Built: American Shipbuilding Co., Toledo, OH; lengthened 120' at Fraser Shipyards, Superior, WI, in '76; converted to a self-unloader at American Shipbuilding Co., Toledo, OH, in '81; repowered in '12 (Edward B. Greene '52-'85, Benson Ford {3} '85-'89)

Lee A. Tregurtha	5385625	SU	1942	D	29,360	826' 00"	75' 00"	39' 00"

Built: Bethlehem Shipbuilding and Drydock Co., Sparrows Point, MD; converted from a saltwater tanker to a Great Lakes bulk carrier in '61; lengthened 96' in '76 and converted to a self-unloader in '78, all at American Shipbuilding Co., Lorain, OH; repowered in '06 (laid down as Mobiloil; launched as Samoset). USS Chiwawa [AO-68] '42-'46, Chiwawa '46-'61, Walter A. Sterling '61-'85, William Clay Ford {2} '85-'89)

I-6	**ISLE ROYALE LINE INC., COPPER HARBOR, MI** *(isleroyale.com)*							
	Isle Royale Queen IV	PA/PK	1980	D	93*	98' 09"	22' 01"	7' 00"

Built: Neuville Boat Works Inc., New Iberia, LA (American Freedom, John Jay, Shuttle V, Danielle G, Harbor Commuter V)

J-1	**J. W. WESTCOTT CO., DETROIT, MI** *(jwwestcott.com)*							
	J. W. Westcott II	MB	1949	D	14*	46' 01"	13' 03"	4' 05"

Built: Paasch Marine Service, Erie, PA; floating post office has its own U.S. ZIP code, 48222

	Joseph J. Hogan	MB	1957	D	16*	40' 00"	12' 05"	5' 00"

Backup mailboat and water taxi for vessels docked at Great Lakes Steel / Zug Island (USCOE Ottawa '57-'95)

J-2	**JEFF FOSTER, SUPERIOR, WI**							
	Sundew	IB	1944	DE	1,025*	180' 00"	37' 05"	17' 04"

Built: Marine Ironworks and Shipbuilding Corp., Duluth, MN; former U.S. Coast Guard cutter WLB-404 was decommissioned in 2004 and turned into a marine museum; vessel was returned to private ownership in 2009

J-3	**JOSEPH B. MARTIN, BEAVER ISLAND, MI**							
	Shamrock	TB	1933	D	60*	64' 00"	18' 00"	7' 03"

Built: Pennsylvania Shipyard Inc., Beaumont, TX

	Tanker II	TK	1964	B	60*	64' 00"	18' 00"	6' 00"

Built: Christy Corp., Sturgeon Bay, WI

J-4	**JUBILEE QUEEN CRUISES, TORONTO, ON** *(jubileequeencruises.ca)*							
	Jubilee Queen	ES	1986	D	269*	122' 00"	23' 09"	5' 05"

(Pioneer Princess III '86-'89)

J-5	**JULIO CONTRACTING CO., HANCOCK, MI**							
	Julio	TB	1941	D	84*	65' 05"	18' 00"	9' 01"
	Winnebago	TW	1945	D	14*	40' 00"	10' 02"	4' 06"

Arthur M. Anderson, with Cason J. Callaway close astern, up at Nine Mile Point on the St. Marys River. (Roger LeLievre)

K

Fleet Name / Vessel Name	IMO #	Vessel Type	Year Built	Engine Type	Cargo Cap. or Gross*	Overall Length	Breadth	Depth
K-1	**KEHOE MARINE CONSTRUCTION CO., LANSDOWNE, ON** *(tiecomarine.com)*							
Houghton		TB	1944	D	15*	45' 00"	13' 00"	6' 00"
Built: Port Houston Iron Works, Houston, TX								
K-2	**KELLEYS ISLAND BOAT LINES, MARBLEHEAD, OH** *(kelleysislandferry.com)*							
Carlee Emily		PA/CF	1987	D	98*	101' 00"	34' 06"	10' 00"
Built: Blount Marine Corp., Warren, RI (Endeavor '87-'02)								
Juliet Alicia		PA/CF	1969	D	95*	88' 03"	33' 00"	6' 08"
Built: Blount Marine Corp., Warren, RI (Kelley Islander)								
Shirley Irene		PA/CF	1991	D	68*	160' 00"	46' 00"	9' 00"
Built: Ocean Group Shipyard, Bayou La Batre, AL								
K-3	**KEWEENAW EXCURSIONS INC., CHARLEVOIX, MI** *(keweenawexcursions.com)*							
Keweenaw Star	631711	ES	1981	D	97*	110' 00"	23' 04"	6' 03"
Built: Camcraft Inc., Crown Point, LA (Atlantic Star, Privateer, De De Bruce)								
K-4	**KINDRA LAKE TOWING LP, CHICAGO, IL** *(kindralake.com)*							
Buckley		TW	1958	D	94*	95' 00"	26' 00"	11' 00"
Built: Parker Bros. Shipyard, Houston, TX (Linda Brooks '58-'67, Eddie B. {2} '67-'95)								
Donald C.	8841967	TB	1962	D	198*	91' 00"	29' 00"	11' 06"
Built: Main Iron Works Inc., Houma, LA (Donald C. Hannah '62-'09)								
Ellie		TB	1970	D	29*	39' 07"	16' 00"	4' 06"
Built: Big River Shipbuilding Inc., Vicksburg, MS (Miss Bissy '09)								
Morgan		TB	1974	D	134*	90' 00"	30' 00"	10' 06"
Built: Peterson Builders Inc., Sturgeon Bay, WI (Donald O'Toole '74-'86, Bonesey B. '86-'95)								
Old Mission		TB	1945	D	94*	85' 00"	23' 00"	10' 04"
Built: Sturgeon Bay Shipbuilding, Sturgeon Bay, WI (U. S. Army ST-880 '45-'47, USCOE Avondale '47-'64, Adrienne B. '64-'95)								
K-5	**KING CO. (THE), HOLLAND, MI** *(kingco.us)*							
Barry J		TB	1943	D	26*	46' 00"	13' 00"	7' 00"
Built: Sturgeon Bay Shipbuilding & Dry Dock Co., Sturgeon Bay, WI								
Buxton II		DR	1976	B	147*	130' 02"	28' 01"	7' 00"
Built: Barbour Boat Works Inc., Holland, MI								
Carol Ann		TB	1981	D	86*	61' 05"	24' 00"	8' 07"
Built: Rodriguez Boat Builders, Bayou La Batre, AL								
John Henry		TB	1954	D	66*	65' 04"	19' 04"	9' 06"
Built: Missouri Valley Steel, Leavenworth, KS (U. S. Army ST-2013 '54-'80)								
Julie Dee		TB	1937	D	64*	68' 08"	18' 01"	7' 06"
Built: Herbert Slade, Beaumont, TX (Dernier, Jerry O'Day, Cindy B)								
Matt Allen		TB	1961	D	146*	80' 04"	24' 00"	11' 03"
Built: Nolty Theriot Inc., Golden Meadow, LA (Gladys Bea '61-'73, American Viking '73-'83, Maribeth Andrie '83-'05)								
Miss Edna		TB	1935	D	13*	36' 08"	11' 02"	4' 08"
Built: Levingston Shipbuilding, Orange, TX								
K-6	**KINGSTON 1,000 ISLANDS CRUISES, KINGSTON, ON** *(1000islandcruises.on.ca)*							
Island Belle I		ES	1988	D	150*	65' 00"	22' 00"	8' 00"
Built: Kettle Creek Boat Works, Port Stanley, ON (Spirit of Brockville '88-'91)								
Island Queen III		ES	1975	D	300*	96' 00"	26' 00"	11' 00"
Built: Marlin Yachts Co. (1974) Ltd., Summerstown, ON								
Papoose III		ES	1968	D	110*	64' 08"	23' 03"	7' 03"
Built: Hike Metal Products Ltd., Wheatley, ON (Peche Island II)								
K-7	**KK INTEGRATED LOGISTICS, MENOMINEE, MI** *(kkwarehousing.com/shipping.html)*							
William H. Donner		CS	1914	B	9,400	524' 00"	54' 00"	30' 00"
Built: Great Lakes Engineering Works, Ashtabula, OH; last operated in 1969; in use as a cargo transfer hull at Marinette, WI								
L-1	**LAFARGE CANADA INC., POINTE-CLAIRE, QC**							
	THE FOLLOWING VESSEL MANAGED BY CANADA STEAMSHIP LINES INC.							
English River	5104382	CC	1961	D	7,450	404' 03"	60' 00"	36' 06"
Built: Canadian Shipbuilding and Engineering Ltd., Collingwood, ON; converted to a self-unloading cement carrier by Port Arthur Shipbuilding, Port Arthur (now Thunder Bay), ON, in '74								
L-2	**LAFARGE NORTH AMERICA INC., BINGHAM FARMS, MI** *(lafargenorthamerica.com)*							
J. B. Ford		CC	1904	R	8,000	440' 00"	50' 00"	28' 00"
Built: American Shipbuilding Co., Lorain, OH; converted to a self-unloading cement carrier in '59; last								

| Fleet Name
Vessel Name | IMO # | Vessel
Type | Year
Built | Engine
Type | Cargo Cap.
or Gross* | Overall
Length | Breadth | Depth |

L

operated Nov. 15, 1985; most recently used as a cement storage and transfer vessel at Superior, WI, and now laid up at that port (Edwin F. Holmes '04-'16, E. C. Collins '16-'59)

THE FOLLOWING VESSELS MANAGED BY ANDRIE INC., MUSKEGON, MI (andrie.com)

Fleet Name / Vessel Name	IMO #	Vessel Type	Year Built	Engine Type	Cargo Cap. or Gross*	Overall Length	Breadth	Depth
G. L. Ostrander	7501106	AT	1976	D	198*	140' 02"	40' 01"	22' 03"

Built: Halter Marine, New Orleans, LA; paired with barge Integrity (Andrew Martin '76-'90, Robert L. Torres '90-'94, Jacklyn M '94-'04)

Fleet Name / Vessel Name	IMO #	Vessel Type	Year Built	Engine Type	Cargo Cap. or Gross*	Overall Length	Breadth	Depth
Innovation	9082336	CC	2006	B	7,320*	460' 00"	70' 00"	37' 00"

Built: Bay Shipbuilding Co., Sturgeon Bay, WI

Fleet Name / Vessel Name	IMO #	Vessel Type	Year Built	Engine Type	Cargo Cap. or Gross*	Overall Length	Breadth	Depth
Integrity	8637213	CC	1996	B	14,000	460' 00"	70' 00"	37' 00"

Built: Bay Shipbuilding Co., Sturgeon Bay, WI

Fleet Name / Vessel Name	IMO #	Vessel Type	Year Built	Engine Type	Cargo Cap. or Gross*	Overall Length	Breadth	Depth
Samuel de Champlain	7433799	AT	1975	D	299*	140' 02"	39' 02"	20' 00"

Built: Mangone Shipbuilding, Houston, TX; paired with barge Innovation (Musketeer Fury '75-'78, Tender Panther '78-'79, Margarita '79-'83, Vortice '83-'99, Norfolk '99-'06)

L-3 LAKE ERIE ISLAND CRUISES LLC, SANDUSKY, OH (goodtimeboat.com)

Fleet Name / Vessel Name	IMO #	Vessel Type	Year Built	Engine Type	Cargo Cap. or Gross*	Overall Length	Breadth	Depth
Goodtime I		ES	1960	D	81*	111' 00"	29' 08"	9' 05"

Built: Blount Marine Corp., Warren, RI

L-4 LAKE EXPRESS LLC, MILWAUKEE, WI (lake-express.com)

Fleet Name / Vessel Name	IMO #	Vessel Type	Year Built	Engine Type	Cargo Cap. or Gross*	Overall Length	Breadth	Depth
Lake Express	9329253	PA/CF	2004	D	96*	179' 02"	57' 07"	16' 00"

Built: Austal USA, Mobile, AL; high-speed ferry service from Milwaukee, WI, to Muskegon, MI; capacity is 250 passengers, 46 autos

L-5 LAKE MICHIGAN CARFERRY SERVICE INC., LUDINGTON, MI (ssbadger.com)

Fleet Name / Vessel Name	IMO #	Vessel Type	Year Built	Engine Type	Cargo Cap. or Gross*	Overall Length	Breadth	Depth
Badger	5033583	PA/CF	1953	S	4,244*	410' 06"	59' 06"	24' 00"

Built: Christy Corp., Sturgeon Bay, WI; traditional ferry service from Ludington, MI, to Manitowoc, WI; capacity is 520 passengers, 180 autos; vessel is the last coal-fired steamship on the Great Lakes

Fleet Name / Vessel Name	IMO #	Vessel Type	Year Built	Engine Type	Cargo Cap. or Gross*	Overall Length	Breadth	Depth
Spartan		PA/CF	1952	S	4,244*	410' 06"	59' 06"	24' 00"

Built: Christy Corp., Sturgeon Bay, WI; last operated Jan. 20, 1979; in long-term lay-up at Ludington, MI

L-6 LAKES PILOTS ASSOCIATION, PORT HURON, MI (lakespilots.com)

Fleet Name / Vessel Name	IMO #	Vessel Type	Year Built	Engine Type	Cargo Cap. or Gross*	Overall Length	Breadth	Depth
Huron Belle		PB	1979	D	38*	50' 00"	15' 07"	7' 09"

Built: Gladding-Hearn Shipbuilding, Somerset, MA; vessel offers pilot service at Port Huron, MI

Fleet Name / Vessel Name	IMO #	Vessel Type	Year Built	Engine Type	Cargo Cap. or Gross*	Overall Length	Breadth	Depth
Huron Maid		PB	1977	D	26*	46' 00"	12' 05"	3' 05"

Built: Hans Hansen Welding Co., Toledo, OH; vessel offers pilot service at Detroit, MI

L-7 LE GROUPE OCÉAN INC., QUÉBEC, QC (groupocean.com)

Fleet Name / Vessel Name	IMO #	Vessel Type	Year Built	Engine Type	Cargo Cap. or Gross*	Overall Length	Breadth	Depth
Basse-Cote	8644620	DB	1932	B	400	201' 00"	40' 00"	12' 00"

Built: Department of Marine and Fisheries Government Shipyard, Sorel, QC (Louis D. '32-'93)

Fleet Name / Vessel Name	IMO #	Vessel Type	Year Built	Engine Type	Cargo Cap. or Gross*	Overall Length	Breadth	Depth
Betsiamites	8644632	SU	1969	B	11,600	402' 00"	75' 00"	24' 00"

Built: Port Weller Dry Docks Ltd., St. Catharines, ON

Fleet Name / Vessel Name	IMO #	Vessel Type	Year Built	Engine Type	Cargo Cap. or Gross*	Overall Length	Breadth	Depth
Jerry G.	8959788	TB	1960	D	202*	91' 06"	27' 03"	12' 06"

Built: Davie Shipbuilding Co., Lauzon, QC

Fleet Name / Vessel Name	IMO #	Vessel Type	Year Built	Engine Type	Cargo Cap. or Gross*	Overall Length	Breadth	Depth
La Prairie	7393585	TB	1975	D	110*	73' 09"	25' 09"	11' 08"

Built: Georgetown Shipyard, Georgetown, PEI

Fleet Name / Vessel Name	IMO #	Vessel Type	Year Built	Engine Type	Cargo Cap. or Gross*	Overall Length	Breadth	Depth
Lac St-Francois		BC	1979	B	1,200	195' 00"	35' 00"	12' 00"

Built: Nashville Bridge Co., Nashhville, TN (TCF 505)

Fleet Name / Vessel Name	IMO #	Vessel Type	Year Built	Engine Type	Cargo Cap. or Gross*	Overall Length	Breadth	Depth
Le Phil D.		TB	1961	D	38*	56' 01"	16' 00"	5' 08"
Navcomar No. 1		DB	1955	B	402*	135' 00"	35' 00"	9' 00"

Built: Sincennes-McNaughton Line Ltd., Montreal, QC (McAllister No. 1 '55-'92)

Fleet Name / Vessel Name	IMO #	Vessel Type	Year Built	Engine Type	Cargo Cap. or Gross*	Overall Length	Breadth	Depth
Océan Abys	8644644	DB	1948	B	1,000	140' 00"	40' 00"	9' 00"

Built: Marine Industries Ltd., Sorel, QC (Omni No. 1 '48-'94)

Fleet Name / Vessel Name	IMO #	Vessel Type	Year Built	Engine Type	Cargo Cap. or Gross*	Overall Length	Breadth	Depth
Océan A. Simard	8000056	TT	1980	D	286*	92' 00"	34' 00"	13' 07"

Built: Georgetown Shipyards Ltd., Georgetown, PEI (Alexis-Simard '80-'11)

Fleet Name / Vessel Name	IMO #	Vessel Type	Year Built	Engine Type	Cargo Cap. or Gross*	Overall Length	Breadth	Depth
Océan Bertrand Jeansonne	9521526	TB	2008	D	402*	94' 05"	36' 05"	17' 02"

Built: East Isle Shipyard, Georgetown, PEI

Fleet Name / Vessel Name	IMO #	Vessel Type	Year Built	Engine Type	Cargo Cap. or Gross*	Overall Length	Breadth	Depth
Océan Bravo	7025279	TB	1970	D	320*	110' 00"	28' 06"	17' 00"

Built: Davie Shipbuilding Co., Lauzon, QC (Takis V. '70-'80, Donald P '80-'80, Nimue '80-'83, Donald P. '83-'98)

Fleet Name / Vessel Name	IMO #	Vessel Type	Year Built	Engine Type	Cargo Cap. or Gross*	Overall Length	Breadth	Depth
Océan Delta	7235707	TB	1973	D	722*	136' 08"	35' 08"	22' 00"

Built: Ulstein Mek. Verksted A.S., Ulsteinvik, Norway (Sistella '73-'78, Sandy Cape '78-'80, Captain Ioannis S. '80-'99)

Fleet Name / Vessel Name	IMO #	Vessel Type	Year Built	Engine Type	Cargo Cap. or Gross*	Overall Length	Breadth	Depth
Océan Express		PB	1999	D	29*	47' 02"	14' 00"	7' 05"

Built: Industries Ocean Inc., Charlevoix, QC (H-2000 '99-'00)

Fleet Name / Vessel Name	IMO #	Vessel Type	Year Built	Engine Type	Cargo Cap. or Gross*	Overall Length	Breadth	Depth
Océan Georgie Bain	9553892	TB	2009	D	204*	75' 02"	29' 09"	12' 09"

Built: Industries Ocean Inc., Ile-Aux-Coudres, QC

Fleet Name / Vessel Name	IMO #	Vessel Type	Year Built	Engine Type	Cargo Cap. or Gross*	Overall Length	Breadth	Depth
Océan Golf	5146354	TB	1959	D	159*	103' 00"	25' 10"	11' 09"
Built: P.K. Harris & Sons, Appledore, England (Launched as Stranton. Helen M. McAllister '59–'97)								
Océan Henry Bain	9420916	TB	2006	D	402*	94' 08"	30' 01"	14' 09"
Built: East Isle Shipyard, Georgetown, PEI								
Océan Hercule	7525346	TB	1976	D	448*	120' 00"	32' 00"	19' 00"
(Stril Pilot '76–'81, Spirit Sky '81–'86, Ireland '86–'89, Irelandia '89–'95, Charles Antoine '95–'97)								
Océan Intrepide	9203423	TT	1998	D	302*	80' 00"	30' 01"	14' 09"
Built: Industries Ocean Inc., Ile-Aux-Coudres, QC								
Océan Jupiter {2}	9220160	TT	1999	D	302*	80' 00"	30' 00"	13' 04"
Built: Industries Ocean Inc., Ile-Aux-Coudres, QC								
Océan K. Rusby	9345556	TB	2005	D	402*	94' 08"	30' 01"	14' 09"
Built: East Isle Shipyard, Georgetown, PEI								
Océan Lima		TB	1977	D	15*	34' 02"	11' 08"	4' 00"
(VM/S St. Louis III '77–'10)								
Océan Raymond Lemay	9420904	TB	2006	D	402*	94' 08"	30' 01"	14' 09"
Built: East Isle Shipyard, Georgetown, PEI								
Océan Ross Gaudreault	9542221	TB	2011	D	402*	94' 04"	36' 05"	17' 00"
Built: East Isle Shipyard, Georgetown, PEI								
Océan Serge Genois	9553907	TB	2010	D	204*	75' 01"	30' 01"	12' 09"
Built: Industries Ocean Inc., Ile-Aux-Coudres, QC								
Océan Traverse Nord	9666534	DR	2012	B	1,165*	210' 00"	42' 03"	14' 07"
Built: Industries Ocean Inc., Ile-Aux-Coudres, QC								
Océan Yvan Desgagnés	9542207	TB	2010	D	402*	94' 04"	36' 05"	17' 00"
Built: East Isle Shipyard, Georgetown, PEI								
Omni-Atlas	8644668	CS	1913	B	479*	133' 00"	42' 00"	10' 00"
Built: Sir William Arrol & Co. Ltd., Glasgow, Scotland								
Omni-Richelieu	6923084	TB	1969	D	144*	83' 00"	24' 06"	13' 06"
Built: Pictou Industries Ltd., Pictou, NS (Port Alfred II '69–'82)								
Rapide Blanc		TB	1951	D	10*	34' 00"	10' 00"	4' 03"
Roxane D		TB	1945	D	50*	60' 06"	16' 06"	6' 07"
Service Boat No. 2		TB	1934	D	78*	65' 02"	17' 00"	8' 01"

L-8 OCÉAN REMORQUAGE TROIS-RIVIÈRES INC. – SUBSIDIARY OF OCÉAN GROUPE INC.

Andre H.	5404172	TB	1963	D	317*	126' 00"	28' 06"	12' 10"
Built: Davie Shipbuilding Co., Lauzon, QC (Foundation Valiant '63–'73, Point Valiant {1} '73–'95)								
Avantage	6828882	TB	1969	D	362*	116' 10"	32' 09"	16' 03"
Built: J. Boel En Zonen, Temse, Belgium (Sea Lion '69–'97)								

Algoway (left) and St. Clair pass downtown Chicago. (Roger LeLievre)

Fleet Name Vessel Name	IMO #	Vessel Type	Year Built	Engine Type	Cargo Cap. or Gross*	Overall Length	Breadth	Depth
Duga	7530030	TB	1977	D	382*	114' 02"	32' 10"	16' 05"

Built: Langsten Slip & Båtbyggeri A/S, Lanste, Norway

Escorte		TT	1964	D	120*	85' 00"	23' 07"	7' 05"

Built: Jakobson Shipyard, Oyster Bay, NY (USS Menasha [YTB / YTM-773, YTM-761] '64-'92, Menasha {1} '92-'95)

Josee H.		PB	1961	D	66*	63' 50"	16' 02"	9' 50"

Built: Ferguson Industries Ltd., Pictou, NS (Le Bic '61-'98)

Océan Charlie	7312024	TB	1973	D	448*	123' 02"	31' 07"	16' 01"

Built: Davie Shipbuilding Co., Lauzon, QC (Leonard W. '73-'98)

Océan Echo II	6913091	AT	1969	D	438*	104' 08"	34' 05"	18' 00"

Built: Port Weller Dry Docks, Port Weller, ON (Atlantic '69-'75, Laval '75-'96)

Océan Foxtrot	7101619	TB	1971	D	700*	170' 10"	38' 09"	11' 11"

Built: Cochrane & Sons Ltd., Selby, England (Polar Shore '71-'77, Canmar Supplier VII '77-'95)

R. F. Grant		TB	1934	D	78*	71' 00"	17' 00"	8' 00"

Built: Canadian Vickers Ltd., Montreal, QC

Service Boat No. 1		PB	1965	D	55*	57' 08"	16' 01"	7' 06"

Built: Three Rivers Boatmen Ltd., St. Antoine de Tilly, QC

Service Boat No. 4		PB	1959	D	26*	39' 01"	14' 02"	6' 03"

Built: Three Rivers Boatmen Ltd., St. Antoine de Tilly, QC

L-9   LOWER LAKES TOWING LTD., PORT DOVER, ON (randlogisticsinc.com)

Cuyahoga	5166392	SU	1943	D	15,675	620' 00"	60' 00"	35' 00"

Built: American Shipbuilding Co., Lorain, OH; converted to a self-unloader by Manitowoc Shipbuilding Co., Manitowoc, WI, in '74; repowered in '01 (J. Burton Ayers '43-'95)

Kaministiqua	8119285	BC	1983	D	34,500	730' 01"	75' 09"	48' 00"

Built: Govan Shipyards, Glasgow, Scotland (Saskatchewan Pioneer '83-'95, Lady Hamilton '95-'06, Voyageur Pioneer '06-'08)

Manitoba {3}	6702301	BC	1967	D	19,093	607' 09"	62' 00"	36' 00"

Built: Collingwood Shipyards, Collingwood, ON (Mantadoc '67-'02, Teakglen '02-'05, Maritime Trader '05-'11)

Michipicoten {2}	5102865	SU	1952	D	22,300	698' 00"	70' 00"	37' 00"

Built: Bethlehem Shipbuilding & Drydock Co., Sparrows Point, MD; lengthened 72' by American Shipbuilding Co., S. Chicago, IL, in '57; converted to a self-unloader by American Shipbuilding Co., Toledo, OH, in '80; repowered in '11 (Elton Hoyt 2nd '52-'03)

Mississagi	5128467	SU	1943	D	15,800	620' 06"	60' 00"	35' 00"

Built: Great Lakes Engineering Works, River Rouge, MI; converted to a self-unloader by Fraser Shipyards, Superior, WI, in '67; repowered in '85 (Hill Annex '43-'43, George A. Sloan '43-'01)

Ojibway	5105831	BC	1952	D	20,668	642' 03"	67' 00"	35' 00"

Built: Defoe Shipbuilding Co., Bay City, MI; repowered in '05 (Charles L. Hutchinson {3} '52-'62, Ernest R. Breech '62-'88, Kinsman Independent '88-'05, Voyageur Independent '05-'08)

Frontenac at sunset on the St. Marys River. (Cathy Kohring)

Saginaw heads for the dock at dusk. (Lee Rowe)

Fleet Name / Vessel Name	IMO #	Vessel Type	Year Built	Engine Type	Cargo Cap. or Gross+	Overall Length	Breadth	Depth
Robert S. Pierson	7366403	SU	1974	D	19,650	630' 00"	68' 00"	36' 11"

Built: American Shipbuilding Co., Lorain, OH (Wolverine {2} '74-'08)

Saginaw {3}	5173876	SU	1953	D	20,200	639' 03"	72' 00"	36' 00"

Built: Manitowoc Shipbuilding Co., Manitowoc, WI, repowered in '08 (John J. Boland {3} '53-'99)

Tecumseh {2}	7225855	BC	1973	D	29,510	641' 00"	78' 00"	45' 03

Built: Lockheed Shipbuilding & Construction Co., Seattle, WA (Sugar Islander '73-'96, Islander '96-'96, Judy Litrico '96-'06, Tina Litrico '06-'11)

L-10   LOWER LAKES TRANSPORTATION CO., WILLIAMSVILLE, NY – DIV. OF LOWER LAKES TOWING LTD.

GRAND RIVER NAVIGATION CO., AVON LAKE, OH – OWNER – AN AFFILIATE OF LOWER LAKES TOWING LTD.

Ashtabula		SU	1982	B	17,982	610' 01"	78' 01"	49' 08"

Built: Bay Shipbuilding Co., Sturgeon Bay, WI (Mary Turner '82-'12)

Calumet {3}	7329314	SU	1973	D	19,650	630' 00"	68' 00"	36' 11"

Built: American Shipbuilding Co., Lorain, OH (William R. Roesch '73-'95, David Z. Norton {3} '95-'07, David Z. '07-'08)

CTC No. 1		CC	1943	R	16,300	620' 06"	60' 00"	35' 00"

Built: Great Lakes Engineering Works, River Rouge, MI; last operated Nov. 12, 1981; former cement storage/transfer vessel is laid up at South Chicago, IL; scheduled to be returned to service at a future date (Launched as McIntyre. Frank Purnell {1} '43-'64, Steelton {3} '64-'78, Hull No. 3 '78-'79, Pioneer {4} '79-'82)

Defiance	8109761	ATB	1982	D	196*	145' 01"	44' 00"	21' 00

Built: Marinette Marine Corp., Marinette, WI; paired with barge Ashtabula (April T. Beker '82-'87, Beverly Anderson '82-'12)

Invincible	7723819	ATB	1979	D	180*	100' 00"	35' 00"	22' 06"

Built: Atlantic Marine Inc., Fort George Island, FL; paired with barge McKee Sons (R. W. Sesler '79-'91)

James L. Kuber	5293341	SU	1953	B	25,500	703' 08"	70' 00"	36' 00"

Built: Great Lakes Engineering Works, River Rouge, MI; lengthened 120' by Fraser Shipyards, Superior, WI, in '75; converted to a self-unloader by Bay Shipbuilding, Sturgeon Bay, WI, in '83; converted to a barge by the owners in '07 (Reserve '53-'08)

Lewis J. Kuber	5336351	SU	1952	B	22,300	616' 10"	70' 00"	37' 00"

Built: Bethlehem Steel Corp., Sparrows Point, MD; lengthened 72' by American Shipbuilding, South Chicago, IL, in '58; converted to a self-unloader by Fraser Shipyards, Superior, WI, in '80; converted to a barge by Erie Shipbuilding, Erie, PA, in '06; (Sparrows Point '52-'90, Buckeye {3} '90-'06)

Manistee	5294307	SU	1943	D	14,900	620' 06"	60' 03"	35' 00"

Built: Great Lakes Engineering Works, River Rouge, MI; converted to a self-unloader by Manitowoc Shipbuilding Co., Manitowoc, WI, in '64; repowered in '76 (Launched as Adirondack. Richard J. Reiss {2} '43-'86, Richard Reiss '86-'05)

Manitowoc	7366398	SU	1973	D	19,650	630' 00"	68' 00"	36' 11"

Built: American Shipbuilding Co., Lorain, OH (Paul Thayer '73-'95, Earl W. Oglebay '95-'07, Earl W. '07-'08)

McKee Sons	5216458	SU	1945	B	19,900	579' 02"	71' 06"	38' 06"

Built: Sun Shipbuilding and Drydock Co., Chester, PA; converted from saltwater vessel to a self-unloading Great Lakes bulk carrier by Maryland Drydock, Baltimore, MD, in '52; completed as a self-unloader by Manitowoc Shipbuilding Co., Manitowoc, WI, in '53; engine removed and converted to a self-unloading barge by Upper Lakes Towing, Escanaba, MI, in '91; owned by Sand Products Corp., Muskegon, MI (USNS Marine Angel '45-'52)

Olive L. Moore	8635227	AT	1928	D	524*	125' 00"	39' 02"	13' 09"

Built: Manitowoc Shipbuilding Co., Manitowoc, WI; paired with barge Lewis J. Kuber (John F. Cushing '28-'66, James E. Skelly '66-'66)

Victory	8003292	TB	1980	D	194*	140' 00"	43' 01"	18' 00"

Built: McDermott Shipyard Inc., Amelia, LA; paired with barge James L. Kuber

L-11   LUEDTKE ENGINEERING CO., FRANKFORT, MI (luedtke-eng.com)

Alan K. Luedtke		TB	1944	D	149*	86' 04"	23' 00"	10' 03"

Built: Allen Boat Co., Harvey, LA (U. S. Army ST-527 '44-'55, USCOE Two Rivers '55-'90)

Ann Marie		TB	1954	D	81*	71' 00"	19' 05"	9' 06"

Built: Smith Basin & Drydock, Pensacola, FL (ST-9684 '54- '80, Lewis Castle '80-'97, Apache '97-'01)

Chris E. Luedtke		TB	1936	D	18*	42' 05"	11' 09"	5' 00"
Erich R. Luedtke		TB	1939	D	18*	42' 05"	11' 09"	5' 00"
Gretchen B		TB	1943	D	18*	41' 09"	12' 05"	6' 00"
Karl E. Luedtke		TB	1928	D	32*	55' 02"	14' 09"	6' 00"

Buit: Leathem D. Smith Dock Co., Sturgeon Bay, WI

Krista S		TB	1954	D	93*	67' 09"	20' 01"	7' 07"

Built: Pascagoula, MS (Sea Wolf '54-'01, Jimmy Wray '01-'08)

Kurt R. Luedtke		TB	1956	D	95*	72' 00"	22' 06"	7' 06"

Built: Lockport Shipyard, Lockport, LA (Jere C. '56-'90)

Fleet Name / Vessel Name	IMO #	Vessel Type	Year Built	Engine Type	Cargo Cap. or Gross*	Overall Length	Breadth	Depth
M-1	**MCM MARINE INC., SAULT STE. MARIE, MI** (mcmmarine.com)							
Beaver State		TB	1935	D	18*	43' 07"	12' 00"	5' 02"
Drummond Islander II		TB	1961	D	97*	65' 00"	36' 00"	9' 00"
Built: Marinette Marine Corp., Marinette, WI								
Mohawk		TB	1945	D	46*	65' 00"	19' 00"	10' 06"
No. 55		DR	1927	DE	721*	165' 00"	42' 08"	12' 00"
No. 56		DS	1928	DE	1,174*	165' 00"	42' 04"	15' 07"
Sioux		DS	1954	B	504*	120' 00"	50' 00"	10' 00"
William C. Gaynor	8423818	TB	1956	D	187*	94' 00"	27' 00"	11' 09"
Built: Defoe Shipbuilding Co., Bay City, MI (William C. Gaynor '56-'88, Captain Barnaby '88-'02)								
M-2	**MacDONALD MARINE LTD., GODERICH, ON** (mactug.com)							
Debbie Lyn		TB	1950	D	10*	45' 00"	14' 00"	10' 00"
Built: Mathieson Boat Works, Goderich, ON (Skipper '50-'60)								
Donald Bert		TB	1953	D	11*	45' 00"	14' 00"	10' 00"
Built: Mathieson Boat Works, Goderich, ON								
Dover		TB	1931	D	70*	84' 00"	17' 00"	6' 00"
Built: Canadian Mead-Morrison Co. Ltd., Welland, ON (Earleejune, Iveyrose)								
Ian Mac		TB	1955	D	12*	45' 00"	14' 00"	10' 00"
Built: Mathieson Boat Works, Goderich, ON								
M-3	**MADELINE ISLAND FERRY LINE INC., LaPOINTE, WI** (madferry.com)							
Bayfield {2}		PA/CF	1952	D	83*	120' 00"	43' 00"	10' 00"
Built: Chesapeake Marine Railway, Deltaville, VA (Charlotte '52-'99)								
Island Queen {2}		PA/CF	1966	D	90*	75' 00"	34' 09"	10' 00"
Madeline		PA/CF	1984	D	94*	90' 00"	35' 00"	8' 00"
Nichevo II		PA/CF	1962	D	89*	65' 00"	32' 00"	8' 09"
M-4	**MALCOLM MARINE, ST. CLAIR, MI** (malcolmmarine.com)							
Debbie Lee		TB	1955	D	13*	32' 00"	11' 00"	4' 04"
Manitou {2}		TB	1942	D	199*	110' 00"	26' 02"	15' 06"
Built: U.S. Coast Guard, Curtis Bay, MD (USCGC Manitou [WYT-60] '43-'84)								
M-5	**MAMMOET-MCKEIL LTD., AYR, ON**							
MM Newfoundland		DB	2011	B	2,165*	249' 06"	72' 00"	16' 01"
Built: Signal International, Pascagoula, MS								
M-6	**MANITOU ISLAND TRANSIT, LELAND, MI** (leelanau.com/manitou)							
Manitou Isle		PA/PK	1946	D	39*	52' 00"	14' 00"	8' 00"
(Namaycush '46-'59)								
Mishe Mokwa		PA/CF	1966	D	49*	65' 00"	17' 06"	8' 00"
M-7	**MARINE RECYCLING CORP., PORT COLBORNE & PORT MAITLAND, ON** (marinerecycling.ca)							
Condarrell	5083605	DH	1953	D	3,017	259' 00"	43' 06"	21' 00"
Built: Canadian Shipbuilding & Engineering, Kingston, ON; in long-term lay-up at Port Maitland, ON (D. C. Everest '53-'81)								
Maumee	5057709	SU	1929	D	12,650	604' 09"	60' 00"	32' 00"
Built: American Shipbuilding Co., Lorain, OH; converted to a self-unloader by Manitowoc Shipbuilding Co., Manitowoc, WI, in '61; repowered in '64; scrapping underway at Port Colborne, ON (William G. Clyde '29-'61, Calcite II '61-'01)								
Provmar Terminal II	5159600	TK	1948	B	6,832	408' 08"	53' 00"	26' 00"
Built: Collingwood Shipyards, Collingwood, ON; last operated in 1986; most recently used as a fuel storage barge at Hamilton, ON; awaiting scrapping at Port Colborne, ON (Imperial Sarnia {2} '48-'89)								
M-8	**MARINE TECH LLC, DULUTH, MN** (marinetechduluth.com)							
Callie M.		TB	1910	D	51*	64' 03"	16' 09"	8' 06"
Built: Houma Shipbuilding Co., Houma, LA (Chattanooga '10-'79, Howard T. Hagen '79-'94, Nancy Ann '94-'01)								
Dean R. Smith		DR	1985	B	338*	120' 00"	48' 00"	7' 00"
(No. 2 '85-'94, B. Yetter '94-'01)								
Miss Laura		TB	1943	D	146*	81' 01"	24' 00"	9' 10"
Built: Lawley & Son Corp., Neponset, MA (DPC-3 '43-'46, DS-43 '46-'50, Fresh Kills '50-'69, Richard K. '69-'93, Leopard '93-'03)								
M-9	**MARIPOSA CRUISE LINE LTD., TORONTO, ON** (mariposacruises.com)							
Capt. Matthew Flinders	8883355	ES	1982	D	746*	144' 00"	40' 00"	8' 06"
Built: North Arm Slipway Pty. Ltd., Port Adelaide, Australia								
Mariposa Belle		ES	1970	D	195*	93' 00"	23' 00"	8' 00"
Built: Hike Metal Products, Wheatley, ON (Niagara Belle '70-'73)								
Northern Spirit I	8870073	ES	1983	D	489*	136' 00"	31' 00"	9' 00"
Built: Blount Marine Corp., Warren, RI (New Spirit '83-'89, Pride of Toronto '89-'92)								

Fleet Name / Vessel Name	IMO #	Vessel Type	Year Built	Engine Type	Cargo Cap. or Gross*	Overall Length	Breadth	Depth
Oriole	8800054	ES	1987	D	200*	75' 00"	23' 00"	9' 00"
Built: Duratug Shipyard Fabricating Ltd., Port Dover, ON								
Rosemary		ES	1960	D	52*	68' 00"	15' 06"	6' 08"
Built: Bender Ship Repairs, Mobile, AL								
Showboat Royal Grace		ES	1988	D	135*	62' 00"	18' 00"	4' 00"
Built: Herb Fraser & Associates Ltd., Port Colborne, ON								

M-10   MAXIMUS CORP., BLOOMFIELD HILLS, MI (boblosteamers.com)

Ste. Claire		PA	1910	R	870*	197' 00"	65' 00"	14' 00"
Built: Toledo Ship Building Co., Toledo, OH; former Detroit to Bob-Lo Island passenger steamer last operated Sept. 2, 1991; undergoing restoration at Detroit, MI								

M-11   McASPHALT MARINE TRANSPORTATION LTD., SCARBOROUGH, ON (mcasphalt.com)

Everlast	7527332	ATB	1976	D	1,361*	143' 04"	44' 04"	21' 04"
Built: Hakodate Dock Co., Hakodate, Japan; paired with barge Norman McLeod (Bilibino '77-'96)								
John J. Carrick	9473444	TK	2008	B	11,613	407' 06"	71' 07"	30' 00"
Built: Penglai Bohai Shipyard Co. Ltd., Penglai, China								
McAsphalt 401	8970768	TK	1966	B	7,399	300' 00"	60' 00"	23' 00"
Built: Todd Shipyards Corp., Houston, TX (Pittson 200 '66-'73, Pointe Levy '73-'87)								
Norman McLeod	8636219	TK	2001	B	6,809*	379' 02"	71' 06"	30' 00"
Built: Jinling Shipyard, Nanjing, China								
Victorious	9473262	ATB	2009	D	1,299	122' 00"	44' 03"	26' 02
Built: Penglai Bohai Shipyard Co. Ltd., Penglai, China; paired with barge John J. Carrick								

M-12   McKEIL MARINE LTD., HAMILTON, ON (mckeilmarine.com)

AGS-359	8636257	DH	1966	B	1,500	187' 00"	35' 00"	11' 00"
Built: Dravo Corp., Neville Island, PA								
Alouette Spirit	8641537	DB	1969	B	10,087*	425' 02"	74' 01"	29' 00"
Built: Gulfport Shipbuilding Co., Port Arthur, TX (KTC 135 '69-'04, Lambert's Spirit '04-'05)								
Blain M	7907099	RV	1981	D	925*	138' 02"	35' 09"	20' 08"
Built: Ferguson Industries, Picton, ON (Wilfred Templeman '81-'11)								
Bonnie B III		TB	1969	D	308*	107' 00"	32' 00"	18' 00"
(Esso Oranjestad '69-'85, Oranjestad '85-'86, San Nicolas '86-'87, San Nicolas I '87-'88)								
Carrol C. 1		TB	1969	D	307*	107' 00"	32' 00"	18' 00"
Built: Gulfport Shipbuilding Corp., Port Arthur, TX (Esso San Nicolas '69-'86, San Nicolas '86-'87, Carrol C '87-'88)								
Erie-West		DB	1951	B	1,800	290' 00"	50' 00"	12' 00"
Built: Dravo Corp., Pittsburgh, PA Dover Light)								
Evans McKeil	8983416	TB	1936	D	284*	110' 00"	25' 06"	14' 07"
Built: Panama Canal Co., Balboa, Panama (Alhajuela '36-'70, Barbara Ann {2} '70-'89)								
Florence M.	5118797	TB	1961	D	236*	96' 03"	29' 03"	9' 00"
Built: P.K. Harris & Sons, Appledore, England (Foundation Vibert '61-'73, Point Vibert '73-'06)								
General Chemical No. 37		TK	1956	D	883*	208' 09"	42' 09"	13' 09"
Built: Todd Shipyard, Houston, TX								
Huron Spirit			1995	B	4,542*	314' 09"	81' 06"	23 05
Built: Jiangdu Shipyard, Changjian, China								
Jarrett M	5030086	TB	1945	D	96*	82' 00"	20' 00"	10' 00"
Built: Russel Brothers Ltd., Owen Sound, ON (Atomic '45-'06)								
Jarrett McKeil	8959776	TB	1956	D	197*	91' 08"	27' 04"	12' 03"
Built: Davie Shipbuilding Co., Lauzon, QC (Robert B. No. 1 '56-'97)								
John Spence	7218735	TB	1972	D	719*	171' 00"	38' 00"	15' 01"
Built: Star Shipyard, New Westminster, BC; paired with barge Niagara Spirit (Mary B. VI '72-'81, Mary B. '81-'82, Mary B. VI '82-'83, Artic Tuktu '83-'94)								
Labrador Spirit		DB	1970	B	4,285*	382' 05"	75' 09"	20' 00"
Built: Bethlehem Steel Corp., San Francisco, CA								
Lac St-Jean		DB	1971	B	771*	150' 00"	54' 09"	10' 06"
Built: Canadian Vickers Ltd., Montreal, QC								
Lambert Spirit	8641525	DB	1968	B	9,645	393' 07"	69' 08"	27' 05"
Built: Avondale Shipyards Inc., Avondale, LA (KTC 115 '68-'06)								
Leonard M.	8519215	TB	1986	D	457*	103' 07"	36' 01"	19' 02"
Built: McTay Marine, Bromborough, England (Point Halifax '86-'12)								
Niagara Spirit		TK	1984	D	418*	340' 00"	78' 00"	19' 00"
Built: FMC Corp., Portland, OR (Alaska Trader '84-'99, Timberjack '99-'08)								
Salvor	5427019	TB	1963	D	407*	120' 00"	31' 00"	18' 06"
Built: Jakobson Shipyard, Oyster Bay, NY (Esther Moran '63-'00)								

U.S. Army Corps of Engineers' tug Hammond Bay. (Roger LeLievre)

Tug Indiana pours on the power assisting Algocanada at Green Bay, Wis. (Daniel J. Fiala)

John M. Selvick and Jimmy L breaking ice for a barge at Marinette, Wis. *(Scott Best)*

Buffalo-based fire tug Edward M. Cotter. *(Alain Gindroz)*

Fleet Name Vessel Name	IMO #	Vessel Type	Year Built	Engine Type	Cargo Cap. or Gross*	Overall Length	Breadth	Depth
S/VM 86		DB	1958	B	487*	161' 01"	40' 00"	10' 00"
Built: Canadian Shipbuilding & Engineering Ltd., Collingwood, ON (S.L.S. 86)								
Tony MacKay	7227786	TB	1973	D	366*	127' 00"	30' 05"	14' 05"
Built: Richard Dunston Ltd., Hessle, England (Point Carroll '73-'01)								
Viateur's Spirit		DB	2004	D	253*	141' 01"	52' 03"	5' 01"
Built: Port Weller Dry Dock, Port Weller, ON (Traverse René Lavasseur '04-'06)								
Wilf Seymour		TB	1961	D	442*	122' 00"	31' 00"	17' 00"
Built: Gulfport Shipbuilding, Port Arthur, TX (M. Moran '61-'70, Port Arthur '70-'72, M. Moran '72-'00, Salvager '00-'04)								
Wyatt M.		TB	1948	D	123*	85' 00"	20' 00"	10' 00"
Built: Russel Brothers Ltd., Owen Sound, ON (P. J. Murer '48-'81, Michael D. Misner '81-'93, Thomas A. Payette '93-'96, Progress '96-'06)								

MONTREAL BOATMEN LTD. – A SUBSIDIARY OF McKEIL MARINE LTD., PORT COLBORNE, ON

Fleet Name Vessel Name	IMO #	Vessel Type	Year Built	Engine Type	Cargo Cap. or Gross*	Overall Length	Breadth	Depth
Aldo H.		PB	1979	D	37*	56' 04"	15' 04"	6' 02"
Boatman No. 3		PB	1965	D	13*	33' 08"	11' 00"	6' 00"
Boatman No. 6		PB	1979	D	39*	56' 07"	18' 07"	6' 03"
Dredge Primrose		DR	1915	B	916*	136' 06"	42' 00"	10' 02"

M-13   McMULLEN & PITZ CONSTRUCTION CO., MANITOWOC, WI (mcmullenandpitz.net)

Fleet Name Vessel Name	IMO #	Vessel Type	Year Built	Engine Type	Cargo Cap. or Gross*	Overall Length	Breadth	Depth
Dauntless		TB	1937	D	25*	52' 06"	15' 06"	5' 03"

M-14   McNALLY CONSTRUCTION INC., HAMILTON, ON (mcnallycorp.com)
A SUBSIDIARY OF WEEKS MARINE INC., CRANFORD, NJ

Fleet Name Vessel Name	IMO #	Vessel Type	Year Built	Engine Type	Cargo Cap. or Gross*	Overall Length	Breadth	Depth
Bagotville		TB	1964	D	65*	65' 00"	18' 05"	8' 03"
Built: Verreault Navigation, Les Méchins, QC								
Beaver Delta II		TB	1959	D	14*	35' 08"	12' 00"	4' 04"
Built: Allied Builders Ltd., Vancouver, BC (Halcyon Bay)								
Beaver Gamma		TB	1960	D	17*	37' 01"	12' 09"	6' 00"
Built: Diesel Sales & Service (Burlington) Ltd., Burlington, ON (Burlington Bertie)								
Beaver Kay		GC	1953	B	614*	115' 01"	60' 00"	9' 05"
Built: George T. Davie & Sons Ltd., Lauzon, QC								
Canadian		DR	1954	B	1,087*	173' 08"	49' 08"	13' 04"
Built: Port Arthur Shipbuilding Co. Ltd., Port Arthur (Thunder Bay), ON								
Canadian Argosy		DS	1978	B	951*	149' 09"	54' 01"	10' 08"
Built: Canadian Shipbuilding & Engineering Ltd., Collingwood, ON								
Cargo Carrier I		DB	1969	B	196*	89' 09"	29' 09"	8' 05"
Built: Halifax Shipyards Ltd., Halifax, NS								
Cargo Master		CS	1964	B	562*	136' 00"	50' 00"	9' 00"
Built: Canadian Shipbuilding & Engineering Ltd., Collingwood, ON								
Carl M.		TB	1957	D	21*	47' 00"	14' 06"	6' 00"
Dapper Dan		TB	1948	D	21*	41' 03"	12' 07"	5' 09"
F. R. McQueen		DB	1959	B	180*	79' 09"	39' 09"	5' 07"
Built: Manitowoc Engineering Corp., Manitowoc, WI								
Greta V		TB	1951	D	14*	44' 00"	12' 00"	5' 00"
Handy Andy		DB	1925	B	313*	95' 09"	43' 01"	10' 00"
Idus Atwell		DS	1962	B	366*	100' 00"	40' 00"	8' 05"
Built: Dominion Bridge Co. Ltd., Toronto, ON								
Island Sauvage		PA	1969	D	381*	86' 03"	61' 04"	9' 03"
Built: Halifax Shipyards Ltd., Halifax, NS (Cargo Carrier II)								
Jamie L.		TB	1988	D	25*	36' 04"	14' 07"	5' 09"
John Holden		DR	1954	B	148*	89' 08"	30' 01"	6' 02"
Built: McNamara Construction Co. Ltd., Toronto, ON								
Lac Como		TB	1944	D	63*	65' 00"	16' 10"	7' 10"
Built: Canadian Bridge Co., Walkerville, ON (Tanac 74 '44-'64)								
Lac Vancouver		TB	1943	D	65*	60' 09"	16' 10"	7' 08"
Built: Central Bridge Co., Trenton, ON (Vancouver '43-'74)								
Mister Joe		TB	1964	D	70*	61' 00"	19' 00"	7' 02"
Built: Russel Brothers Ltd., Owen Sound, ON (Churchill River -'99)								
Oshawa		TB	1969	D	24*	42' 09"	13' 08"	5' 04"
Sandra Mary		TB	1962	D	97*	80' 00"	21' 00"	10' 09"
Built: Russel Brothers Ltd., Owen Sound, ON (Flo Cooper '62-'00)								
Whitby		TB	1978	D	24*	42' 19"	13' 08"	6' 05"
William B. Dilly		DR	1957	B	473*	116' 00"	39' 10"	9' 01"
Built: Canadian Shipbuilding & Engineering Ltd., Collingwood, ON								
Willmac		TB	1959	D	16*	40' 00"	13' 00"	3' 07"

Fleet Name Vessel Name	IMO #	Vessel Type	Year Built	Engine Type	Cargo Cap. or Gross*	Overall Length	Breadth	Depth

M

M-15 MENASHA TUGBOAT CO., SARNIA, ON

Menasha {2}		TB	1949	D	132*	78' 00"	24' 00"	9' 08"

Built: Bludworth Marine, Houston, TX (W. C. Harms '49-'54, Hamilton '54-'86, Ruby Casho '86-'88, W. C. Harms '88-'97)

M-16 MICHIGAN DEPARTMENT OF NATURAL RESOURCES, LANSING, MI *(michigan.gov/dnr)*

Channel Cat		RV	1968	D	24*	46' 00"	13' 06"	4' 00"
Lake Char		RV	2006	D	26*	56' 00"	16' 00"	4' 05"
Steelhead		RV	1967	D	70*	63' 00"	16' 04"	6' 06"

M-17 MICHIGAN TECHNOLOGICAL UNIVERSITY, HOUGHTON, MI

Agassiz		RV	2002	D	14*	36' 00"	13' 00"	4' 00"

M-18 MIDLAND TOURS INC., PENETANGUISHENE, ON *(midlandtours.com)*

Miss Midland	7426667	ES	1974	D	106*	68' 07"	19' 04"	6' 04"

M-19 MIDWEST MARITIME CORP., MILWAUKEE, WI

Leona B.		TB	1972	D	99*	59' 08"	24' 01"	10' 03"

(Kings Squire '72-'89, Juanita D. '78-'89, Peggy Ann '89-'93, Mary Page Hannah {2} '93-'04)

M-20 MILLER BOAT LINE, PUT-IN-BAY, OH *(millerferry.com)*

Islander {3}		PA/CF	1983	D	92*	90' 03"	38' 00"	8' 03"
Put-in-Bay {3}		PA/CF	1997	D	97*	136 00"	38' 06"	9' 06"

Built: Sturgeon Bay Shipbuilding Co., Sturgeon Bay, WI; lengthened by 40' at Cleveland, OH, in '09

South Bass		PA/CF	1989	D	95*	96' 00"	38' 06"	9' 06"
Wm. Market		PA/CF	1993	D	95*	96' 00"	38' 06"	8' 09"

Built: Peterson Builders Inc., Sturgeon Bay, WI

M-21 MILWAUKEE BOAT LINE, MILWAUKEE, WI *(mkeboat.com)*

Iroquois		PA	1922	D	91*	61' 09"	21' 00"	6' 04"
Vista King		ES	1978	D	60*	78' 00"	23' 00"	5' 02"
Voyageur		PA	1988	D	94*	67' 02"	21' 00"	7' 04"

M-22 MILWAUKEE HARBOR COMMISSION, MILWAUKEE, WI *(city.milwaukee.gov/port)*

Harbor Seagull		TB	1961	D	23*	44' 05"	16' 04"	5' 00"
Joey D.		TB	2011	D		60' 00"	20' 06"	6' 06"

Built: Great Lakes Shipyard, Cleveland, OH

M-23 MILWAUKEE RIVER CRUISE LINE, MILWAUKEE, WI *(edelweissboats.com)*

Edelweiss II		ES	1989	D	95*	73' 08"	20' 00"	2' 08"

M-24 MINISTRY OF TRANSPORTATION, DOWNSVIEW, ON *(www.mto.gov.on.ca)*

Cassiopeia IV		PA	1957	Gas	40*	50' 00"	24' 00"	3' 070"

Built: Russel-Hipwell Engines Ltd., Owen Sound, ON

Frontenac II	5068875	PA/CF	1962	D	666*	181' 00"	45' 00"	10' 00"

Built: Chantier Maritime de Saint-Laurent, Saint-Laurent, QC (Charlevoix {2} '62-'92)

Frontenac Howe Islander		PF/CF	2004	D	130*	100' 00"	32' 03"	5' 05"

Built: Heddle Marine Service Inc., Hamilton, ON

Glenora	5358074	PA/CF	1952	D	189*	127' 00"	33' 00"	9' 00"

Built: Erieau Shipbuilding & Drydock Co. Ltd., Erieau, ON (The St. Joseph Islander '52-'74)

Jiimaan	9034298	PA/CF	1992	D	2,807*	176' 09"	42' 03"	13' 06"

Built: Port Weller Drydock, Port Weller, ON

Pelee Islander	5273274	PA/CF	1960	D	334*	145' 00"	32' 00"	10' 00"

Built: Erieau Shipbuilding & Drydock Co. Ltd., Erieau, ON

Quinte Loyalist	5358062	PA/CF	1954	D	204*	127' 00"	32' 00"	8' 00"

Built: Erieau Shipbuilding & Drydock Co. Ltd., Erieau, ON

Wolfe Islander III	7423079	PA/CF	1975	D	985*	205' 00"	68' 00"	6' 00"

Built: Port Arthur Shipbuilding Co., Port Arthur, ON

M-25 MONTREAL PORT AUTHORITY, MONTREAL, QC *(port-montreal.com)*

Denis M		TB	1942	D	21*	46' 07"	12' 08"	4' 01"

Built: Russel Brothers Ltd., Owen Sound, ON (Marcel D.)

Maisonneuve	7397749	PA	1972	D	84*	63' 10"	20' 07"	9' 03"

Built: Fercraft Marine Inc., Ste. Catherine D'Alexandrie, QC

M-26 MUNISING BAY SHIPWRECK TOURS INC., MUNISING, MI *(shipwrecktours.com)*

Miss Munising		ES	1967	D	50*	60' 00"	14' 00"	4' 04"

Michipicoten departing Duluth, Minn., harbor. (Mike Sipper)

Fleet Name / Vessel Name	IMO #	Vessel Type	Year Built	Engine Type	Cargo Cap. or Gross*	Overall Length	Breadth	Depth
M-27 MUSIQUE AQUATIQUE CRUISE LINES INC., TORONTO, ON (citysightseeingtoronto.com)								
Harbour Star		ES	1978	D	45*	63' 06"	15' 09"	3' 09"
Built: Eastern Equipment Ltd., LaSalle, QC (K. Wayne Simpson '78-'95)								
M-28 MUSKOKA STEAMSHIP & HISTORICAL SOCIETY, GRAVENHURST, ON (segwun.com)								
Segwun		PA	1887	R	308*	128' 00"	24' 00"	7' 06"
Built: Melancthon Simpson, Toronto, ON (Nipissing {2} 1887-'25)								
Wanda III		PA	1915	R	60*	94' 00"	12' 00"	5' 00"
Built: Poulson Iron Works Ltd., Toronto, ON								
Wenonah II	8972003	PA	2001	D	447*	127' 00"	28' 00"	6' 00"
Built: McNally Construction Inc., Belleville, ON								
M-29 M/V ZEUS LC, CHESAPEAKE CITY, MD								
Zeus	9506071	TB	1964	D	98*	104' 02"	29' 03"	13' 05"
Built: Houma Shipbuilding Co., Houma, LA; usually paired with barge Robert F. Deegan, Fleet U-14								
M-30 MYSTIC BLUE CRUISES INC., CHICAGO, IL (mysticbluecruises.com)								
Mystic Blue		PA	1998	D	97*	138' 09"	36' 00"	10' 05"
Built: Chesapeake Shipbuilding Corp., Salisbury, MD								
N-1 NADRO MARINE SERVICES LTD., PORT DOVER, ON (nadromarine.com)								
Ecosse	8624682	TB	1979	D	142*	91' 00"	26' 00"	8' 06"
Built: Hike Metal Products Ltd., Wheatley, ON (R & L No. 1 '79-'96)								
Intrepid III		TB	1976	D	39*	66' 00"	17' 00"	7' 06"
Built: Halter Marine Ltd., Chalmette, LA								
Lac Manitoba		TB	1944	D	51*	64' 00"	16' 07"	7' 10"
Built: Central Bridge Co., Trenton, ON (Tanac 75 '44-'52, Manitoba '52-'57)								
Molly M. 1	5118838	TB	1962	D	207*	98' 06"	27' 10"	12' 02"
Built: Davie Shipbuilding Co., Lauzon, QC (Foundation Vigour '62-'74, Point Vigour '74-'07)								
Seahound		TB	1941	D	57*	65' 00"	18' 00"	8' 00"
Built: Equitable Equipment Co., New Orleans, LA ([Unnamed] '41-'56, Sea Hound '56-'80, Carolyn Jo '80-'00)								
Stormont	8959893	TB	1953	D	108*	80' 00"	20' 00"	15' 00"
Built: Canadian Dredge & Dock Co., Kingston, ON								
Vac		TB	1942	D	36*	65' 00"	20' 04"	4' 03"
Built: George Gamble, Port Dover, ON								
Vigilant I		TB	1944	D	111*	79' 06"	20' 11"	10' 02"
Built: Russell Brothers Ltd., Owen Sound, ON (HMCS Glenlivet [W-43] '44-'75, Glenlivet II '75-'77, Canadian Franko '77-'82, Glenlivet II '82-'00)								
N-2 NAUTICA QUEEN CRUISE DINING, CLEVELAND, OH (nauticaqueen.com)								
Nautica Queen		ES	1981	D	95*	124' 00"	31' 02"	8' 09"
Built: Blount Marine Corp., Warren, RI (Bay Queen '81-'85, Arawanna Queen '85-'88, Star of Nautica '88-'92)								
N-3 NAUTICAL ADVENTURES, TORONTO, ON (nauticaladventure.com)								
Empire Sandy	5071561	ES/3S	1943	D/W	338*	140' 00"	32' 08"	14' 00"
Built: Clellands Ltd., Wellington-Quay-on-Tyne, England (Empire Sandy '43-'48, Ashford '48-'52, Chris M. '52-'79)								
Wayward Princess		ES	1976	D	325*	92' 00"	26' 00"	10' 00"
Built: Marlin Yacht Co., Summerstown, ON (Cayuga II '76-'82)								
N-4 NEW YORK POWER AUTHORITY, LEWISTON, NY								
Breaker		TB	1962	D	29*	43' 03"	14' 03"	5' 00"
Daniel Joncaire		TB	1979	D	25*	43' 03"	15' 00"	5' 00"
Havasu II		CS	2010	B	114*	80' 00"	34' 00"	5' 00"
N-5 NEW YORK DEPT. OF ENVIRONMENTAL QUALITY, LAKE ONTARIO UNIT, CAPE VINCENT, NY								
Seth Green		RV	1985	D	50*	47' 00"	17' 00"	8' 00"
Built: Newport Offshore, Newport, RI								
N-6 NEW YORK STATE MARINE HIGHWAY TRANSPORTATION CO., TROY, NY (nysmarinehighway.com)								
Benjamin Elliot		TB	1960	D	27*	47 07"	15' 02"	7' 02
Built: Gladding-Hearn Shipbuilding, Somerset, MA (El-Jean)								
Margot	5222043	TB	1958	D	141*	90' 00"	25' 00"	10' 00"
Built: Jakobson Shipyard, Oyster Bay, NY (Jolene Rose, Margot Moran)								
N-7 NORTH SHORE SCENIC CRUISES, SILVER BAY, MN (scenicsuperior.com)								
Wenonah		ES	1960	D	91*	70' 07"	19' 04"	9' 07"
Built: Dubuque Boat & Boiler, Dubuque, IA (Jamaica '60-'64)								

Fleet Name / Vessel Name	IMO #	Vessel Type	Year Built	Engine Type	Cargo Cap. or Gross*	Overall Length	Breadth	Depth
N-8 **NORTHERN MARINE TRANSPORTATION INC., SAULT STE. MARIE, MI**								
Empire State		PB	1951	D	21*	41' 09"	12' 04"	6' 06"
David Allen		PB	1964	D	32*	56' 04"	13' 03"	6' 00"
Linda Jean		PB	1950	D	17*	38' 00"	10' 00"	5' 00"
O-1 **OAK GROVE & MARINE TRANSPORTATION INC., CLAYTON, NY**								
Maple Grove		PK	1954	D	55*	73' 07"	20' 00"	9' 00"
O-2 **OHIO DEPARTMENT OF NATURAL RESOURCES, COLUMBUS, OH** (dnr.state.oh.us)								
Explorer II		RV	1999	D		53' 00"	15' 05"	4' 05"
Grandon		RV	1990	D	47*	47' 00"	16' 00"	5' 05"
O-3 **OLSON DREDGE & DOCK CO., ALGONAC, MI**								
Anchor Bay		TB	1930	D	264*	112' 01"	36' 02"	7' 02"
Built: Great Lakes Engineering Works, Ecorse, MI (Dupuis No. 12)								
John Michael		TB	1913	D	41*	55' 04"	15' 01"	7' 06"
Built: Cowles Shipyard Co., Buffalo, NY (Colonel Ward, Ross Coddington, Joseph J. Olivieri)								
O-4 **OLYMPIA CRUISE LINE INC., THORNHILL, ON** (torontocruises.com)								
Enterprise 2000		ES	1998	D	370*	121' 06"	35' 00"	6' 00"
O-5 **ONTARIO MINISTRY OF NATURAL RESOURCES, PETERBOROUGH, ON** (mnr.gov.on.ca)								
Erie Explorer		RV	1981	D	72*	53' 05"	20' 01"	4' 08"
Built: Hopper Fisheries Ltd., Port Stanley, ON (Janice H.X. '81-'97)								
Huron Explorer I		RV	2010	D	112*	62' 00"	21' 03"	6' 00"
Built: Hike Metal Products Ltd., Wheatley, ON								
Keenosay		RV	1957	D	68*	51' 04"	20' 07"	2' 07"
Built: S.G. Powell Shipyard Ltd., Dunnville, ON								
Nipigon Osprey		RV	1990	D	33*	42' 04"	14' 09"	6' 08"
Built: Kanter Yachts Corp., St. Thomas, ON								
Ontario Explorer		RV	2009	D	84*	64' 09"	21' 03"	6' 00"
Built: Hike Metal Products Ltd., Wheatley, ON								
O-6 **ONTARIO POWER GENERATION INC., TORONTO, ON**								
Niagara Queen II		IB	1992	D	58*	56' 01"	18' 00"	6' 08"
Built: Hike Metal Products Ltd., Wheatley, ON								
O-7 **OSBORNE MATERIALS CO., GRAND RIVER, OH** (osbornecompaniesinc.com)								
Emmett J. Carey		SC	1948	D	900	114' 00"	23' 00"	11' 00"
Built: Hugh E. Lee Iron Works, Saginaw, MI; laid up at Fairport, OH (Beatrice Ottinger '48-'63, James B. Lyons '63-'88)								
F. M. Osborne {2}		SC	1910	D	500	150' 00"	29' 00"	11' 03"
Built: J. Baterman & T. Horn, Buffalo, NY (Grand Island {1} '10-'58, Lesco '58-'75)								
O-8 **OWEN SOUND TRANSPORTATION CO. LTD., OWEN SOUND, ON** (ontarioferries.com)								
Chi-Cheemaun	7343607	PA/CF	1974	D	6,991*	365' 05"	61' 00"	21' 00"
Built: Canadian Shipbuilding and Engineering Ltd., Collingwood, ON								
P-1 **PENNZOIL-QUAKER STATE CANADA INC., CALGARY, AB**								
Arca	5411761	RT	1963	D	1,296	175' 00"	36' 00"	14' 00"
Built: Port Weller Dry Docks, Port Weller, ON; serves vessels near Montreal, QC (Imperial Lachine '63-'03, Josee M. '03-'03)								
P-2 **PERE MARQUETTE SHIPPING CO., LUDINGTON, MI** (pmship.com)								
Pere Marquette 41	5073894	SU	1941	B	3,413*	403' 00"	58' 00"	23' 05"
Built: Manitowoc Shipbuilding Co., Manitowoc, WI; converted from powered train/car ferry to a self-unloading barge in '97 (City of Midland 41 '41-'97)								
Undaunted	8963210	AT	1943	DE	569*	143' 00"	38' 00"	18' 00"
Built: Gulfport Boiler/Welding, Port Arthur, TX; paired with barge Pere Marquette 41 (USS Undaunted [ATR-126, ATA-199] '44-'63, USMA Kings Pointer '63-'93, Krystal K. '93-'97)								
P-3 **PICTURED ROCKS CRUISES INC., MUNISING, MI** (picturedrocks.com)								
Grand Island {2}		ES	1989	D	52*	68' 00"	16' 01"	7' 01"
Grand Portal		ES	2004	D	76*	64' 08"	20' 00"	8' 08"
Miners Castle		ES	1974	D	82*	68' 00"	16' 06"	6' 04"
Miss Superior		ES	1984	D	83*	68' 00"	16' 09"	10' 04"
Pictured Rocks		ES	1972	D	53*	55' 07"	13' 07"	4' 04"
P-4 **PLAUNT TRANSPORTATION CO. INC., CHEBOYGAN, MI** (bbiferry.com)								
Kristen D		CF	1987	D	83*	64' 11"	36' 00"	4' 06"

Fleet Name / Vessel Name	IMO #	Vessel Type	Year Built	Engine Type	Cargo Cap. or Gross*	Overall Length	Breadth	Depth

P-5 PORT CITY CRUISE LINE INC., NORTH MUSKEGON, MI *(portcityprincesscruises.com)*

Port City Princess		ES	1966	D	79*	64' 09"	30' 00"	5' 06"

Built: Blount Marine Corp., Warren, RI (Island Queen {1} '66-'87)

P-6 PORTOFINO ON THE RIVER, WYANDOTTE, MI *(portofinoontheriver.com)*

Friendship		ES	1968	D	76*	85' 00"	23' 04"	7' 03"

Built: Hike Metal Products Ltd., Wheatley, ON (Peche Island V '68-'71, Papoose V '71-'82)

P-7 PRESQUE ISLE BOAT TOURS, ERIE, PA *(piboattours.com)*

Lady Kate {2}		ES	1952	D	11*	59' 03"	15' 00"	3' 09"

Built: J. W. Nolan & Sons, Erie, PA (G. A. Boeckling II, Cedar Point III, Island Trader '89-'97)

P-8 PROVMAR FUELS INC., HAMILTON, ON *(provmar.com)*
A DIVSION OF STERLING FUELS, WINDSOR, ON

Hamilton Energy	6517328	RT	1965	D	1,282	201' 05"	34' 01"	14' 09"

Built: Grangemouth Dockyard Co., Grangemouth, Scotland; scheduled to be retired in 2013
(Partington '65-'79, Shell Scientist '79-'81, Metro Sun '81-'85)

Provmar Terminal	5376521	TK	1959	B	7,300	403' 05"	55' 06"	28' 05"

Built: Sarpsborg Mek, Verksted, Norway; last operated in 1984; formerly in use as a fuel storage barge at
Hamilton, ON, and now laid up there (Varangnes '59-'70, Tommy Wiborg '70-'74, Ungava Transport '74-'85)

Sterling Energy	9277058	RT	2002	D	749*	226' 03"	32' 10"	14' 09"

Built: Selahattan Alsan Shipyard, Istanbul Turkey; serves vessels in the vicinity of Hamilton and
Toronto, ON, as well as the Welland Canal (Melisa D '02-'13)

P-9 PURE MICHIGAN BOAT CRUISES LLC, MUNISING, MI

Isle Royale Queen III		PA	1959	D	88*	74' 03"	18' 04"	6' 05"

Built: T.D. Vinette Co., Escanaba, MI (Isle Royale Queen II)

P-10 PURVIS MARINE LTD., SAULT STE. MARIE, ON *(purvismarine.com)*

Adanac III		TB	1913	D	108*	80' 03"	19' 03"	9' 10"

Built: Western Drydock & Shipbuilding Co., Port Arthur, ON (Edward C. Whalen '13-'66, John McLean '66-'95)

Algonorth	7028104	BC	1971	D	28,750	729' 10"	75' 02"	42' 11"

Built: Upper Clyde Shipbuilders, Govan, Scotland; awaiting scrapping at Sault Ste. Mare, ON
(Temple Bar '71-'76, Lake Nipigon '76-'84, Laketon {2} '84-'86, Lake Nipigon '86-'87)

Anglian Lady	5141483	TB	1953	D	398*	132' 00"	31' 00"	14' 00"

Built: John I. Thorneroft & Co., Southampton, England (Hamtun '53-'72, Nathalie Letzer '72-'88)

Avenger IV	5401297	TB	1962	D	291*	120' 00"	30' 00"	19' 00"

Built: Cochrane & Sons Ltd., Selby, Yorkshire, England (Avenger '62-'85)

G.L.B. No. 2		DB	1953	B	3,215	240' 00"	50' 00"	12' 00"

Built: Ingalls Shipbuilding Corp., Birmingham, AL (Jane Newfield '53-'66, ORG 6502 '66-'75)

Malden		DB	1946	B	1,075	150' 00"	41' 09"	10' 03"

Built: Russel Brothers Ltd., Owen Sound, ON

Martin E. Johnson		TB	1959	D	26*	47' 00"	16' 00"	7' 00"

Built: Russel Brothers Ltd., Owen Sound, ON

PML 357		DB	1932	B	363*	138' 00"	38' 00"	11' 00"
PML 2501		TK	1980	B	1,954*	302' 00"	52' 00"	17' 00"

Built: Cenac Shipyard, Houma, LA (CTCO 2505 '80-'96)

PML 9000		DB	1968	B	4,285*	400' 00"	76' 00"	20' 00"

Built: Bethlehem Steel – Shipbuilding Division, San Francisco, CA (Palmer '68-'00)

PML Alton		DB	1933	B	150	93' 00"	30' 00"	8' 00"

Built: McClintic- Marshall, Sturgeon Bay, WI

PML Ironmaster		DB	1962	B	7,437*	360' 00"	75' 00"	25' 00"

Built: Yarrows Ltd., Esquimalt, BC (G.T. Steelmaster, Ceres, American Gulf VII, Seaspan 241, G.T. Ironmaster)

PML Tucci		CS	1958	B	601*	150' 00"	52' 00"	10' 00"

Built: Calumet Shipyard & Drydock Co., Chicago, IL (MCD '58-'73, Minnesota '73-'88, Candace Andrie '88-'08)

PML Tucker		DS	1971	B	477*	140' 00"	50' 00"	9' 00"

Built: Twin City Shipyard, St. Paul, MN (Illinois '71-'02, Meredith Andrie '02-'08)

Reliance	7393808	TB	1974	D	708*	148' 03"	35' 07"	21' 07"

Built: Ulstein Hatlo A/S, Ulsteinvik, Norway (Sinni '74-'81, Irving Cedar '81-'96, Atlantic Cedar '96-'02)

Rocket		TB	1901	D	40*	73' 00"	16' 00"	7' 00"

Built: Buffalo Shipbuilding Co., Buffalo, NY

Sheila P.		TB	1940	D	15*	40' 00"	14' 00"	5' 00"
Tecumseh II		DB	1976	B	2,500	180' 00"	54' 00"	12' 00"
Wilfred M. Cohen	7629271	TB	1947	D	284*	102' 06"	28' 00"	15' 00"

Built: Newport News Shipbuilding and Drydock Co., Newport News, VA (A. T. Lowmaster '48-'75)

Algoma Provider – marking its 50th birthday in 2013 – only made a few trips last year, fitting out late in the season for the grain trade. Here she is upbound in the Welland Canal. *(John C. Knecht)*

Fleet Name / Vessel Name	IMO #	Vessel Type	Year Built	Engine Type	Cargo Cap. or Gross*	Overall Length	Breadth	Depth
W. I. Scott Purvis	5264819	TB	1938	D	203*	96' 00"	26' 00"	10' 00"

Built: Marine Industries, Sorel, QC (Orient Bay '38-'75, Guy M. No. 1 '75-'90)

W.J. Isaac Purvis		TB	1962	D	71*	72' 00"	19' 00"	12' 00"

Built: McNamara Marine Ltd., Toronto, ON (Angus M. '62-'92, Omni Sorel '92-'02, Joyce B. Gardiner '02-'09)

W. J. Ivan Purvis	5217218	TB	1938	D	190*	100' 00"	26' 00"	10' 00"

Built: Marine Industries, Sorel, QC (Magpie '38-'66, Dana T. Bowen '66-'75)

Yankcanuck {2}	5409811	CS	1963	D	4,760	324' 03"	49' 00"	26' 00"

Built: Collingwood Shipyards, Collingwood, ON; in lay-up at Sault Ste. Marie, ON, since 2008.

P-11 PUT-IN-BAY BOAT LINE CO., PORT CLINTON, OH *(jet-express.com)*

Jet Express		PF/CA	1989	D	93*	92' 08"	28' 06"	8' 04"
Jet Express II		PF/CA	1992	D	85*	92' 06"	28' 06"	8' 04"
Jet Express III		PF/CA	2001	D	70*	78' 02"	27' 06"	8' 02"
Jet Express IV		PF/CA	1995	D	71*	77' 02"	28' 05"	7' 07"

(Monmouth, Theodore Roosevelt, Grey Lady)

Q-1 QUEBEC PORT AUTHORITY, QUÉBEC, QC *(portquebec.ca)*

Le Cageux		TB	2011	D	24*	42' 06"	16' 01"	7' 07"

R-1 ROCKPORT BOAT LINE LTD., ROCKPORT, ON *(rockportcruises.com)*

Chief Shingwauk		ES	1965	D	109*	70' 00"	24' 00"	4' 06"
Ida M.		ES	1970	D	29*	55' 00"	14' 00"	3' 00"
Ida M. II		ES	1973	D	121*	63' 02"	22' 02"	5' 00"
Sea Prince II		ES	1978	D	172*	83' 00"	24' 02"	6' 08"

R-2 ROEN SALVAGE CO., STURGEON BAY, WI *(roensalvage.com)*

Chas. Asher		TB	1967	D	39*	49' 02"	17' 06"	6' 10"

Built: Sturgeon Bay Shipbuilding Co., Sturgeon Bay, WI

John R. Asher		TB	1943	D	93*	68' 09"	20' 00"	8' 00"

Built: Platzer Boat Works, Houston, TX (U. S. Army ST-71 '43-'46, Russell 8 '46-'64, Reid McAllister '64-'67, Donegal '67-'85)

Louie S.		TB	1956	D	10*	37' 00"	12' 00"	4' 05"
Spuds		TB	1944	D	19*	42' 00"	12' 05"	5' 04"
Stephan M. Asher		TB	1954	D	60*	65' 00"	19' 01"	5' 04"

Built: Burton Shipyard Inc., Port Arthur, TX (Captain Bennie '54-'82, Dumar Scout '82-'87)

Timmy A.		TB	1953	D	12*	33' 06"	10' 08"	5' 02"

R-3 RUSSELL ISLAND TRANSIT CO., ALGONAC, MI

Islander {2}		PA/CF	1967	D	38*	41' 00"	15' 00"	3' 06"

R-4 RYBA MARINE CONSTRUCTION CO., CHEBOYGAN, MI *(rybamarine.com)*

Amber Mae		TB	1922	D	67*	65' 00"	14' 01"	10' 00"

Built: Glove Shipyard Inc., Buffalo, NY (E. W. Sutton '22-'52, Venture '52- '00)

Kathy Lynn	8034887	TB	1944	D	140*	85' 00"	24' 00"	9' 06"

Built: Decatur Iron & Steel Co., Decatur, AL (U. S. Army ST-693 '44-'79, Sea Islander '79-'91)

Rochelle Kaye		TB	1963	D	52*	51' 06"	19' 04"	7' 00"

Built: St. Charles Steel Works Inc., Thibodeaux, LA (Jaye Anne '63-?, Katanni ?-'97)

Tenacious	5238004	TB	1960	D	149*	79' 01"	25' 06"	12' 06"

Built: Ingalls Shipbuilding Corp., Pascagoula, MS (Mobil 8 '60-'91, Tatarrax '91-'93, Nan McKay '93-'95)

S-1 SAND PRODUCTS CORP., MUSKEGON, MI

LAKE SERVICE SHIPPING, MUSKEGON, MI

McKee Sons	*(Vessel operated by Grand River Navigation Co., see fleet L-11)*							

MICHIGAN-OHIO BARGE LLC, MUSKEGON, MI

Cleveland Rocks		SU	1957	B	6,280*	390' 00"	71' 00"	27' 00"

Built: Todd Shipyards Corp., Houston, TX (M-211 '57-'81, Virginia '81-'88, C-11 '88-'93, Kellstone 1 '93-'04)

PORT CITY MARINE SERVICES, MUSKEGON, MI

St. Marys Conquest	5015012	CC	1937	B	8,500	437' 06"	55' 00"	28' 00"

Built: Manitowoc Shipbuilding Co., Manitowoc, WI; converted from a powered tanker to a self-unloading cement barge by Bay Shipbuilding, Sturgeon Bay, WI, in '87
(Red Crown '37-'62, Amoco Indiana '62-'87, Medusa Conquest '87-'99, Southdown Conquest '99-'04)

PORT CITY STEAMSHIP SERVICES INC., MUSKEGON, MI

St. Marys Challenger	5009984	CC	1906	S	10,250	552' 01"	56' 00"	31' 00"

Built: Great Lakes Engineering Works, Ecorse, MI; repowered in '50; converted to a self-unloading cement carrier by Manitowoc Shipbuilding Co., Manitowoc, WI, in '67; (William P. Snyder '06-'26, Elton Hoyt II {1} '26-'52, Alex D. Chisholm '52-'66, Medusa Challenger '66-'99, Southdown Challenger '99-'04)

Fleet Name / Vessel Name	IMO #	Vessel Type	Year Built	Engine Type	Cargo Cap. or Gross*	Overall Length	Breadth	Depth

PORT CITY TUG INC., MUSKEGON, MI

Bradshaw McKee	7644312	ATB	1977	D	174*	121' 06"	34' 06"	18' 02"

Built: Toche Enterprises Inc., Ocean Springs, MS (Lady Elda '77-'78, Kings Challenger '78-'78, ITM No. 1 '78-'81, Kings Challenger '81-'86, Susan W. Hannah '86-'11)

Prentiss Brown	7035547	TB	1967	D	197*	123' 05"	31' 06"	19' 00"

Built: Gulfport Shipbuilding, Port Arthur, TX; paired with barge St. Marys Conquest (Betty Culbreath, Micheala McAllister)

S-2   SEA SERVICE LLC, SUPERIOR, WI

Sea Bear		PB	1959	D	28*	45' 08"	13' 08"	7' 00"

Built: Gladding-Hearn Shipbuilding, Somerset, MA (Narrows)

S-3   SELVICK MARINE TOWING CORP., STURGEON BAY, WI

Carla Anne Selvick	5298389	TB	1908	D	191*	96' 00"	23' 00"	11' 02"

Built: Skinner Shipbuilding & Dry Dock Co., Baltimore, MD (S.O. Co. No. 19 '08-'16, S.T. Co. No. 19 '16-'18, Socony 19 '18-'47, Esso Tug No. 4 '47-'53, McAllister 44 '53-'55, Roderick McAllister '55-'84)

Cameron O.		TB	1955	D	26*	50' 00"	15' 00"	7' 03"

Built: Peterson Builders Inc., Sturgeon Bay, WI (Escort II '55-'06)

Jacquelyn Nicole		TB	1913	D	96*	71' 00"	20' 01"	11' 02"

Built: Great Lakes Towing Co., Cleveland, OH (Michigan {4} '13-'78, Ste. Marie II '78-'81, Dakota '81-'92, Ethel E. '92-'02)

Jimmy L.		TB	1939	D	148*	110' 00"	25' 00"	13' 00"

Built: Defoe Shipbuilding Co., Bay City, MI (USCGC Naugatuck [WYT / WYTM-92] '39-'80, Timmy B. '80-'84)

Mary Page Hannah {1}	7436234	TB	1950	DE	461*	143' 00"	33' 01"	14' 06"

Built: Levingston Shipbuilding, Orange, TX (U. S. Army ATA-230 '49-'72, G. W. Codrington '72-'73, William P. Feeley {2} '73-'73, William W. Stender '73-'78)

Sharon M. Selvick		TB	1945	D	28*	45' 05"	12' 10"	7' 01"

Built: Kewaunee Shipbuilding & Engineering, Kewaunee, WI (USACE Judson)

Susan L.		TB	1944	D	133*	86' 00"	23' 00"	10' 04"

Built: Equitable Equipment Co., New Orleans, LA (U. S. Army ST-709 '44-'47, USCOE Stanley '47-'99)

William C. Selvick		TB	1944	D	142*	85' 00"	23' 00"	9' 07"

Built: Platzer Boat Works, Houston, TX (U. S. Army ST-500 '44-'49, Sherman H. Serre '49-'77)

S-4   SHEPARD MARINE CONSTRUCTION, CLINTON TOWNSHIP, MI

Robin Lynn	7619769	TB	1952	D	148*	85' 00"	25' 00"	11' 00"

Built: Alexander Shipyard Inc., New Orleans, LA (Bonita '52-'85, Susan Hoey {2} '85-'95, Blackie B '95-'97, Susan Hoey {3} '97-'98)

S-5   SHEPLER'S MACKINAC ISLAND FERRY, MACKINAW CITY, MI *(sheplersferry.com)*

Capt. Shepler		PF	1986	D	71*	84' 00"	21' 00"	7' 10"
Felicity		PF	1972	D	65*	65' 00"	18' 01"	8' 03"
Sacre Bleu		PK	1959	D	98*	94' 10"	31' 00"	9' 09"
The Hope		PF	1975	D	87*	77' 00"	20' 00"	8' 03"
The Welcome		PF	1969	D	66*	60' 06"	16' 08"	8' 02"
Wyandot		PF	1979	D	83*	77' 00"	20' 00"	8' 00"

S-6   SHORELINE CHARTERS, GILLS ROCK, WI *(shorelinecharters.net)*

The Shoreline		ES	1973	D	12*	33' 00"	11' 4"	3' 00"

S-7   SHORELINE CONTRACTORS INC., WELLINGTON, OH *(shorelinecontractors.com)*

Eagle		TB	1943	D	31*	57' 09"	14' 05"	6' 10"

Built: Defoe Shipbuilding Co., Bay City, MI

S-8   SHORELINE SIGHTSEEING CO., CHICAGO, IL *(shorelinesightseeing.com)*

Cap Streeter		ES	1987	D	28*	63' 06"	24' 04"	7' 07"
Evening Star		ES	2001	D	93*	83' 00"	23' 00"	7' 00"
Marlyn		ES	1961	D	70*	65' 00"	25' 00"	7' 00"
Shoreline II		ES	1987	D	89*	75' 00"	26' 00"	7' 01"
Star of Chicago {2}		ES	1999	D	73*	64' 10"	22' 08"	7' 05"
Voyageur		CF	1983	D	98*	65' 00"	35' 00"	7' 00"

S-9   SOCIÉTÉ DES TRAVERSIERS DU QUÉBEC, QUÉBEC, QC *(traversiers.gouv.qc.ca)*

Alphonse-Desjardins	7109233	CF	1971	D	1,741*	214' 00"	71' 06"	20' 00"

Built: Davie Shipbuilding Co., Lauzon, QC

Armand-Imbeau	7902269	CF	1980	D	1,285*	203' 07"	72' 00"	18' 04"

Built: Marine Industries Ltd., Sorel, QC

Camille-Marcoux	7343578	CF	1974	D	6,122*	310' 09"	62' 09"	39' 00"

Built: Marine Industries Ltd., Sorel, QC

Joseph L. Block passes Hon. James L. Oberstar in fog below Mission Point on the St. Marys River. (Chanda McClain)

Fleet Name / Vessel Name	IMO #	Vessel Type	Year Built	Engine Type	Cargo Cap. or Gross*	Overall Length	Breadth	Depth
Catherine-Legardeur	8409355	CF	1985	D	1,348*	205' 09"	71' 10"	18' 10"
Built: Davie Shipbuilding Co., Lauzon, QC								
Felix-Antoine-Savard	9144706	CF	1997	D	2,489*	272' 00"	70' 00"	21' 09"
Built: Davie Shipbuilding Co., Lauzon, QC								
Grue-des-Iles	8011732	CF	1981	D	447*	155' 10"	41' 01"	12' 06"
Built: Bateaux Tur-Bec Ltd., Ste-Catherine, QC								
Ivan-Quinn	9554028	CF	2008	D	241*	83' 07"	26' 09"	11' 03"
Built: Meridien Maritime Reparation Inc., Matane, QC								
Jos-Deschenes	391571	CF	1980	D	1,287*	203' 07"	72' 00"	18' 04"
Built: Marine Industries Ltd., Sorel, QC								
Joseph-Savard	8409343	CF	1985	D	1,445*	206' 00"	71' 10"	18' 10"
Built: Davie Shipbuilding Co., Lauzon, QC								
Lomer-Gouin	7109221	CF	1971	D	1,741*	214' 00"	71' 06"	20' 00"
Built: Davie Shipbuilding Co., Lauzon, QC								
Lucien-L.	6721981	CF	1967	D	867*	220' 10"	61' 06"	15' 05"
Built: Marine Industries Ltd., Sorel, QC								
Radisson {1}		CF	1954	D	1,037*	164' 03"	72' 00"	10' 06"
Built: Davie Shipbuilding Co., Lauzon, QC								

S-10 SOO LOCKS BOAT TOURS, SAULT STE. MARIE, MI (soolocks.com)

Fleet Name / Vessel Name	IMO #	Vessel Type	Year Built	Engine Type	Cargo Cap. or Gross*	Overall Length	Breadth	Depth
Bide-A-Wee {3}		ES	1955	D	99*	64' 07"	23' 00"	7' 11"
Built: Blount Marine Corp., Warren, RI								
Hiawatha {2}		ES	1959	D	99*	64' 07"	23' 00"	7' 11"
Built: Blount Marine Corp., Warren, RI								
Holiday		ES	1957	D	99*	64' 07"	23' 00"	7' 11"
Built: Blount Marine Corp., Warren, RI								
Le Voyageur		ES	1959	D	70*	65' 00"	25' 00"	7' 00"
Built: Sturgeon Bay Shipbuilding and Drydock Co., Sturgeon Bay, WI								
Nokomis		ES	1959	D	70*	65' 00"	25' 00"	7' 00"
Built: Sturgeon Bay Shipbuilding and Drydock Co., Sturgeon Bay, WI								

S-11 SOO MARINE SUPPLY INC., SAULT STE. MARIE, MI (soomarinesupply.com)

Fleet Name / Vessel Name	IMO #	Vessel Type	Year Built	Engine Type	Cargo Cap. or Gross*	Overall Length	Breadth	Depth
Ojibway		SB	1945	D	53*	53' 00"	28' 00"	7' 00"
Built: Great Lakes Engineering Works, Ashtabula, OH								

S-12 SPIRIT CRUISES LLC, CHICAGO, IL (spiritcruises.com)

Fleet Name / Vessel Name	IMO #	Vessel Type	Year Built	Engine Type	Cargo Cap. or Gross*	Overall Length	Breadth	Depth
Spirit of Chicago		ES	1988	D	92*	156' 00"	35' 00"	7' 01"
Built: Blount Marine Corp., Warren, RI								

S-13 SPIRIT OF THE SOUND SCHOONER CO., PARRY SOUND, ON (spiritofthesound.ca)

Fleet Name / Vessel Name	IMO #	Vessel Type	Year Built	Engine Type	Cargo Cap. or Gross*	Overall Length	Breadth	Depth
Chippewa III		PA	1954	D	47*	65' 00"	16' 00"	6' 06"
Built: Russel-Hipwell Engines Ltd., Owen Sound, ON (Maid of the Mist III '54-'56, Maid of the Mist '56-'92)								

S-14 ST. JAMES MARINE CO. / FOGG TOWING & MARINE, ST. JAMES, MI (stjamesmarine.com)

Fleet Name / Vessel Name	IMO #	Vessel Type	Year Built	Engine Type	Cargo Cap. or Gross*	Overall Length	Breadth	Depth
American Girl		TB	1922	D	63*	62' 00"	14' 00"	6' 05"
Wendy Anne		TB	1955	D	89*	71' 00"	20' 00"	8' 05"
Built: Smith Basin Drydock, Port Everglades, FL (ST-2199, Four Point)								

S-15 ST. LAWRENCE CRUISE LINES INC., KINGSTON, ON (stlawrencecruiselines.com)

Fleet Name / Vessel Name	IMO #	Vessel Type	Year Built	Engine Type	Cargo Cap. or Gross*	Overall Length	Breadth	Depth
Canadian Empress		PA	1981	D	463*	108' 00"	30' 00"	8' 00"
Built: Algan Shipyards Ltd., Gananoque, ON								

S-16 ST. LAWRENCE SEAWAY DEVELOPMENT CORP., MASSENA, NY (seaway.dot.gov)

Fleet Name / Vessel Name	IMO #	Vessel Type	Year Built	Engine Type	Cargo Cap. or Gross*	Overall Length	Breadth	Depth
Grasse River		GL	1958	GL		150' 00"	65' 08"	5' 06"
Performance		TB	1997	D		50' 00"	16' 06"	7' 05"
Built: Marine Builders Inc., Utica, IN								
Robinson Bay		TB	1958	DE	213*	103' 00"	26' 10"	14' 06"
Built: Christy Corp., Sturgeon Bay, WI								

S-17 ST. LAWRENCE SEAWAY MANAGEMENT CORP., CORNWALL, ON (greatlakes-seaway.com)

Fleet Name / Vessel Name	IMO #	Vessel Type	Year Built	Engine Type	Cargo Cap. or Gross*	Overall Length	Breadth	Depth
VM/S Hercules		GL	1962	D	2,107*	200' 00"	75' 00"	18' 08"
VM/S Maisonneuve		SV	1974	D	56*	58' 03"	20' 03"	6' 05"
VM/S St. Lambert		TB	1974	D	20*	30' 08"	13' 01"	6' 05"

S-18 ST. MARYS CEMENT INC. (CANADA), TORONTO, ON (stmaryscement.com)

Fleet Name / Vessel Name	IMO #	Vessel Type	Year Built	Engine Type	Cargo Cap. or Gross*	Overall Length	Breadth	Depth
Sea Eagle II	7631860	ATB	1979	D	560*	132' 00"	35' 00"	19' 00"
Built: Modern Marine Power Co., Houma, LA; paired with barge St. Marys Cement II								
(Sea Eagle '79-'81, Canmar Sea Eagle '81-'91)								

Fleet Name Vessel Name	IMO #	Vessel Type	Year Built	Engine Type	Cargo Cap. or Gross*	Overall Length	Breadth	Depth
St. Marys Cement		CC	1986	B	9,400	360' 00"	60' 00"	23' 03"
Built: Merce Industries East, Cleveland, OH								
St. Marys Cement II	8879914	CC	1978	B	19,513	496' 06"	76' 00"	35' 00"
Built: Galveston Shipbuilding Co., Galveston, TX (Velasco '78-'81, Canmar Shuttle '81-'90)								

THE FOLLOWING VESSEL CHARTERED BY ST. MARYS CEMENT CO. FROM GREAT LAKES & INTERNATIONAL TOWING & SALVAGE CO., BURLINGTON, ON

Petite Forte	6826119	TB	1969	D	368*	127' 00"	32' 00"	14' 06"
Built: Cochrane and Sons Ltd., Selby, Yorkshire, England; paired with barge St. Marys Cement								
(E. Bronson Ingram '69-'72, Jarmac 42 '72-'73, Scotsman '73-'81, Al Battal '81-'86)								

S-19	**STAR LINE MACKINAC ISLAND FERRY, ST. IGNACE, MI** *(mackinacferry.com)*							
Anna May		ES	1947	D	94*	64' 10"	30' 00"	7' 03"
Built: Sturgeon Bay Shipbuilding Co., Sturgeon Bay, WI (West Shore '47-'12)								
Cadillac {5}		PF	1990	D	73*	64' 07"	20' 00"	7' 07"
Joliet {3}		PF	1993	D	83*	64' 08"	22' 00"	8' 03"
La Salle {4}		PF	1983	D	55*	65' 00"	20' 00"	7' 05"
Marquette II {2}		PF	2005	D	65*	74' 00"	23' 06"	8' 00"
Radisson {2}		PF	1988	D	97*	80' 00"	23' 06"	7' 00"

T-1	**TALL SHIP ADVENTURES OF CHICAGO, CHICAGO, IL** *(tallshipadventuresofchicago.com)*							
Red Witch		ES/2S	1986	W	41*	77' 00"	17' 06"	6' 05"
Built: Nathaniel Zirlott, Bayou La Batre, AL								
Windy		ES/4S	1996	W	75*	148' 00"	25' 00"	8' 00"
Built: Detyens Shipyards Inc., Charleston, SC								

T-2	**T.F. WARREN GROUP, BRANTFORD, ON** *(tfwarrengroup.com)*							
PHOENIX STAR SHIPPING CO.								
Phoenix Star	6821937	BC	1968	D	28,400	730' 00"	75' 00"	39' 08"
Built: Collingwood Shipyards, Collingwood, ON (Algocen '68-'05, Valgocen '05-'08, J.W. Shelley '08-'12)								
PHOENIX SUN SHIPPING CO.								
Phoenix Sun	8506529	BC	1987	D	28,901	610' 03"	75' 10"	46' 11"
Built: Fincantieri-Cant. Nav. Italiani S.p.A. - Ancona, Italy (Sagittarius '87-'09, Beststar '09-'11, VSL Centurion '11-'12)								

T-3	**TGL MARINE HOLDINGS ULC, TORONTO, ON**							
Jane Ann IV	7802809	ATB	1978	D	954*	150' 11"	42' 08"	21' 04"
Built: Mitsui Engineering & Shipbuilding Co., Tokyo, Japan; paired with barge Sarah Spencer; in long-term lay-up at								
Detroit, MI; (Ouro Fino '78-'81, Bomare '81-'93, Tignish Sea '93-'98)								
Sarah Spencer	5002223	SU	1959	B	21,844	693' 10"	72' 00"	40' 00"
Built: Manitowoc Shipbuilding Co., Manitowoc, WI; engine removed, converted to a self-unloading barge by								
Halifax Dartmouth Industries, Halifax, NS, in '89; in long-term lay-up at Detroit, MI (Adam E. Cornelius {3} '59-'89,								
Capt. Edward V. Smith '89-'91, Sea Barge One '91-'96)								

T-4	**THOUSAND ISLANDS & SEAWAY CRUISES, BROCKVILLE, ON** *(1000islandscruises.com)*							
General Brock III		ES	1977	D	56*	56' 05"	15' 04"	5' 02"
Built: Gananoque Boat Line Ltd., Gananoque, ON (Miss Peterborough)								
Sea Fox II		ES	1988	D	55*	39' 08"	20' 00"	2' 00"

T-5	**THUNDER BAY TUG SERVICES LTD., THUNDER BAY, ON**							
Glenada		TB	1943	D	107*	80' 06"	25' 00"	10' 01"
Built: Russel Brothers Ltd., Owen Sound, ON (HMCS Glenada [W-30] '43-'45)								
Keewanis		DB	1959	B	165*	79' 10"	35' 00"	6' 04"
Miseford		TB	1915	D	116*	85' 00"	20' 00"	9' 06"
Built: M. Beatty & Sons Ltd., Welland, ON								
Paul Becotte Sr.		DB	1963	B	167*	79' 10"	35' 00"	6' 04"
Point Valour		TB	1958	D	246*	97' 08"	28' 02"	13' 10"
Built: Davie Shipbuilding Co., Lauzon, QC (Foundation Valour '58-'83)								
Robert W.		TB	1949	D	48*	60' 00"	16' 00"	8' 06"
Built: Russel Brothers Ltd., Owen Sound, ON								
Rosalee D.		TB	1943	D	22*	55' 00"	12' 07"	4' 11"

T-6	**TNT DREDGING INC., CALEDONIA, MI**							
Joyce Marie		TB	1960	D	36*	46' 02"	15' 02"	6' 03"
Built: Kremer Motor Co. (Kendee '60-'71, Morelli, Michelle B, Debra Ann '98-'03)								

T-7	**TORONTO BOAT CRUISES, TORONTO, ON** *(torontoboatcruises.com)*							
Aurora Borealis		ES	1983	D	277*	108' 00"	24' 00"	6' 00"
Built: Ralph Hurley, Port Burwell, ON								

American Courage navigates Cleveland's twisty Cuyahoga River. (Paul Magyar)

Fleet Name Vessel Name	IMO #	Vessel Type	Year Built	Engine Type	Cargo Cap. or Gross*	Overall Length	Breadth	Depth
T-8	**TORONTO BRIGANTINE INC., TORONTO, ON** *(tallshipadventures.on.ca)*							
Pathfinder		W/TV	1963	D/W	35*	53' 00"	15' 00"	6' 09"
Built: Canadian Shipbuilding & Engineering Ltd., Collingwood, ON								
Playfair		W/TV	1973	D/W	41*	53' 07"	15' 00"	7' 04"
Built: Canadian Dredge & Co. Ltd., Kingston, ON								
T-9	**TORONTO DRYDOCK LTD., TORONTO, ON** *(torontodrydock.com)*							
M. R. Kane		TB	1945	D	51*	60' 06"	16' 05"	6' 07"
Built: Central Bridge Co. Ltd., Trenton, ON (Tanac V-276 '45-'47)								
Menier Consol		FD	1962	B	2,575*	304' 05"	49' 06"	25' 06"
Built: Davie Shipbuilding Co., Lauzon, QC; former pulpwood carrier is now a floating dry dock at Toronto, ON								
Salvage Monarch	5308275	TB	1959	D	219*	97' 09"	29' 00"	13' 06"
Built: P.K. Harris Ltd., Appledore, England								
T-10	**TORONTO FIRE DEPARTMENT, TORONTO, ON** *(toronto.ca/fire)*							
Wm. Lyon Mackenzie	6400575	FB	1964	D	102*	81' 01"	20' 00"	10' 00"
Built: Russel Brothers Ltd., Owen Sound, ON								
T-11	**TORONTO PADDLEWHEEL CRUISES LTD., NORTH YORK, ON** *(pioneercruises.com)*							
Pioneer Princess		ES	1984	D	96*	56' 00"	17' 01"	3' 09"
Built: Robin Lane Hanson, Oromocto, NB								
Pioneer Queen		ES	1968	D	110*	85' 00"	30' 06"	7' 03"
Built: Hike Metal Products, Wheatley, ON (Peche Island III '68-'71, Papoose IV '71-'96)								
T-12	**TORONTO PORT AUTHORITY, TORONTO, ON** *(torontoport.com)*							
Brutus I		TB	1992	D	10*	36' 01"	11' 09"	4' 04"
David Hornell VC		PA/CF	2006	D	219*	95' 10"	37' 07"	7' 05"
Built: Hike Metal Products, Wheatley, ON (TCCA 2 '09-'10)								
Maple City		PA/CF	1951	D	135*	70' 06"	36' 04"	5' 11"
Built: Muir Brothers Dry Dock Co. Ltd., Port Dalhousie, ON								
Marilyn Bell I		PA/CF	2009	D	270*	95' 10"	37' 07"	7' 05"
Built: Hike Metal Products, Wheatley, ON (TCCA 2 '09-'10)								
William Rest		TB	1961	D	62*	65' 00"	18' 06"	10' 06"
Built: Erieau Shipbuilding & Drydock Co. Ltd., Erieau, ON								
Windmill Point		PA/CF	1954	D	118*	65' 00"	36' 00"	10' 00"
Built: Kingston Shipyards Ltd., Kingston, ON								

The last lake vessels powered by Skinner Uniflow steam engines are the carferry Badger (this page) and the bulk cement carrier St. Marys Challenger (opposite).

Jim Hoffman

Fleet Name / Vessel Name	IMO #	Vessel Type	Year Built	Engine Type	Cargo Cap. or Gross*	Overall Length	Breadth	Depth
T-13 TORONTO TOURS LTD., TORONTO, ON *(torontotours.com)*								
Miss Kim Simpson		ES	1960	D	33*	90' 02"	13' 04"	3' 09"
Built: Molenaar's Scheepswerf, Zaandam, Netherlands								
New Beginnings		ES	1961	D	28*	41' 09"	13' 01"	4' 09"
Built: J.J. Taylor & Sons Ltd., Toronto, ON (Harry J. Kimber)								
Shipsands		ES	1972	D	23*	58' 03"	12' 01"	4' 07"
Built: Cliff Richardson Boats Ltd., Meaford, ON								
T-14 TRANSPORT NANUK INC., MONTREAL, QC *(neas.ca)*								
THE FOLLOWING VESSELS CHARTERED TO NUNAVUT EASTERN ARCTIC SHIPPING INC.								
Vessels offer service between St. Lawrence River ports and the Canadian Arctic between July and November								
Aivik	7908445	HL	1980	D	4,860	359' 08"	63' 08"	38' 09"
Built: ACH - Construction Navale, Le Havre, France (Mont Ventoux '80-'90, Aivik '90-'91, Unilifter '91-'92)								
Avataq	8801618	GC	1989	D	9,653	370' 07"	62' 00"	37' 00"
Built: Miho Shipbuilding Co. Ltd., Shimizu Shizuoka Prefecture, Japan; operated by Spliethoff's, Amsterdam (Poleca, Mekhanik Volkosh, Tiger Speed, Lootsgracht)								
Qamutik	9081289	GC	1995	D	12,760	446' 00"	62' 00"	38' 02"
Built: Frisian Shipbuilding Welgelegen B.V., Harlingen, Netherlands; operated by Spliethoff's, Amsterdam (Edisongracht)								
Umiavut	8801591	GC	1988	D	9,653	370' 07"	63' 01"	37' 00"
Built: Miho Shipbuilding Co. Ltd., Shimizu Shizuoka Prefecture, Japan; operated by Spliethoff's, Amsterdam, Netherlands (Completed as Newca; Kapitan Silin '88-'92, Lindengracht '92-'00)								
T-15 TRAVERSE TALL SHIP CO., TRAVERSE CITY, MI *(tallshipsailing.com)*								
Manitou {1}		ES/2S	1983	W	78*	114' 00"	21' 00"	9' 00"
Built: Steel Ship Corp., Portsmouth, NH								
T-16 30,000 ISLANDS CRUISE LINES INC., PARRY SOUND, ON *(island-queen.com)*								
Island Queen V		ES	1990	D	526*	130' 00"	35' 00"	6' 06"
Built: Herb Fraser & Associates Ltd., Port Colborne, ON								
T-17 TRIDENT MARINE CORP., CLEVELAND, OH *(holidaycleveland.com)*								
Holiday		PA	1964	D	25*	60' 00"	16' 01"	5' 06"
U-1 UNCLE SAM BOAT TOURS, ALEXANDRIA, NY *(usboattours.com)*								
Alexandria Belle		ES	1988	D	92*	82' 00"	32' 00"	8' 00"
Island Duchess		ES	1988	D	73*	90' 03"	27' 08"	9' 00"

Jeff Mast

Fleet Name Vessel Name	IMO #	Vessel Type	Year Built	Engine Type	Cargo Cap. or Gross*	Overall Length	Breadth	Depth
Island Wanderer		ES	1971	D	57*	62' 05"	22' 00"	7' 02"
Uncle Sam 7		ES	1976	D	55*	60' 04"	22' 00"	7' 01"

U-2 U.S. ARMY CORPS OF ENGINEERS – GREAT LAKES AND OHIO RIVER DIV., CINCINNATI, OH
(usace.army.mil) **U.S. ARMY CORPS OF ENGINEERS – BUFFALO DISTRICT**

Cheraw		TB	1970	D	356*	109' 00"	30' 06"	16' 03"

Built: Southern Shipbuilding Corp., Slidell, LA (USS Cheraw [YTB-802] '70-'96)

McCauley		CS	1948	B		112' 00"	52' 00"	4' 25"
Simonsen		CS	1954	B		142' 00"	58' 00"	5' 00"

U.S. ARMY CORPS OF ENGINEERS – DETROIT DISTRICT, LAKE MICHIGAN AREA OFFICE, KEWAUNEE SUB-OFFICE

Kenosha		TB	1954	D	82*	70' 00"	20' 00"	9' 08"

Built: Missouri Valley Bridge & Iron Works, Leavenworth, KS (U. S. Army ST-2011 '54-'65)

Manitowoc		CS	1976	B		132' 00"	44' 00"	8' 00"
Racine		TB	1931	D	61*	66' 03"	18' 05"	7' 08"

Built: Marine Iron & Shipbuilding Company, Duluth MN

U.S. ARMY CORPS OF ENGINEERS – DETROIT DISTRICT, DETROIT AREA OFFICE

Demolen		TB	1974	D	356*	109' 00"	30' 06"	16' 03"

Built: Marinette Marine Corp., Marinette, WI (USS Metacom [YTB-829] '74-'01, Metacom '01-'02)

Veler		CS	1991	B	613*	150' 00"	46' 00"	10' 06"

U.S. ARMY CORPS OF ENGINEERS – DETROIT DISTRICT, DULUTH AREA OFFICE

D. L. Billmaier		TB	1968	D	356*	109' 00"	30' 06"	16' 03"

Built: Southern Shipbuilding Corp., Slidell, LA (USS Natchitoches [YTB-799] '68-'95)

H. J. Schwartz		DB	1995	B		150' 00"	48' 00"	11' 00"
Hammond Bay		TB	1953	D	23*	45' 00"	13' 00"	7' 00"

Walter J. McCarthy Jr. arriving at the Duluth, Minn., entry. (Mike Sipper)

Fleet Name / Vessel Name	IMO #	Vessel Type	Year Built	Engine Type	Cargo Cap. or Gross*	Overall Length	Breadth	Depth
U.S. ARMY CORPS OF ENGINEERS – DETROIT DISTRICT, SOO AREA OFFICE								
Harvey		DB	1961	B		120' 00"	40' 00"	8' 00"
Nicolet		DB	1971	B		120' 00"	40' 00"	8' 00"
Owen M. Frederick		TB	1942	D	56*	65' 00"	17' 00"	7' 06"
Built: Sturgeon Bay Shipbuilding Co., Sturgeon Bay, WI								
Paul Bunyan		GL	1945	B		150' 00"	65' 00"	12' 06"
Built: Wiley Manufacturing Co., Port Deposit, MD								
Whitefish Bay		TB	1953	D	23*	45' 00"	13' 00"	7' 00"

U-3 **U.S. COAST GUARD 9TH COAST GUARD DISTRICT, CLEVELAND, OH** *(uscg.mil/d9)*								
Alder [WLB-216]		BT	2004	D	2,000*	225' 09"	46' 00"	19' 08"
Built: Marinette Marine Corp., Marinette, WI; stationed at Duluth, MN								
Biscayne Bay [WTGB-104]		IB	1979	D	662*	140' 00"	37' 06"	12' 00"
Built: Tacoma Boatbuilding Co., Tacoma, WA; stationed at St. Ignace, MI								
Bristol Bay [WTGB-102]		IB	1979	D	662*	140' 00"	37' 06"	12' 00"
Built: Tacoma Boatbuilding Co., Tacoma, WA; stationed at Detroit, MI								
Buckthorn [WLI-642]		BT	1963	D	200*	100' 00"	24' 00"	4' 08"
Built: Mobile Ship Repair Inc., Mobile, AL; stationed at Sault Ste. Marie, MI								
CGB-12001		BT	1991	B	700*	120' 00"	50' 00"	6' 00"
CGB-12002		BT	1992	B	700*	120' 00"	50' 00"	6' 00"
Hollyhock [WLB-214]		BT	2003	D	2,000*	225' 09"	46' 00"	19' 08"
Built: Marinette Marine Corp., Marinette, WI; stationed at Port Huron, MI								
Katmai Bay [WTGB-101]		IB	1978	D	662*	140' 00"	37' 06"	12' 00"
Built: Tacoma Boatbuilding Co., Tacoma, WA; stationed at Sault Ste. Marie, MI								
Mackinaw [WLBB-30]		IB	2005	D	3,407*	240' 00"	58' 00"	15' 05"
Built: Marinette Marine Corp., Marinette, WI; stationed at Cheboygan, MI								

Fleet Name Vessel Name	IMO #	Vessel Type	Year Built	Engine Type	Cargo Cap. or Gross*	Overall Length	Breadth	Depth
Mobile Bay **[WTGB-103]**		IB	1979	D	662*	140' 00"	37' 06"	12' 00"

Built: Tacoma Boatbuilding Co., Tacoma, WA; stationed at Sturgeon Bay, WI

Morro Bay **[WTGB-106]**		IB	1979	D	662*	140' 00"	37' 06"	12' 00"

Built: Tacoma Boatbuilding Co., Tacoma, WA; stationed at Cleveland, OH

Neah Bay **[WTGB-105]**		IB	1980	D	662*	140' 00"	37' 06"	12' 00"

Built: Tacoma Boatbuilding Co., Tacoma, WA; stationed at Cleveland, OH

U-4   **U.S. ENVIRONMENTAL PROTECTION AGENCY, DULUTH, MN & CHICAGO, IL** *(epa.gov)*

Lake Explorer II		RV	1966	D	150*	86' 09"	22' 00"	7' 02"

Built: Jackobson Shipyard, Oyster Bay, New York (NOAA Rude '66-'08)

Lake Guardian	8030609	RV	1981	D	282*	180' 00"	40' 00"	11' 00"

Built: Halter Marine Inc., Moss Point MS (Marsea Fourteen '81-'90)

U-5   **U.S. FISH & WILDLIFE SERVICE, JORDAN RIVER NATIONAL FISH HATCHERY, ELMIRA, MI**

Spencer F. Baird		RV	2006	D	256*	95' 00"	30' 00"	9' 05"

Built: Conrad Industries, Inc., Morgan City, LA

U-6   **U.S. NAT'L PARK SERVICE - ISLE ROYALE NAT'L PARK, HOUGHTON, MI** *(nps.gov)*

Greenstone II		TK	2003	B	114*	70' 01"	24' 01"	8' 00"

Built: Fraser Shipyards Inc., Superior, WI

Ranger III	7618234	PK	1958	D	648*	152' 08"	34' 00"	13' 00"

Built: Christy Corp., Sturgeon Bay, WI

U-7   **U.S. NAVAL SEA CADET CORPS** *(seacadets.org)*

Grayfox **[TWR-825]**		TV	1985	D	213*	120' 00"	25' 00"	12' 00"

Built: Marinette Marine, Marinette, WI; based at Port Huron, MI (USS TWR-825 '85-'97)

Manatra **[YP-671]**		TV	1974	D	67*	80' 05"	17' 09"	5' 04"

Based at Chicago, IL; name stands for MArine NAvigation and TRaining Association (USS YP-671 '74-'89)

Pride of Michigan **[YP-673]**		TV	1977	D	70*	80' 06"	17' 08"	5' 03"

Built: Peterson Builders Inc., Sturgeon Bay, WI; based at Mount Clemens, MI (USS YP-673 '77-'89)

U-8   **U.S. VENTURE INC., APPLETON, WI** *(usoil.com)*

Great Lakes {2}		TK	1982	B	5,024*	414' 00"	60' 00"	30' 00"

Built: Bay Shipbuilding Co., Sturgeon Bay, WI (Amoco Great Lakes '82-'85)

Michigan {10}	8121795	AT	1982	D	292*	107' 08"	34' 00"	16' 00"

Built: Bay Shipbuilding Co., Sturgeon Bay, WI (Amoco Michigan '82-'85)

U-9   **UNIVERSITY OF MINNESOTA-DULUTH, DULUTH, MN** *(d.umn.edu)*

Blue Heron		RV	1985	D	175*	87' 00"	23' 00"	11' 00"*

Built: Goudy and Stevens, E. Boothbay, ME (Fairtry '85-'97)

U-10   **UNIVERSITY OF WISCONSIN, GREAT LAKES WATER INSTITUTE, MILWAUKEE, WI** *(glwi.uwm.edu)*

Neeskay		RV	1952	D	75*	71' 00"	17' 06"	7' 06"

Built: Higgins Industries, New Orleans LA (T-494)

U-11   **UNIVERSITY OF WISCONSIN, SUPERIOR, WI** *(uwsuper.edu)*

L. L. Smith Jr.		RV	1950	D	38*	57' 06"	16' 06"	6' 06"

U-12   **UPPER LAKES GROUP INC., TORONTO, ON** *(upperlakes.com)*

LES GRAINS LAC SUPERIOR LTEE., TROIS-RIVIÈRES, QC

BIG 503		BC	2000	B	902*	190' 06"	35' 00"	14' 00"

Built: Jeffboat LLC, Jeffersonville, IN

BIG 543, BIG 546, BIG 548, BIG 549 and **BIG 551**

Built: Trinity Marine Products, Ashland City, TN		BC	2003	B	916*	191' 00"	35' 00"	14' 00"
BIG 9708 B		BC	1996	B	958*	191' 09"	35' 00"	14' 00"

Built: Trinity Marine Products, Ashland City, TN

BIG 9917 B		BC	1999	B	958*	191' 09"	35' 00"	14' 00"

Built: Trinity Marine Products, Ashland City, TN

U-13   **UPPER LAKES TOWING CO., ESCANABA, MI**

Joseph H. Thompson		SU	1944	B	21,200	706' 06"	71' 06"	38' 06"

Built: Sun Shipbuilding & Drydock Co., Chester, PA; converted from a saltwater vessel to a Great Lakes bulk carrier by Maryland Dry Dock, Baltimore, MD, and American Shipbuilding Co., South Chicago, IL, in '52; converted to a self-unloading barge by the owners in '91 (USNS Marine Robin '44-'52)

Joseph H. Thompson Jr.		ATB	1990	D	841*	146' 06"	38' 00"	30' 00"

Built: At Marinette, WI, from steel left over from the conversion of Joseph H. Thompson (above)

Tecumseh unloading canola at the ADM Elevator in Windsor, Ont. (Roger LeLievre)

Fleet Name Vessel Name	IMO #	Vessel Type	Year Built	Engine Type	Cargo Cap. or Gross*	Overall Length	Breadth	Depth
U-14	**USS GREAT LAKES LLC, NEW YORK, NY**							
Robert F. Deegan		TK	1968	B	2,424*	225' 08"	60' 00"	18' 00"
Built: Wyatt Industries, Houston, TX; usually paired with tug Zeus, Fleet M-26								
V-1	**VANENKEVORT TUG & BARGE INC., ESCANABA MI** *(vtbarge.com)*							
GREAT LAKES MARINE LEASING LLC, PORTLAND, OR – OWNER								
Great Lakes Trader	8635966	SU	2000	B	39,600	740' 00"	78' 00"	45' 00"
Built: Halter Marine, Pearlington, MS								
Joyce L. VanEnkevort	8973033	AT	1998	D	1,179*	135' 04"	50' 00"	26' 00"
Built: Bay Shipbuilding Co., Sturgeon Bay, WI; paired with barge Great Lakes Trader								
V-2	**VIC POWELL WELDING LTD., DUNNVILLE, ON**							
Toni D		TB	1959	D	15*	46' 00"	15' 07"	4' 01"
V-3	**VICTORIAN PRINCESS CRUISE LINES INC., ERIE, PA** *(victorianprincess.com)*							
Victorian Princess		ES	1985	D	46*	67' 00"	24' 00"	4' 05"
Built: Mid-City Steel Fabricating Inc., La Crosse, WI (Rosie 1, Rosie O'Shea)								
V-4	**VIKING I LLC, MENOMINEE, MI**							
Manitowoc		DB	1926	B	3,080*	371' 03"	67' 03"	22' 06"
Built: Manitowoc Shipbuilding Co., Manitowoc, WI; laid up at Menominee, MI								
Snohomish		TB	1943	DE	195*	110' 00"	26' 06"	12' 06"
Built: Ira S. Bushey & Sons Inc., Brooklyn, NY; laid up at Menominee, MI (WYTM-98 Snohomish, Dami Dew)								
Viking I	5018246	CF	1925	D	2,713*	360' 00"	56' 03"	21' 06"
Built: Manitowoc Shipbuilding Co., Manitowoc, WI; laid up at Menominee, MI (Ann Arbor No. 7 '25-'64, Viking {2} '64-'96)								
V-5	**VISTA FLEET, DULUTH, MN** *(vistafleet.com)*							
Vista Queen		ES	1987	D	97*	64' 00"	16' 00"	6' 02"
Built: Mid-City Steel Fabricating Inc., La Crosse, WI (Queen of Excelsior)								
Vista Star		ES	1987	D	95*	91' 00"	24' 09"	5' 02"
Built: Freeport Shipbuilding Inc., Freeport, FL (Island Empress '87-'88)								
V-6	**VOIGHT'S MARINE SERVICES LTD., ELLISON BAY AND GILLS ROCK, WI** *(islandclipper.com)*							
Island Clipper {2}		ES	1987	D	71*	65' 00"	20' 00"	8' 00"
Yankee Clipper		ES	1971	D	41*	46' 06"	17' 00"	6' 00"
W-1	**WALPOLE-ALGONAC FERRY LINE, PORT LAMBTON, ON** *(walpolealgonacferry.com)*							
City of Algonac		CF	1990	D	82*	62' 06"	27' 09"	5' 09"
Built: Duratug Shipyard & Fabricating Ltd., Port Dover, ON								
Walpole Islander		CF	1986	D	72*	54' 05"	27' 09"	6' 03"
W-2	**WALSTROM MARINE, HARBOR SPRINGS, MI** *(walstrom.com)*							
DePere		DB	1924	B	172*	118' 06"	32' 00"	5' 02"
Elizabeth		TB	1945	D	21*	42' 02"	12' 01"	5' 05"
Built: Burger Boat Co., Manitowoc, WI (Charles F. Liscomb, Jason, Lydie Rae)								
W-3	**WHITE LAKE DOCK & DREDGE INC., MONTAGUE, MI** *(wlddi.com)*							
Captain George		TB	1929	D	61*	60' 09"	16' 07"	7' 07"
Built: Charles Ward Engine Works at Charleston, WV (Captain George '29-'73, Kurt R. Luedtke '73-'91)								
W-4	**WARNER PETROLEUM CORP., CLARE, MI** *(warnerpetroleum.com)*							
Coloma L. Warner	7337892	TB	1955	D	134*	86' 00"	24' 00"	10' 00"
Built: Sturgeon Bay Shipbuilding, Sturgeon Bay, WI; paired with the barge Warner Provider (Harbor Ace '55-'61, Gopher State '61-'71, Betty Gale '71-'93, Hannah D. Hannah '93-'10)								
Warner Provider		RT	1962	B	1,698*	264' 00"	52' 05"	12' 00"
Built: Port Houston Iron Works, Houston, TX (Hannah 2903)								
William L. Warner	7322055	RT	1973	D	492*	120' 00"	40' 00"	14' 00"
Built: Halter Marine, New Orleans, LA; (Jos. F. Bigane '73-'04)								
W-5	**WASHINGTON ISLAND FERRY LINE INC., WASHINGTON ISLAND, WI** *(wisferry.com)*							
Arni J. Richter		PA/CF	2003	D	92*	104' 00"	38' 06"	10' 11"
Built: Bay Shipbuilding Co., Sturgeon Bay, WI								
Eyrarbakki		PA/CF	1970	D	95*	87' 00"	36' 00"	7' 06"
Built: Bay Shipbuilding Co., Sturgeon Bay, WI								
Robert Noble		PA/CF	1979	D	97*	90' 04"	36' 00"	8' 03"
Built: Peterson Builders Inc., Sturgeon Bay, WI								
Washington {2}		PA/CF	1989	D	97*	100' 00"	37' 00"	9' 00"
Built: Peterson Builders Inc., Sturgeon Bay, WI								

Fleet Name Vessel Name	IMO #	Vessel Type	Year Built	Engine Type	Cargo Cap. or Gross*	Overall Length	Breadth	Depth
W-6 **WENDELLA BOAT TOURS, CHICAGO, IL** *(wendellaboats.com)*								
Linnea		ES	2010	D	77*	85' 05"	30' 00"	7' 01"
Ouilmette		ES	2001	D	43*	65' 00"	22' 04"	4' 05"
Sunliner		ES	1961	D	35*	62' 00"	14' 04"	6' 04"
Wendella		ES	2007	D	77*	85' 05"	30' 00"	7' 01"
Wendella LTD		ES	1992	D	66*	68' 00"	20' 00"	4' 09"
W-7 **WILLY'S CONTRACTING CO., SOUTHAMPTON, ON** *(willyscontracting.com)*								
Pride		TB	1957	D	47*	52' 06"	29' 08"	5' 01"
Built: Strege Fisheries Inc., Racine, WI								
W-8 **WINDSOR RIVER CRUISES LTD., WINDSOR, ON** *(windsorrivercruises.com)*								
Macassa Bay	8624709	ES	1986	D	210*	93' 07"	29' 07"	10' 04"
Built: Boiler Pump & Marine Works Ltd., Hamilton, ON								
W-9 **WOHLLEB-SOCIE CO., TOLEDO, OH**								
Bessie B		TB	1947	D	30*	52' 03"	13' 09"	5' 05"
W-10 **WISCONSIN DEPARTMENT OF NATURAL RESOURCES, BAYFIELD AND STURGEON BAY, WI**								
Coregonus		RV	2011	D	37*	60' 00"	16' 00"	5' 09"
Gaylord Nelson		RV	1992	D	12*	45' 09"	16' 00"	5' 05"
Hack Noyes		RV	1947	D	50*	56' 00"	14' 05"	4' 00"
Z-1 **ZINKS MARINE TOWING LLC, WESTLAKE, OH**								
Apalachee		TB	1943	DE	224*	110' 00"	26' 04"	15' 01"
Built: Ira S. Bushey & Sons Inc., Brooklyn, NY (Apalachee WYTM-71)								

Indiana Harbor meets Roger Blough below the Soo Locks. (Sam Lapinski)

The Maritime Academy of Toledo Foundation

One Maritime Plaza
Toledo, OH 43604
Phone: 419-244-9999
Fax: 419-244-9898

www.themaritimefoundation.us

Leading the way in Maritime Education and Job Retraining in Northwest Ohio

Offering USCG-approved Professional Mariner Courses

- STCW Basic Safety Training
- Radar Observer Recertification
- Radar Observer (Unlimited)
- Crowd Management
- Crisis Management & Human Behavior

Ask about our Professional Mariner Development Training

Overnight and Extended-Stay Facilities Available
Conference / Meeting Rooms, Pool, Fitness Center, Theater,
Teaching Galley and Commercial Laundry Facilities

E-mail us at: **info@themaritimefoundation.us**

GROH'S PHOTOGRAPHY

(920) 918-3402
www.grohs-photography.com

FULL LINE OF GREAT LAKES FREIGHTER IMAGES

1906-'37

1906: St. Marys Challenger *(re:'67)*
1936: J.A.W. Iglehart *(re:'65)**
1937: St. Marys Conquest *(re:'87)*

1941-'49

1941: Pere Marquette 41 *(re:'97)*
1942: Alpena *(re:'91)*, American Victory *(re:'61,'82)***
Lee A. Tregurtha *(re:'61)*
1943: Algoma Transfer *(re:'98)*, Cuyahoga *(re:'74)*,
Manistee *(re:'64)*, Mississagi *(re:'67)*
1944: Joseph H. Thompson *(re'52,'91)*,
McKee Sons *(re:'53,'91)*
1945: Paul H. Townsend *(re:'52)**
1949: Wilfred Sykes

1950-'59

1952: Arthur M. Anderson *(re:'75,'82)*, Kaye E. Barker
(re:'76, '81), Cason J. Callaway *(re:'74,'82)*, Philip R.
Clarke *(re:'74,'82)*, Lewis J. Kuber *(re:'06)*, Michipicoten
(re:'57,'80), Ojibway, John G. Munson
1953: American Valor *(re:'74,'82)***, American
Fortitude *(re:'81)***, Badger, James J. Kuber *(re:'07)*,
Pathfinder *(re:'98)*, Saginaw
1958: John Sherwin**
1959: Cedarglen *(re:'77)*, Hon. James L. Oberstar *(re:'72,
'81)*, Herbert C. Jackson *(re:'75)*, Sarah Spencer *(re:'89)***

1960-'69

1960: Edward L. Ryerson**
1961: English River *(re:'74)*
1962: Catherine Desgagnés, Algoma Montrealais
1963: Algoma Provider, Algoma Quebecois,
Yankcanuck**
1965: Stephen B. Roman *(re:'83)*
1966: Algosteel *(re:'89)*
1967: Tim S. Dool *(re:'96)*, Canadian Navigator *(re:'80,
'97)*, John D. Leitch *(re:'02)*, Manitoba
1968: Algomarine *(re:'89)*, Algorail, Algoma Progress,
Frontenac *(re:'73)*, Phoenix Star
1969: CSL Tadoussac *(re:'01)*

1972-'79

1972: Algoway, Roger Blough, CSL Niagara *(re:'99)*,
Stewart J. Cort
1973: Adam E. Cornelius, Calumet, Manitowoc, John
J. Boland, Rt. Hon. Paul J. Martin *(re:'00)*, Presque Isle,
Tecumseh

1974: Algosoo, H. Lee White, Robert S. Pierson
1975: Melissa Desgagnés, Sam Laud
1976: James R. Barker, Joseph L. Block, Algoma
Olympic, Amelia Desgagnés, Thalassa Desgagnés,
St. Clair
1977: Algoeast, Algolake, CSL Assiniboine *(re:'05)*, CSL
Laurentien *(re:'01)*, Walter J. McCarthy Jr., Mesabi Miner
1978: Radcliffe R. Latimer *(re:'09)*, Algosar, American
Integrity, American Spirit, Buffalo
1979: American Courage, Algoma Enterprise, Algoma
Transport, Edwin H. Gott, Indiana Harbor

1980-'87

1980: American Mariner, Burns Harbor, Salarium, Edgar
B. Speer, Oakglen, Richelieu
1981: Algowood *(re:'00)*, American Century, Great
Republic, Capt. Henry Jackman *(re:'96)*, Mapleglen,
Saguenay, Paul R. Tregurtha
1982: Atlantic Superior, Camilla Desgagnés, Peter
R. Cresswell *(re:'98)*, Michigan, Véga Desgagnés,
Ashtabula
1983: John B. Aird, Birchglen, Spruceglen, Kaministiqua
1984: Atlantic Huron *(re:'89,'03)*
1985: Atlantic Erie, Pineglen
1986: Anna Desgagnés, Algoma Spirit
1987: Algoma Discovery, Algoma Guardian,
Phoenix Sun

1992-'99

1992: Dara Desgagnés, Esta Desgagnés
1993: Jana Desgagnés
1996: Integrity
1998: Algosea
1999: Maria Desgagnés

2000-'13

2000: Great Lakes Trader
2001: Norman McLeod
2004: Algoscotia, Lake Express
2006: Innovation
2007: Rosaire A. Desgagnés
2008: Algocanada, Algonova, John J. Carrick,
Zelada Desgagnés
2009: Sedna Desgagnés
2011: Algoma Mariner, Claude A. Desgagnés
2012: Lakes Contender, Bella Desgagnés, Baie St. Paul
2013: Algoma Equinox, Thunder Bay, Whitefish Bay,
Baie Comeau, Algoma Harvester

(re = major rebuild; * storage barge; ** long-term lay-up)

ENGINES – *Great Lakes & Seaway Vessels*

Vessel Name	Engine Manufacturer & Model #	Engine Type	Total Engines	Total Cylinders	Rated HP	Total Props	Speed MPH
Adam E. Cornelius	GM EMD - 20-645-E7B	Diesel	2	20	7,200 bhp	1 cpp	16.1
Alder (USCG)	Caterpillar - 3608TA	Diesel	2	6	3,100 bhp	1 cpp	
Algocanada	MaK - 9M32C	Diesel	1	9	6,118 bhp	1 cpp	16.1
Algoeast	B&W - 6K45GF	Diesel	1	6	5,300 bhp	1 cpp	15.8
Algolake	Pielstick - 10PC2-2V-400	Diesel	2	10	9,000 bhp	1 cpp	17.3
Algoma Dartmouth	M.A.N.-B&W - 6L23/30A	Diesel	2	6	2,310 bhp	2 cpp	13.3
Algoma Discovery	Sulzer - 6RTA62	Diesel	1	6	15,499 bhp	1 cpp	16.4
Algoma Enterprise	M.A.N. - 7L40/45	Diesel	2	7	8,804 bhp	1 cpp	13.8
Algoma Equinox	Wartsila 5RT-flex50-D	Diesel	1	5	9,349 bhp	1 cpp	16.1
Algoma Guardian	Sulzer - 6RTA62	Diesel	1	6	15,499 bhp	1 cpp	16.4
Algoma Harvester	Wartsila 5RT-flex50-D	Diesel	1	5	9,349 bhp	1 cpp	16.1
Algoma Mariner	M.A.N.-B&W - 6L48/60CR	Diesel	1	6	9,792 bhp	1 cpp	
Algoma Montrealais	Canadian General Electric Co. Ltd.	Turbine	1	**	9,900 shp	1	19.0
Algoma Navigator	Doxford Engines Ltd. - 76J4	Diesel	1	4	9,680 bhp	1	16.7
Algoma Olympic	M.A.N. - 8L40/54A	Diesel	2	8	10,000 bhp	1 cpp	15.0
Algoma Progress	Caterpillar - 3612-TA	Diesel	2	12	9,000 bhp	1 cpp	15.5
Algoma Provider	John Inglis Co. Ltd.	Turbine	1	**	10,000 shp	1	17.3
Algoma Quebecois	Canadian General Electric Co. Ltd.	Turbine	1	**	9,900 shp	1	19.0
Algoma Spirit	Sulzer - 6RTA62	Diesel	1	6	11,284 bhp	1 cpp	16.4
Algoma Transfer	Sulzer - 5RND68	Diesel	1	5	6,100 bhp	1 cpp	18.4
Algoma Transport	M.A.N. - 8L40/45	Diesel	2	8	10,000 bhp	1 cpp	13.8
Algomarine	Sulzer - 6RND76	Diesel	1	6	9,600 bhp	1 cpp	17.0
Algonova	MaK - 9M32C	Diesel	1	9	6,118 bhp	1 cpp	16.1
Algorail	Fairbanks Morse - 10-38D8-1/8	Diesel	4	10	6,662 bhp	1 cpp	13.8
Algosar	Alco - 16V251E	Diesel	2	16	5,150 bhp	2	14.4
Algoscotia	Wartsila - 6L46C	Diesel	1	6	8,445 bhp	1 cpp	16.0
Algosoo	Pielstick - 10PC2-V-400	Diesel	2	10	9,000 bhp	1 cpp	15.0
Algosea	Wartsila - 6L46A	Diesel	1	6	6,434 bhp	1 cpp	15.0
Algosteel	Sulzer - 6RND76	Diesel	1	6	9,599 bhp	1	17.0
Algoway	Fairbanks Morse - 10-38D8-1/8	Diesel	4	10	6,662 bhp	1 cpp	13.8
Algowood	MaK - 6M552AK	Diesel	2	6	10,200 bhp	1 cpp	13.8
Alpena	De Laval Steam Turbine Co.	Turbine	1	**	4,400 shp	1	14.1
Amelia Desgagnés	Allen - 12PVBCS12-F	Diesel	2	12	4,000 bhp	1 cpp	16.1
American Century	GM - EMD - 20-645-E7B	Diesel	4	20	14,400 bhp	2 cpp	17.3
American Courage	GM - EMD - 20-645-E7	Diesel	2	20	7,200 bhp	1 cpp	16.1
American Fortitude	General Electric Co.	Turbine	1	**	7,700 shp	1	16.7
American Integrity	GM EMD - 20-645-E7	Diesel	4	20	14,400 bhp	2 cpp	18.4
American Mariner	GM EMD - 20-645-E7	Diesel	2	20	7,200 bhp	1 cpp	15.0
American Spirit	Pielstick - 16PC2-2V-400	Diesel	2	16	16,000 bhp	2 cpp	17.3
American Valor	Westinghouse Elec. Corp.	Turbine	1	**	7,700 shp	1	16.1
American Victory	Bethlehem Steel Corp.	Turbine	1	**	7,700 shp	1	19.0
Amundsen (CCG)	Alco - 16V251F	Diesel	6	16	17,700 bhp	2	18.6
Anglian Lady *	Deutz - SBA12M528	Diesel	2	12	3,480 bhp	2 cpp	15.5
Anna Desgagnés	M.A.N. - K5SZ70/125B	Diesel	1	5	10,332 bhp	1	17.8
Arctic	M.A.N. - 14V52/55A	Diesel	1	14	14,769 bhp	1	17.8
Arthur M. Anderson	Westinghouse Elec. Corp.	Turbine	1	**	7,700 shp	1	16.1
Atlantic Erie	Sulzer - 6RLB66	Diesel	1	6	11,100 bhp	1 cpp	16.1
Atlantic Huron	Sulzer - 6RLB66	Diesel	1	6	11,094 bhp	1 cpp	17.3
Atlantic Superior	Sulzer - 6RLA66	Diesel	1	6	11,095 bhp	1 cpp	17.3
Avenger IV *	British Polar	Diesel	1	9	2,700 bhp	1 cpp	12.0
Badger **	Skinner Engine Co. - Steeple Compound Uniflow	Steam	2	4	8,000 ihp	2	18.4
Baie Comeau	MAN-B&W - 6S50ME-B9	Diesel	1	6	10,680 bhp	1	15.5
Baie St. Paul	MAN-B&W - 6S50ME-B9	Diesel	1	6	10,680 bhp	1	15.5
Barbara Andrie *	GM EMD 16-645-EF	Diesel	1	16	2,000 bhp	1	

* = tug   ** = ferry

bhp: brake horsepower, a measure of diesel engine output measured at the crankshaft before entering gearbox or any other power take-out device

ihp: indicated horsepower, based on an internal measurement of mean cylinder pressure, piston area, piston stroke and engine speed; used for reciprocating engines

shp: shaft horsepower, a measure of engine output at the propeller shaft at the output of the reduction gearbox; used for steam and diesel-electric engines

cpp: controllable pitch propeller

Vessel Name	Engine Manufacturer & Model #	Engine Type	Total Engines	Total Cylinders	Rated HP	Total Props	Speed MPH
Bella Desgagnés	Wartsila - 9L20CR	Diesel	4	9	8,320 bhp	2 azimuth	17.3
Birchglen	Sulzer 4RLB76	Diesel	1	4	10,880 bhp	1cpp	13.8
Biscayne Bay (USCG)	Fairbanks Morse - 10-38D8-1/8	Diesel	2	10	2,500 bhp	1	13.8
Bradshaw McKee *	GM EMD - 12-645-E5	Diesel	2	12	4,320 bhp	2	11.5
Bristol Bay (USCG)	Fairbanks Morse - 10-38D8-1/8	Diesel	2	10	2,500 bhp	1	13.8
Buffalo	GM EMD - 20-645-E7	Diesel	2	20	7,200 bhp	1 cpp	16.1
Burns Harbor	GM EMD - 20-645-E7	Diesel	4	20	14,400 bhp	2 cpp	18.4
Calumet	Alco - 16V251E	Diesel	2	16	5,600 bhp	1	16.1
Camilla Desgagnés	Werkspoor - 12TM410	Diesel	1	12	7,797 bhp	1 cpp	
Capt. Henry Jackman	MaK - 6M552AK	Diesel	2	6	9,465 bhp	1 cpp	17.3
Cason J. Callaway	Westinghouse Elec. Corp.	Turbine	1	**	7,700 shp	1	16.1
Catherine Desgagnés	Sulzer - 6SAD60	Diesel	1	6	3,841 bhp	1	15.5
Cedarglen	B&W - 7-74VTBF-160	Diesel	1	7	8,750 bhp	1 cpp	15.5
Chi-Cheemaun **	Caterpillar - C280-6	Diesel	4	6	9,280 bhp	2	
Claude A. Desgagnés	MaK/Caterpillar - 6M43C	Diesel	1	6	7,342 bhp	1 cpp	17.8
Commodore Straits *	Werkspoor	Diesel	2		3,470 bhp	2	13.8
CSL Assiniboine	Pielstick - 10PC2-2V-400	Diesel	2	10	9,000 bhp	1 cpp	15.0
CSL Laurentien	Pielstick - 10PC2-2V-400	Diesel	2	10	9,000 bhp	1 cpp	16.1
CSL Niagara	Pielstick - 10PC2-2V-400	Diesel	2	10	9,000 bhp	1 cpp	15.0
CSL Tadoussac	Sulzer - 6RND76	Diesel	1	6	9,600 bhp	1	17.0
Cuyahoga	Caterpillar - 3608	Diesel	1	8	3,000 bhp	1 cpp	12.6
Dara Desgagnés	B&W - 6L35MC	Diesel	1	6	5,030 bhp	1 cpp	14.4
Defiance *	GM EMD - 20-645-E7	Diesel	2	20	7,200 bhp	2	15.0
Des Groseilliers (CCG)	Alco - 16V251F	Diesel	6	16	17,700 bhp	2	18.6
Dorothy Ann *	GM EMD - 20-645-E7B	Diesel	2	20	7,200 bhp	2 Z-drive cpp	16.1
Ecosse *	GM Detroit - 16V92 N	Diesel	2	16	1,800 bhp	2	13.8
Edgar B. Speer	Pielstick - 18PC2-3V-400	Diesel	2	18	19,260 bhp	2 cpp	17.0
Edward L. Ryerson	General Electric Co.	Turbine	1	**	9,900 shp	1	19.0
Edwin H. Gott	MaK - 8M43C	Diesel	2	8	19,578 bhp	2 ccp	16.7
English River	Werkspoor - TMAB-390	Diesel	1	8	1,850 bhp	1 cpp	13.8
Esta Desgagnés	B&W - 6L35MC	Diesel	1	6	5,030 bhp	1 cpp	14.4
Evans McKeil *	GM EMD - 16-645C	Diesel	1	16	2,150 bhp	1	11.5
Everlast *	Daihatsu - 8DSM-32	Diesel	2	8	6,000 bhp	2	16.5
Federal Agno	Sulzer - 6RTA58	Diesel	1	6	9,500 bhp	1	16.7
Federal Asahi	B&W - 6S46MC-C	Diesel	1	6	10,710 bhp	1	16.1
Federal Hudson	B&W - 6S46MC-C	Diesel	1	6	10,710 bhp	1	15.5
Federal Hunter	B&W - 6S46MC-C	Diesel	1	6	10,710 bhp	1	15.5
Federal Kivalina	B&W - 6S46MC-C	Diesel	1	6	10,710 bhp	1	16.1
Federal Kumano	B&W - 6S46MC-C	Diesel	1	6	10,710 bhp	1	16.1
Federal Kushiro	Mitsubishi - 6UEC52LA	Diesel	1	6	9,626 bhp	1	16.6
Federal Maas	B&W - 6S50MC	Diesel	1	6	11,640 bhp	1	16.1
Federal Mackinac	B&W - 6S46MC-C	Diesel	1	6	10,540 bhp	1	16.1
Federal Margaree	B&W - 6S46MC-C	Diesel	1	6	10,686 bhp	1	16.1
Federal Nakagawa	B&W - 6S46MC-C	Diesel	1	6	10,710 bhp	1	16.1
Federal Oshima	B&W - 6S46MC-C	Diesel	1	6	10,710 bhp	1	16.1
Federal Rhine	B&W - 6S50MC	Diesel	1	6	11,640 bhp	1	16.1
Federal Rideau	B&W - 6S46MC-C	Diesel	1	6	10,710 bhp	1	16.1
Federal Saguenay	B&W - 6S50MC	Diesel	1	6	11,665 bhp	1	16.1
Federal Sakura	Mitsubishi - 6UEC52LA	Diesel	1	6	8,663 bhp	1	16.6
Federal Schelde	B&W - 6S50MC	Diesel	1	6	11,640 bhp	1	16.1
Federal Seto	M.A.N.-B&W - 6S46MC-C	Diesel	1	6	10,711 bhp	1	16.7
Federal Shimanto	Mitsubishi - 6UEC52LA	Diesel	1	6	9,600 bhp	1	16.6
Federal St. Laurent	B&W - 6S50MC	Diesel	1	6	11,640 bhp	1	16.1
Federal Welland	B&W - 6S46MC-C	Diesel	1	6	10,710 bhp	1	16.1
Federal Weser	B&W - 6S46MC-C	Diesel	1	6	10,686 bhp	1	18.0
Federal Yoshino	Mitsubishi - 6UEC52LA	Diesel	1	6	9,600 bhp	1	16.6
Federal Yukina	M.A.N.-B&W - 6S46MC-C	Diesel	1	6	8,960 bhp	1	16.1
Federal Yukon	B&W - 6S46MC-C	Diesel	1	6	10,710 bhp	1	15.5
Florence M *	Fairbanks Morse - 8-28D8-1/4	Diesel	2	8	1,450 bhp	2	
Frontenac	Sulzer - 6RND76	Diesel	1	6	9,600 bhp	1 cpp	17.0
G.L. Ostrander *	Caterpillar - 3608-DITA	Diesel	2	8	6,008 bhp	2	17.3
Great Republic	GM EMD - 20-645-E7	Diesel	2	20	7,200 bhp	2 cpp	15.0
Grayfox (USNCS)	Caterpillar - 3512 TAC	Diesel	2	12	2,350 bhp.	2	20.7
H. Lee White	GM EMD - 20-645-E7B	Diesel	2	20	7,200 bhp	1 cpp	15.0

Vessel Name	Engine Manufacturer & Model #	Engine Type	Total Engines	Total Cylinders	Rated HP	Total Props	Speed MPH
Hamilton Energy	GM EMD - 12-534-E6	Diesel	1	12	1,500 bhp	1 cpp	13.8
Herbert C. Jackson	General Electric Co.	Turbine	1	**	6,600 shp	1	16.0
Hollyhock (USCG)	Caterpillar - 3608TA	Diesel	2	6	3,100 bhp	1	
Hon. James L. Oberstar	Rolls-Royce Bergen - B32:40L6P	Diesel	2	6	8,160 shp	1 ccp	17.0
Indiana Harbor	GM EMD - 20-645-E7	Diesel	4	20	14,400 bhp	2 cpp	16.1
Invincible *	GM EMD - 16-645-E7B	Diesel	2	16	5,750 bhp	2	13.8
J. A. W. Iglehart	De Laval Steam Turbine Co.	Turbine	1	**	4,400 shp	1	15.0
J. S. St. John	GM EMD - 8-567	Diesel	1	8	850 bhp	1	11.5
James R. Barker	Pielstick - 16PC2-2V-400	Diesel	2	16	16,000 bhp	2 cpp	15.5
Jana Desgagnés	B&W - 6L35MC	Diesel	1	6	5,030 bhp	1 cpp	14.4
Jane Ann IV *	Pielstick - 8PC2-2L-400	Diesel	2	8	8,000 bhp	2	15.8
Jiimaan **	Ruston Paxman Diesels Ltd. - 6RK215	Diesel	2	6	2,839 bhp	2 cpp	15.0
John B. Aird	MaK - 6M552AK	Diesel	2	6	9,460 bhp	1 cpp	13.8
John D. Leitch	B&W - 5-74VT2BF-160	Diesel	1	5	7,500 bhp	1 cpp	16.1
John G. Munson	General Electric Co.	Turbine	1	**	7,700 shp	1	17.3
John J. Boland	GM EMD - 20-645-E7B	Diesel	2	20	7,200 bhp	1 cpp	15.0
John Sherwin	Conversion from steam to diesel begun in 2008 but suspended due to economy						
John Spence *	GM EMD 16-567-C	Diesel	2	16	3,280 bhp	2	13.8
Joseph H. Thompson Jr. *	Caterpillar	Diesel	2			1	
Joseph L. Block	GM EMD - 20-645-E7	Diesel	2	20	7,200 bhp	1 cpp	17.3
Joyce L. VanEnkevort *	Caterpillar - 3612	Diesel	2	12	10,200 bhp	2 cpp	
Kaministiqua	Sulzer - 4RLB76	Diesel	4	4	10,880 bhp	1cpp	15.5
Karen Andrie *	GM EMD - 8-710G7C	Diesel	2	8	4,000 bhp	2	19
Katmai Bay (USCG)	Fairbanks Morse - 10-38D8-1/8	Diesel	2	10	2,500 bhp	1	13.8
Kaye E. Barker	Rolls-Royce Bergen - B32:40L6P	Diesel	2	6	8,160 shp	1 ccp	17.0
Ken Boothe Sr.*	Cat-MaK - 8M32C	Diesel	2	8	10,876 bhp	2 cpp	18.4
Lake Express **	M.T.U. - 16V4000M70	Diesel	4	16	12,616 bhp	4 water jet	40.0
Lee A. Tregurtha	Rolls-Royce Bergen B32:40L6P	Diesel	2	6	8,160 shp	1 ccp	17.0
Mackinaw (USCG)	Caterpillar - 3612	Diesel	3	12	9,119 bhp	2 Azipod	17.3
Manistee	GM EMD - 20-645-E6	Diesel	1	20	2,950 bhp	1	
Manitoba	Fairbanks Morse - 8-38D8-1/8	Diesel	4	8	5,332 bhp	1 cpp	16.1
Manitowoc	Alco - 16V251E	Diesel	2	16	5,600 bhp	1	16.1
Mapleglen	B&W - 6K67GF	Diesel	1	6	11,600 bhp	1	16.1
Maria Desgagnés	B&W - 6S42MC	Diesel	1	6	8,361 bhp	1 cpp	16.1
Martha L. Black (CCG)	Alco - 16V251F	Diesel	3	16	8,973 bhp	2	13.8
Mary E. Hannah *	GM EMD - 16-567C	Diesel	2	16	3,200 bhp	2	15.0
Mary Page Hannah *	GM -12-278A	Diesel	2	12	1,850 bhp	2	
Melissa Desgagnés	Allen - 12PVBCS12-F	Diesel	2	12	4,000 bhp	1 cpp	13.8
Mesabi Miner	Pielstick - 16PC2-2V-400	Diesel	2	16	16,000 bhp	2 cpp	15.5
Michigan *	GM EMD - 20-645-E6	Diesel	2	16	3,900 bhp	2	13.2
Michipicoten	MaK - 6M32C	Diesel	2	6	8,160 bhp	1	14.0
Mississagi	Caterpillar - 3612-TA	Diesel	1	12	4,500 bhp	1 cpp	13.8
Mobile Bay (USCG)	Fairbanks Morse - 10-38D8-1/8	Diesel	2	10	2,500 bhp	1	13.8
Morro Bay (USCG)	Fairbanks Morse - 10-38D8-1/8	Diesel	2	10	2,500 bhp	1	13.8
Neah Bay (USCG)	Fairbanks Morse - 10-38D8-1/8	Diesel	2	10	2,500 bhp	1	13.8
Nordik Express	GM EMD - 20-645-E7	Diesel	2	20	7,200 bhp	2 ccp	16.0
Oakglen	B&W - 6K67GF	Diesel	1	6	11,600 bhp	1	15.5
Ojibway	GE - 7FDM EFI	Diesel	1	16	4,100 bhp	1 cpp	
Olive L. Moore *	Alco - 16V251	Diesel	2	16	5,830 bhp	1	
Paul H. Townsend	Nordberg - TSM-216	Diesel	1	6	2,150 bhp	1	12.1
Paul R. Tregurtha	MaK - M43C	Diesel	2	6	16,080 bhp	2 cpp	
Pelee Islander **	Caterpillar - 3408	Diesel	2	8	910 bhp	2	
Peter R. Cresswell	MaK - 6M552AK	Diesel	2	6	9,460 bhp	1 cpp	13.8
Petite Forte *	Ruston - 8ATC	Diesel	2	8	4,200 bhp	2	15.5
Philip R. Clarke	Westinghouse Elec. Corp.	Turbine	1	**	7,700 shp	1	16.1
Phoenix Star	Fairbanks Morse -10-38D8-1/8	Diesel	4	10	7,999 bhp	1cpp	13.8
Phoenix Sun	Sulzer - 4RTA58	Diesel	1	4	8,640 bhp	1	17.8
Pierre Radisson (CCG)	Alco - 16V251F	Diesel	6	16	17,700 bhp	2	18.4
Pineglen	MaK - 6M601AK	Diesel	1	6	8,158 bhp	1 cpp	15.5
Point Valour *	Fairbanks Morse - 8-38D8-1/8	Diesel	1	8	1,280 bhp	1	13.0
Prentiss Brown *	GM EMD - 12-645-E2	Diesel	2	12	3,900 bhp	1	
Presque Isle *	Mirrlees Blackstone Ltd. - KVMR-16	Diesel	2	16	14,840 bhp	2 cpp	
Quinte Loyalist **	Caterpillar - 3196	Diesel	2	6	770 bhp		
Radcliffe R. Latimer	MaK - 8M32C	Diesel	2	8	10,442 bhp	1 cpp	
Rebecca Lynn *	GM EMD - 16-567-BC	Diesel	2	16	3,600 bhp	2	

Vessel Name	Engine Manufacturer & Model #	Engine Type	Total Engines	Total Cylinders	Rated HP	Total Props	Speed MPH
Reliance *	A.B. Nohab - SVI 16VS-F	Diesel	2	16	5,600 bhp	1 cpp	17.6
Richelieu	B&W - 6K67GF	Diesel	1	6	11,600 bhp	1	15.4
Robert S. Pierson	Alco - 16V251E	Diesel	2	16	5,600 bhp	1	17.8
Roger Blough	Pielstick - 16PC2V-400	Diesel	2	16	14,200 bhp	1 cpp	16.7
Rosaire A. Desgagnés	MaK/Caterpillar - 6M43	Diesel	1	6	7,344 bhp	1 cpp	17.8
Rt. Hon. Paul J. Martin	Pielstick - 10PC2-V-400	Diesel	2	10	9,000 bhp	1 cpp	15.0
Saginaw	MaK - 6M43C	Diesel	1	6	8,160 bhp	1 cpp	16.1
Saguenay	B&W - 6K67GF	Diesel	1	6	11,600 bhp	1	16.1
Salarium	Pielstick - 10PC2-2V-400	Diesel	2	10	10,700 bhp	1 cpp	13.8
Salvor *	GM EMD - 16-645-E7	Diesel	2	16	5,750 bhp	2	13.8
Sam Laud	GM EMD - 20-645-E7	Diesel	2	20	7,200 bhp	1 cpp	16.1
Samuel deChamplain *	GM EMD - 20-645-E5	Diesel	2	20	7,200 bhp	2 cpp	17.3
Samuel Risley (CCG)	Wartsila - VASA 16V22HF	Diesel	2	16	7,590 bhp	2 cpp	17.3
Sarah Desgagnés	MaK - 7M43	Diesel	1	7	9,517 bhp	1 cpp	15.0
Sea Eagle II *	GM EMD - 20-645-E7	Diesel	2	20	7,200 bhp	2	13.8
Sedna Desgagnés	MaK/Caterpillar - 6M43	Diesel	1	6	7,344 bhp	1 cpp	17.8
Spruceglen	Sulzer - 4RLB76	Diesel	1	4	10,880 bhp	1 cpp	13.8
St. Clair	GM EMD - 20-645-E7	Diesel	3	20	10,800 bhp	1 cpp	16.7
St. Marys Challenger	Skinner Engine Co.	Uniflow	1	4	3,500 ihp	1	12.0
Stephen B. Roman	Total	Diesel			5,996 bhp	1 cpp	18.4
(Center)	Fairbanks Morse - 10-38D8-1/8	Diesel	2	10	3,331 bhp		
(Wing)	Fairbanks Morse - 8-38D8-1/8	Diesel	2	8	2,665 bhp		
Stewart J. Cort	GM EMD - 20-645-E7	Diesel	4	20	14,400 bhp	2 cpp	18.4
Sugar Islander II **	Caterpillar - 3412	Diesel	2	12	1,280 bhp		
Tecumseh	Pielstick - 12PC-2V-400	Diesel	2	12	12,000 bhp	1 cpp	16.1
Thalassa Desgagnés	B&W - 8K42EF	Diesel	1	8	5,000 bhp	1 cpp	16.4
Tim S. Dool	MaK - 8M43C	Diesel	1	8	10,750 bhp	1 cpp	17.3
Tony MacKay *	Ruston - 12C-5VM	Diesel	1	12	2,800 bhp	1 cpp	15.0
Thunder Bay	MAN-B&W - 6S50ME-B9	Diesel	1	6	10,680 bhp	1	15.5
Umiak I	M.A.N.-B&W - 7S70ME-C	Diesel	1	7	29,598 bhp	1 cpp	16.5
Umiavut	Hanshin - 6LF58	Diesel	1	6	6,000 bhp	1 cpp	16.2
Undaunted *	Cummins K38-M	Diesel	2		Repowered winter 2013		
Véga Desgagnés	Wartsila - 9R32	Diesel	2	9	7,560 bhp	1 cpp	16.1
Victorious *	MaK - 6M25	Diesel	2	6	5,384 bhp	2 cpp	12.1
Victory *	MaK - 6MU551AK	Diesel	2	6	7,880 bhp	2	16.1
Walter J. McCarthy Jr.	GM EMD - 20-645-E7B	Diesel	4	20	14,400 bhp	2 cpp	16.1
Whitefish Bay	MAN-B&W - 6S50ME-B9	Diesel	1	6	10,680 bhp	1	15.5
Wilfred Sykes	Westinghouse Elec. Corp.	Turbine	1	**	7,700 shp	1	16.1
Wilf Seymour *	GM EMD - 16-645-E7	Diesel	2	16	5,750 bhp	2	13.8
William J. Moore *	GM EMD 16-645-E	Diesel	2	16	4,000 bhp	2 cpp	15.5
Wolfe Islander III **	Caterpillar - 3412E	Diesel	4	12	2,284 bhp	2 x 2	13.8
Yankcanuck	Cooper-Bessemer Corp.	Diesel	1	8	1,860 bhp	1	11.5
Zélada Desgagnés	MaK/Caterpillar - 6M43	Diesel	1	6	7,344 bhp	1 cpp	17.8
Zeus *	Caterpillar - D399	Diesel	2	8	2,250 bhp	2	

Solina makes the turn into the Rock Cut, below the Soo Locks. (Roger LeLievre)

Elbeborg in the St. Marys River, headed for Lake Superior. (Roger LeLievre)

Saltwater Fleets

Federal Asahi enters Lock 7 on the Welland Canal. (Roger LeLievre)

Fleet Name / Vessel Name	IMO #	Vessel Type	Year Built	Engine Type	Cargo Cap. or Gross*	Overall Length	Breadth	Depth
IA-1 **AKSAY DENIZCILIK VE TICARET ANONIM SIRKETI, ISTANBUL, TURKEY** *(aksay.org)*								
Chem Pegasus	9121754	TK	1995	D	16,150	454' 09"	71' 07"	39' 08"
(Spring Leo '95-'03, Kerim '03-'10)								
IA-2 **ALVTANK REDERI AB, DONSO, SWEDEN** *(alvtank.se)*								
Ramira	9362152	TK	2008	D	12,164	472' 07"	75' 07"	40' 08"
IA-3 **AMALTHIA MARINE INC., ATHENS, GREECE** *(www.amalmar.gr)*								
Seneca	8200486	BC	1983	D	28,788	606' 11"	75' 09"	48' 02"
*(**Mangal Desai** '83-'98, **Millenium Eagle** '98-'02, **Stokmarnes** '02-'05)*								
Tuscarora	8120698	BC	1983	D	28,031	639' 09"	75' 09"	46' 11"
*(Manila Spirit '83-'86, **Rixta Oldendorff** '86-'06)*								
IA-4 **ARDMORE SHIPPING LTD., CORK, IRELAND** *(ardmoreshipping.com)*								
Ardmore Calypso	8116984	TK	1983	D	12,334	423' 03"	65' 08"	36' 09"
(Samho Leader '83-'11)								
IA-5 **ATLANTSKA PLOVIDBA D.D., DUBROVNIK, REPUBLIC OF CROATIA** *(atlant.hr)*								
FOLLOWING VESSEL UNDER CHARTER TO FEDNAV LTD.								
Orsula	9110901	BC	1996	D	34,372	656' 02"	77' 01"	48' 10"
*(**Federal Calumet** {2} '96-'97)*								
IB-2 **BERGESEN WORLDWIDE LIMITED, OLSO, NORWAY** *(bergesen.no)*								
Bold World	9141417	TK	1998	D	19,125	486' 10"	75' 06"	42' 04"
(Cambridgeshire '98-'98, Stolt Kent '98-'07, Stolt Bold World '07-'08)								
IB-3 **BERNHARD SCHULTE GROUP OF COMPANIES, HAMBURG, GERMANY** *(schultegroup.com)*								
Elisalex Schulte	9439876	TK	2011	D	16,418	476' 05"	76' 05"	41' 00"
Ruth Schulte	9332420	TK	2007	D	12,956	417' 04"	66' 11"	37' 09"
(Swartberg '07-'07, Ruth Schulte '07-'07, Clipper Tasmania '07-'10)								
IB-4 **BESIKTAS LIKID TASIMACILIK DENIZCILIK TICARET, ISTANBUL, TURKEY** *(besiktasgroup.com)*								
Mainland	9431056	TK	2008	D	7,724	402' 05"	56' 05"	28' 10"
Purple Gem	9403827	TK	2009	D	6,824	390' 09"	55' 05"	27' 07"
IB-5 **BIGLIFT SHIPPING BV, AMSTERDAM, NETHERLANDS** *(www.bigliftshipping.com)*								
Happy River	9139294	HL	1997	D	15,593	452' 09"	74' 10"	42' 06"
Happy Rover	9139309	HL	1997	D	15,593	452' 09"	74' 10"	42' 06"
Tracer	9204702	HL	2000	D	8,874	329' 09"	73' 06"	26' 11"
Tramper	9204697	HL	2000	D	8,874	329' 09"	73' 06"	26' 11"
Transporter	9204714	HL	1999	D	8,469	329' 09"	80' 01"	36' 05"
IB-6 **BLOUNT SMALL SHIP ADVENTURES, WARREN, RHODE ISLAND, USA** *(blountsmallshipadventures.com)*								
Grande Caribe	8978631	PA	1997	D	97*	182' 07"	39' 01"	9' 10"
Grande Mariner	8978643	PA	1998	D	97*	182' 07"	39' 01"	9' 10"
Niagara Prince	8978629	PA	1994	D	99*	174' 00"	40' 00"	9' 00"
IB-7 **BLYSTAD TANKERS INC., OSLO, NORWAY** *(blystad.no)*								
FOLLOWING VESSELS UNDER CHARTER TO SONGA SHIPMANAGEMENT								
Songa Diamond	9460459	TK	2009	D	17,596	472' 05"	74' 02"	41' 00"
Songa Eagle	9461714	TK	2008	D	13,250	423' 03"	67' 00"	37' 09"
Songa Emerald	9473937	TK	2009	D	17,596	472' 05"	74' 02"	41' 00"
Songa Jade	9473925	TK	2009	D	17,596	472' 05"	74' 02"	41' 00"
Songa Opal	9473913	TK	2009	D	17,596	472' 05"	74' 02"	41' 00"
Songa Pearl	9444455	TK	2008	D	17,596	472' 05"	74' 02"	41' 00"
Songa Ruby	9444479	TK	2008	D	17,596	472' 05"	74' 02"	41' 00"
Songa Sapphire	9444467	TK	2008	D	17,596	472' 05"	74' 02"	41' 00"
Songa Topaz	9460461	TK	2009	D	17,596	472' 05"	74' 02"	41' 00"
IB-8 **BRIESE SCHIFFFAHRTS GMBH & CO. KG, LEER, GERMANY** *(briese.de)*								
BBC Amazon	9303302	GC	2007	D	17,348	469' 07"	75' 11"	42' 08"
BBC Austria	9433327	GC	2009	D	7,530	393' 00"	66' 03"	32' 02"
BBC Balboa	9501667	GC	2012	D	8,129	423' 01"	54' 02"	32' 10"
BBC Elbe	9347059	GC	2006	D	17,348	469' 07"	75' 11"	42' 08"
(Horumersiel '06-'06)								

Fleet Name / Vessel Name	IMO #	Vessel Type	Year Built	Engine Type	Cargo Cap. or Gross*	Overall Length	Breadth	Depth
BBC Ems	9347035	GC	2006	D	17,348	469' 07"	75' 11"	42' 08"
BBC Europe	9266308	GC	2003	D	7,409	391' 09"	66' 03"	32' 02"
BBC Greenland	9427079	GC	2007	D	7,530	393' 00"	66' 03"	32' 02"
BBC Houston	9331593	GC	2005	D	7,530	393' 00"	66' 03"	32' 02"
(BBC Australia '05-'05, Wesier Hiede '05-'05, BBC Australia '05-'10)								
BBC Jade	9421116	GC	2007	D	12,000	469' 00"	62' 00"	35' 11"
BBC Mississippi	9347061	GC	2006	D	17,348	469' 07"	75' 11"	42' 08"
(Greetsiel '06-'07)								
BBC Sweden	9278600	GC	2003	D	4,325	324' 06"	45' 03"	24' 03"
BBC Volga	9436329	GC	2009	D	17,300	469' 07"	74' 10"	43' 08"
(Ocean Breeze '09-'09)								
Kurt Paul	9435856	GC	2009	D	17,300	469' 07"	74' 10"	43' 08"
Sjard	9303314	GC	2007	D	17,348	469' 07"	75' 11"	42' 08"

IB-9 BROSTROM AB, GOTEBORG, SWEDEN *(brostrom.se)*

Bro Alma	9356610	TK	2008	D	17,000	472' 05"	75' 06"	40' 08"
(Ganstar '07-'08)								

IC-1 CANADIAN FOREST NAVIGATION CO. LTD., MONTREAL, QUEBEC, CANADA *(canfornav.com)*

At press time, Canadian Forest Navigation Co. Ltd. had the following vessels under long or short-term charter. Please consult their respective fleets for details: **Andean, Apollon, Barnacle, Blacky, Bluebill, Bluewing, Brant, Chestnut, Cinnamon, Eider, Gadwall, Garganey, Greenwing, Maccoa, Mandarin, Mottler, Pochard, Puffin, Redhead, Ruddy, Shoveler, Torrent, Tufty, Tundra, Whistler, Wigeon.**

IC-2 CANDLER SCHIFFAHRT GMBH, BREMEN, GERMANY *(candler-schiffahrt.de)*

Alert	9177789	GC	1999	D	12,947	420' 01"	69' 07"	37' 01"

IC-3 CHEMFLEET SHIPPING LTD., ISTANBUL, TURKEY *(chemfleet.org)*

Mehmet A	9418822	TK	2011	D	20,000	530' 04"	73' 06"	34' 01"
(Aldemar '11-'11)								
Sakarya	9425356	TK	2007	D	11,258	426' 06"	65' 00"	34' 01"
(Sakarya-D '07-'08)								
Zeynep A	9424223	TK	2007	D	10,500	425' 08"	64' 04"	34' 01"

IC-4 CHEMIKALIEN SEETRANSPORT GMBH, HAMBURG, GERMANY *(chemikalien-seetransport.de)*

Chemtrans Alster	9439319	TK	2010	D	13,073	421' 11"	66' 11"	37' 09"
Chemtrans Elbe	9439345	TK	2008	D	13,073	421' 11"	66' 11"	37' 09"
Chemtrans Ems	9439321	TK	2008	D	13,073	421' 11"	66' 11"	37' 09"
Chemtrans Havel	9439333	TK	2009	D	13,073	421' 11"	66' 11"	37' 09"
Chemtrans Mabuhay	9232369	TK	2000	D	17,427	455' 01"	66' 11"	39' 04"
Chemtrans Oste	9435557	TK	2008	D	13,073	421' 11"	66' 11"	37' 09"
Chemtrans Weser	9439307	TK	2009	D	13,073	421' 11"	66' 11"	37' 09"

IC-5 CHEMNAV INC., ATHENS, GREECE *(chemnav.gr)*

Commencement	9388211	TK	2008	D	13,091	421' 11"	66' 11"	37' 09"

IC-6 CLIPPER GROUP AS, COPENHAGEN, DENMARK *(clipper-group.com)*

Clipper Aki	9505974	TK	2010	D	14,732	440' 07"	73' 06"	39' 08"
Clipper Anne	9453793	BC	2010	D	12,000	454' 05"	68' 11"	36' 01"
(Marselisborg '10-'12)								

EDITOR'S NOTE: Observers will likely spot saltwater vessels not included in this book. These may be newcomers to the Great Lakes/Seaway system, recent renames or new construction. This is not meant to be an exhaustive listing of every saltwater vessel that could potentially visit the Great Lakes and St. Lawrence Seaway. To attempt to do so, given the sheer number of world merchant ships, would be space and cost prohibitive.

This list reflects vessels whose primary trade routes are on saltwater but which also regularly visit Great Lakes and St. Lawrence Seaway ports above Montreal. Fleets listed may operate other vessels worldwide than those included herein; additional vessels may be found on fleet Web sites, which have been included where available. Former names listed in **boldface type** indicate the vessel visited the Seaway system under that name.

Vikingbank, with its unusual bow design, on the St. Marys River. (Roger LeLievre)

Fleet Name / Vessel Name	IMO #	Vessel Type	Year Built	Engine Type	Cargo Cap. or Gross*	Overall Length	Breadth	Depth
Clipper Gemini	9557800	TK	2012	D	9,500	393' 02"	66' 11"	36' 05"
(Clipper Sigrun '12-'12)								
Clipper Katja	9340922	TK	2006	D	11,255	382' 03"	65' 09"	37' 05"
Clipper Klara	9340910	TK	2004	D	11,259	382' 03"	66' 07"	38' 05"
Clipper Lancer	9363182	TK	2006	D	10,098	388' 04"	62' 04"	33' 02"
Clipper Leander	9334430	TK	2006	D	10,098	388' 04"	62' 04"	33' 02"
Clipper Legacy	9307437	TK	2005	D	10,098	388' 04"	62' 04"	33' 02"
Clipper Mari	9422677	TK	2009	D	19,822	481' 00"	77' 10"	42' 08"
Clipper Oceanica	9317262	TK	2005	D	12,099	406' 10"	65' 07"	36' 09"
(Panam Oceanica '05-'07)								

At press time, Clipper Group AS also had the following vessels under charter. Please consult their respective fleets for details: **Eships Eagle, Eships Nahyan, Clipper Magdalena, Clipper Marinus, Clipper Marlene.**

IC-7 COASTAL SHIPPING LTD., GOOSE BAY, NEWFOUNDLAND, CANADA *(woodwards.nf.ca)*

Alsterstern	9053220	TK	1994	D	17,078	528' 03"	75' 06"	38' 05"
Havelstern	9053218	TK	1994	D	17,078	528' 03"	75' 06"	38' 05"

IC-8 COLUMBIA SHIPMANAGEMENT, HAMBURG, GERMANY *(csm-d.com)*

Cape Egmont	9262819	TK	2003	D	12,950	417' 04"	67' 00"	37' 09"

IC-9 CONCORD SHIPPING GMBH & CO., JORK, GERMANY *(concord-shipping.de)*

Anke	9570632	BC	2011	D	7,909	427' 02"	54' 02"	37' 09"
(Anke '11-'11, BBC Christina '11-'11)								

IC-10 CORSO LOGISTIC SOLUTIONS, SLIEMA, MALTA

Corso Dream	9008122	BC	1992	D	6,273	365' 02"	57' 01"	24' 11"
(Putyatin '92-'92, Socofl Pearl '92-'04, CIC Brasil '04-'11)								

IC-11 CSL GROUP INC., MONTREAL, QUEBEC, CANADA *(csl.ca)*

CSL Spirit	9138111	SU	2001	D	41,428	708' 05"	105' 06"	64' 09"

MARBULK SHIPPING INC. – MANAGED BY CSL INTERNATIONAL INC. *(cslint.com)*
PARTNERSHIP BETWEEN CSL INTERNATIONAL INC. AND ALGOMA CENTRAL CORP.

Pioneer	7925613	SU	1981	D	37,448	730' 00"	75' 10"	50' 00"
*Built: Port Weller Dry Docks, Port Weller, ON (**Canadian Pioneer** '81-'86)*								

ID-1 DAIICHI CHUO KISEN KAISHA, TOKYO, JAPAN *(www.firstship.co.jp)*

Federal Yukina	9476977	BC	2010	D	35,868	656' 01"	78' 01"	48' 09"

ID-2 DANSER VAN GENT, DELFZIJL, NETHERLANDS *(danservangent.nl)*
FOLLOWING VESSELS UNDER CHARTER TO WAGENBORG SHIPPING

Marietje Deborah	9481594	BC	2011	D	8,200	413' 10"	50' 06"	30' 02"
Marietje Marsilla	9458248	BC	2010	D	8,200	413' 10"	50' 06"	30' 02"

ID-3 DE POLI TANKERS BV, SPIJKENISSE, NETHERLANDS *(www.depoli-tankers.nl)*

Alessandro DP	9384162	TK	2007	D	17,096	453' 01"	75' 06"	40' 02"
Giovanni DP	9261516	TK	2003	D	16,875	453' 01"	75' 06"	40' 02"
Laguna D	9192375	TK	2000	D	15,200	446' 02"	75' 06"	40' 02"
(Jo Laguna D '00-'05)								
Miro D	9243382	TK	2002	D	16,875	453' 01"	75' 06"	40' 02"

ID-4 DOUN KISEN CO. LTD., OCHI EHIME PREFECTURE, JAPAN

Bright Laker	9228265	BC	2001	D	30,778	606' 11"	77' 05"	48' 11"

IE-1 EITZEN CHEMICAL ASA, OSLO, NORWAY *(eitzen-chemical.com)*

North Contender	9352585	TK	2005	D	19,998	481' 00"	77' 09"	42' 08"
North Fighter	9352597	TK	2006	D	19,998	481' 00"	77' 09"	42' 08"
Sichem Beijing	9397042	TK	2007	D	13,073	421' 11"	66' 11"	37' 09"
Sichem Challenge	9196448	TK	1998	D	17,485	382' 06"	62' 04"	33' 02"
*(Queen of Montreaux '98-'99, **North Challenge** '99-'06, Songa Challenge '06-'07)*								
Sichem Contestor	9416020	TK	2007	D	19,998	481' 00"	77' 09"	42' 08"
Sichem Defiance	9244374	TK	2001	D	17,369	442' 11"	74' 10"	41' 00"
*(**North Defiance** '01-'06, **Songa Defiance** '06-'07)*								
Sichem Dubai	9376933	TK	2007	D	12,956	417' 04"	67' 00"	37' 09"

Fleet Name Vessel Name	IMO #	Vessel Type	Year Built	Engine Type	Cargo Cap. or Gross*	Overall Length	Breadth	Depth
Sichem Edinburgh	9352066	TK	2007	D	13,073	421' 11"	66' 11"	37' 09"
Sichem Hiroshima	9361483	TK	2008	D	13,073	421' 11"	66' 11"	37' 09"
Sichem Hong Kong	9397054	TK	2007	D	13,073	421' 11"	66' 11"	37' 09"
Sichem Manila	9322097	TK	2007	D	13,125	421' 11"	67' 00"	37' 09"
Sichem Melbourne	9376921	TK	2007	D	12,936	417' 04"	67' 00"	37' 09"
Sichem Montreal	9404900	TK	2008	D	13,073	421' 11"	66' 11"	37' 09"
Sichem Mumbai	9322085	TK	2006	D	13,141	421' 11"	66' 11"	37' 09"
Sichem New York	9337834	TK	2007	D	12,956	417' 04"	67' 00"	37' 09"
Sichem Onomichi	9361471	TK	2005	D	13,091	421' 11"	66' 11"	37' 09"
Sichem Paris	9404895	TK	2008	D	13,073	421' 11"	66' 11"	37' 09"

IE-2 ELBE SHIPPING GMBH, DROCHTERSEN, GERMANY *(reederei-elbe-shipping.de)*

BBC Rhine	9368338	GC	2008	D	12,782	468' 06"	70' 06"	43' 08"
(Beluga Fusion '06-'11)								
BBC Steinhoeft	9358046	GC	2006	D	12,744	452' 11"	68' 11"	36' 01"
(Beluga Fusion '06-'11)								

IE-3 EMIRATES SHIP INVESTMENT CO. LLC, ABU DHABI, UNITED ARAB EMIRATES *(eships.ae)*

Eships Eagle	9353905	TK	2007	D	13,147	418' 06"	67' 00"	38' 05"
Eships Nahyan	9321809	TK	2005	D	8,657	387' 07"	61' 08"	31' 10"

IE-4 EMPIRE CHEMICAL TANKERS, PIRAEUS, GREECE *(empiretankers.com)*

Miramis	9421271	GC	2008	D	17,526	472' 05"	74' 03"	41' 00"
(Montello '08-'08, Empire Pajararan '08-'10)								

IE-5 ENERGY SHIPPING SPA, GENOA, ITALY *(energycoal.com)*

Sunflower E	9549669	GC	2009	D	13,000	393' 08"	72' 02"	36' 01"

IE-6 ENZIAN SHIPPING AG, BERNE, SWITZERLAND *(www.enzian-shipping.com)*

Celine	9214185	BC	2001	D	8,600	423' 03"	52' 00"	32' 00"
Nirint Neerlandia	9314375	BC	2006	D	12,680	459' 03"	70' 06"	38' 03"
(Leman '06-'06, Safmarine Leman '06-'10, SCL Leman '10-'11								
Sabina	9205718	BC	2000	D	9,231	416' 08"	52' 00"	32' 00"
SCL Bern	9304461	BC	2005	D	12,680	459' 03"	70' 06"	38' 03"

Marietje Marsilla departing Duluth, Minn. *(Glenn Blaszkiewicz)*

Fleet Name / Vessel Name	IMO #	Vessel Type	Year Built	Engine Type	Cargo Cap. or Gross*	Overall Length	Breadth	Depth
IF-1 FAIRFIELD CHEMICAL CARRIERS, WILTON, CONNECTICUT, USA (fairfieldchemical.com)								
Fairchem Colt	9304344	TK	2005	D	19,998	477' 04"	77' 10"	43' 10"
Fairchem Stallion	9311256	TK	2004	D	19,998	477' 04"	77' 10"	43' 10"
Fairchem Steed	9311256	TK	2005	D	19,998	477' 04"	77' 10"	43' 10"
IF-2 FEDNAV LTD., MONTREAL, QUEBEC, CANADA (fednav.com)								
CANARCTIC SHIPPING CO. LTD. – DIVISION OF FEDNAV LTD.								
Arctic	7517507	GC	1978	D	26,440	692' 04"	75' 05"	49' 05"
Built: Port Weller Dry Docks, Port Weller, ON								
Umiak I	9334715	BC	2006	D	31,992	619' 04"	87' 02"	51' 50"
Built: Universal Shipbuilding Corp., Kawasaki, Japan								
FEDNAV INTERNATIONAL LTD. - DIVISION OF FEDNAV LTD.								
Federal Agno	8316522	BC	1985	D	29,643	599' 09"	76' 00"	48' 07"
(*Federal Asahi* {1} '85-'89)								
Federal Asahi {2}	9200419	BC	2000	D	36,563	656' 02"	77' 11"	48' 09"
Federal Fuji	8321931	BC	1986	D	29,643	599' 09"	76' 00"	48' 07"
Federal Hudson {3}	9205902	BC	2000	D	36,563	656' 02"	77' 11"	48' 09"
Federal Hunter {2}	9205938	BC	2001	D	36,563	656' 02"	77' 11"	48' 09"
Federal Kivalina	9205885	BC	2000	D	36,563	656' 02"	77' 11"	48' 09"
Federal Kumano	9244257	BC	2001	D	32,787	624' 08"	77' 05"	49' 10"
Federal Kushiro	9284702	BC	2003	D	32,787	624' 08"	77' 05"	49' 10"
Federal Maas {2}	9118135	BC	1997	D	34,372	656' 02"	77' 01"	48' 10"
Federal Mackinac	9299460	BC	2004	D	27,000	606' 11"	77' 09"	46' 25"
Federal Margaree	9299472	BC	2005	D	27,000	606' 11"	77' 09"	46' 25"
Federal Mayumi	9529578	BC	2012	D	35,300	655' 06"	78' 09"	48' 09"
Federal Nakagawa	9278791	BC	2005	D	36,563	656' 02"	77' 11"	48' 09"
Federal Oshima	9200330	BC	1999	D	36,563	656' 02"	77' 11"	48' 09"
Federal Rhine {2}	9110925	BC	1997	D	34,372	656' 02"	77' 01"	48' 10"
Federal Rideau	9200445	BC	2000	D	36,563	656' 02"	77' 11"	48' 09"
Federal Saguenay {2}	9110913	BC	1996	D	34,372	656' 02"	77' 01"	48' 10"
Federal Satsuki	9529578	BC	2012	D	35,300	655' 06"	78' 09"	48' 09"
Federal Schelde {3}	9118147	BC	1997	D	34,372	656' 02"	77' 01"	48' 10"
Federal Seto	9267209	BC	2004	D	36,563	656' 02"	77' 11"	48' 09"

Polish-flagged Lubie in the Welland Canal. (Matt Miner)

Fleet Name Vessel Name	IMO #	Vessel Type	Year Built	Engine Type	Cargo Cap. or Gross*	Overall Length	Breadth	Depth
Federal Shimanto	9218404	BC	2001	D	32,787	624' 08"	77' 05"	49' 10"
Federal St. Laurent {3}	9110896	BC	1996	D	34,372	656' 02"	77' 01"	48' 10"
Federal Welland	9205926	BC	2000	D	36,563	656' 02"	77' 11"	48' 09"
Federal Weser	9229972	BC	2002	D	37,372	652' 11"	78' 05"	50' 02"
Federal Yoshino	9218416	BC	2001	D	32,787	624' 08"	77' 05"	49' 10"
Federal Yukon	9205897	BC	2000	D	36,563	656' 02"	77' 11"	48' 09"

At press time, FedNav Ltd. also had the following vessels under charter. Please consult their respective fleets for details: **Federal Elbe, Federal Ems, Federal Katsura, Federal Leda Federal Mattawa, Federal Miramichi, Federal Power, Federal Sakura, Federal Yukina, Orsula**

IF-3	**FINBETA, SAVONA, ITALY** (www.finbeta.com)							
Acquamarina	9268631	TK	2004	D	12,004	447' 10"	66' 11"	33' 10"
Sapphire	9114969	TK	1997	D	14,015	467' 06"	72' 02"	36' 01"

IF-4	**FLINTER SHIPPING BV, BARENDRECHT, THE NETHERLANDS** (flinter.nl)							
Citadel	9361380	GC	2008	D	4,500	363' 05"	45' 11"	24' 07"
Flinter Arctic	9504126	GC	2010	D	11,000	434' 08"	52' 01"	35' 04"
Flinterduin	9213882	GC	2000	D	6,359	364' 01"	49' 02"	26' 09"
Flintereems	9180865	GC	2000	D	6,200	366' 07"	48' 08"	26' 09"
Flinterland	9352339	GC	2007	D	7,705	393' 08"	49' 10"	27' 11"
Flintermaas	9180877	GC	2000	D	6,200	366' 07"	48' 10"	26' 10"
Flintermar	9327322	GC	2006	D	7,750	393' 00"	50' 07"	27' 11"
(Flintermar '06-'06, UAL Malabo '06-'09)								
Flinterrebecca	9361108	GC	2008	D	5,756	324' 02"	45' 11"	27' 11"
Flinterspirit	9229049	GC	2001	D	6,358	366' 07"	48' 08"	26' 09"
Flinterstar	9243758	GC	2002	D	9,122	424' 06"	55' 09"	32' 10"
(Flinterstar '02-'03, UAL Africa '03-'11)								
Flinterstream	9415040	GC	2009	D	9,122	424' 06"	55' 09"	32' 10"

Welland Canal Flight Locks, viewed from the Polish vessel Wicko. (Alain Gindroz)

Fleet Name Vessel Name	IMO #	Vessel Type	Year Built	Engine Type	Cargo Cap. or Gross*	Overall Length	Breadth	Depth
Flintersun	9243746	GC	2002	D	9,122	424' 06"	55' 09"	32' 10"
Zeus	9190212	GC	2000	D	9,150	427' 01"	52' 01"	33' 06"

IF-5 FRANCO COMPANIA NAVIERA SA, ATHENS, GREECE *(franco.gr)*

Barbro	8307686	BC	1984	D	29,692	599' 09"	75' 09"	48' 07"
(Olympic Dignity '84-'92, Alam Sejahtera '92-'07)								
Stefania I	8406925	BC	1985	D	28,269	584' 08"	75' 11"	48' 05"
(Astral Ocean '85-'95, Sea Crystal '95 '97, Stefania '97-'98)								

IF-6 FREESE SHIPPING, STADE, GERMANY *(freeseship.com)*

BBC Minnesota	9260378	GC	2004	D	12,828	452' 09"	68' 11"	36' 01"
(Nordwind '04-'04, BBC Maryland '04-'04, Beluga Elegance '04-'11, Freesia '04-'12)								
BBC Washington	9283954	GC	2004	D	12,806	452' 09"	68' 11"	36' 01"
(Beluga Efficiency '04-'06, BBC Carolina '06-'07, Beluga Efficiency '07-'11, Lilia '11-'11, Freese Scan '11-'12)								
Pacific Huron	9546796	GC	2010	D	30,000	623' 04"	77' 11"	47' 11"
(Seven Islands '10-'10)								
Three Rivers	9546784	GC	2010	D	30,000	623' 04"	77' 11"	47' 11"

IG-1 G. BROS MARITIME S.A., PIRAEUS, GREECE

Bulk Sunset	9151395	BC	1997	D	18,315	486' 03"	74' 10"	40' 00"
(Rubin Halcyon '97-'04, Rubin Nacre '04-'08, Porto Cayo '08-'12)								

IG-2 GIUSEPPE MESSINA S.R.L., GENOA, ITALY

Rapallo	9480655	BC	2010	D	8,476	377' 04"	62' 04"	26' 03"

IG-3 GOLDEX FORTUNE LTD., MONROVIA, LIBERIA

Asphodel	8316467	BC	1984	D	28,303	580' 08"	75' 09"	47' 07"
(Vamand Wave '84-'07, Yamaska '07-'09)								

IH-1 HACI ISMAIL KAPTANOGLU GROUP OF COMPANIES, ISTANBUL, TURKEY *(www.kaptanoglu.com)*

Eylul K	9394222	BC	2007	D	21,057	518' 00"	76' 09"	41' 00"

IH-2 HAMMONIA REEDEREI GMBH & CO., HAMBURG, GERMANY *(www.hammonia-reederei.de)*

HR Resolution	9267754	BC	2005	D	10,536	441' 04"	70' 06"	30' 06"
(Beluga Resolution '05-'11)								

IH-3 HANSA HEAVY LIFT GMBH, BREMEN, GERMANY *(harren-partner.de)*

HHL Amazon	9466996	GC	2009	D	12,700	453' 00"	68' 11"	36' 01"
(Beluga Fairy '09-'11)								
HHL Amur	9435753	HL	2007	D	12,744	452' 11"	68' 11"	36' 01"
(Beluga Fidelity '07-'11)								
HHL Congo	9467005	GC	2011	D	12,700	453' 00"	68' 11"	36' 01"
(Beluga Fealty '11-'11)								
HHL Nile	9443669	GC	2009	D	12,700	453' 00"	68' 11"	36' 01"
(Beluga Faculty '09-'11)								
HHL Volga	9381392	GC	2007	D	12,744	452' 11"	68' 11"	36' 01"
(Beluga Family '07-'11)								

IH-4 HARREN & PARTNER SCHIFFAHRTS GMBH, BREMEN, GERMANY *(harren-partner.de)*
FOLLOWING VESSELS UNDER CHARTER TO COMBI LIFT

Palabora	9501875	HL	2010	D	10,052	436' 04"	75' 06"	37' 05"
Palau	9501899	HL	2010	D	10,052	436' 04"	75' 06"	37' 05"
Palembang	9501887	HL	2010	D	10,052	436' 04"	75' 06"	37' 05"
Palmerton	9501863	HL	2009	D	10,052	436' 04"	75' 06"	37' 05"
Panagia	9305295	HL	2004	D	7,846	393' 00"	66' 03"	32' 02"
Pangani	9318943	HL	2004	D	7,846	393' 00"	66' 03"	32' 02"

FOLLOWING VESSELS UNDER CHARTER TO CANADIAN FOREST NAVIGATION LTD.

Pochard	9262534	BC	2003	D	37,384	655' 10"	77' 09"	50' 02"
Puffin	9262522	BC	2003	D	37,384	655' 10"	77' 09"	50' 02"

IH-5 HARTMAN SEATRADE, URK, NETHERLANDS *(hartmanseatrade.com)*

Deo Volente	9391658	BC	2006	D	3,500	343' 10"	51' 02"	24' 03"

Fleet Name / Vessel Name	IMO #	Vessel Type	Year Built	Engine Type	Cargo Cap. or Gross*	Overall Length	Breadth	Depth
IH-6	**HELD BEREEDERUNGS GMBH & CO, HAREN-EMS, GERMANY**							
BBC Naples	9484223	GC	2010	D	9,755	433' 09"	52' 01"	31' 08"
(Beluga Novation '10-'11)								
IH-7	**HELLESPONT SHIP MANAGEMENT GMBH, HAMBURG, GERMANY** *(www.hellespont.com)*							
Hellespont Centurion	9433303	TK	2009	D	16,850	472' 05"	74' 02"	42' 00"
Hellespont Charger	9436381	TK	2009	D	16,850	472' 05"	74' 02"	42' 00"
Hellespont Chieftain	9436393	TK	2010	D	16,850	472' 05"	74' 02"	42' 00"
IH-8	**HELLAS MARINE SERVICES LTD., PIRAEUS, GREECE** *(hellasmarine.gr)*							
Sir Henry	9151383	BC	1996	D	18,315	486' 03"	74' 10"	40' 00"
(Rubin Lark '96-'05)								
IH-9	**HERMANN BUSS GMBH, LEER, GERMANY** *(bussgruppe.de)*							
BBC Carolina	9402043	GC	2007	D	12,744	452' 11"	68' 11"	36' 01"
(Beluga Fantastic '07-'11)								
Mellum Trader	9204934	BC	1999	D	6,265	327' 09"	55' 09"	30' 06"
(Catherine Scan '99-'12)								
IH-10	**HERNING SHIPPING AS, HERNING, DENMARK** *(herning-shipping.dk)*							
Charlotte Theresa	9400708	TK	2008	D	11,000	424' 10"	63' 00"	27' 11"
Ina Theresa	9449455	TK	2010	D	12,592	399' 07"	67' 00"	39' 00"
(Rio Delaware '10-'10)								
Ida Theresa	9449417	TK	2009	D	12,592	399' 07"	67' 00"	39' 00"
Irene Theresa	9449443	TK	2010	D	12,592	399' 07"	67' 00"	39' 00"
Jette Theresa	9406582	TK	2009	D	11,000	424' 10"	63' 00"	27' 11"
II-1	**INTERSEE SCHIFFAHRTS-GESELLSCHAFT MBH & CO. , HAREN-EMS, GERMANY** *(intersee.de)*							
Alexia	9369083	GC	2008	D	11,211	477' 09"	60' 03"	33' 10"
Amalia	9312717	GC	2006	D	5,726	348' 02"	47' 03"	26' 07"
(Francesca '04-'06)								
Annalisa	9213727	GC	2000	D	8,737	433' 10"	52' 01"	31' 08"
(Malte Rainbow '00-'03)								
Carola	9214173	GC	2000	D	9,000	424' 08"	52' 00"	33' 04"

Amstelborg along the St. Lawrence Seaway. *(Ronald Dole Jr.)*

Fleet Name / Vessel Name	IMO #	Vessel Type	Year Built	Engine Type	Cargo Cap. or Gross*	Overall Length	Breadth	Depth
Hermann Schoening	9413901	BC	2010	D	29,635	622' 04"	77' 05"	47' 11"
Jana	9255725	GC	2001	D	8,994	433' 09"	52' 01"	31' 08'
Julietta	9217151	GC	2002	D	10,500	468' 02"	59' 10"	33' 04"
Katja	9235490	GC	2000	D	9,000	424' 08"	52' 00"	33' 04"
(Katja '00-'01, MSC Apapa '01-'02)								
Leandra	9438585	GC	2008	D	11,211	477' 09"	60' 03"	33' 10"
Luebbert	9415167	BC	2010	D	29,635	622' 04"	77' 05"	47' 11"
Maxima	9369071	GC	2007	D	11,211	477' 09"	60' 03"	33' 10"
(Maxima '07-'07, Nordana Maxima '07-'08)								
Rebecca	9239288	GC	2002	D	10,500	468' 02"	59' 10"	33' 04"
Sabrina	9240471	GC	2002	D	10,500	468' 02"	59' 10"	33' 04"
(Sabrina '02-'02 , MSC Rades '02-'04 , Sabrina '04-'04 , SCM Olympic '04-'05)								
Serena	9294977	GC	2004	D	10,500	468' 02"	59' 10"	33' 04"
Sofia	9312690	GC	2005	D	5,726	348' 02"	47' 03"	26' 07"
Tatjana	9235488	GC	2000	D	9,000	424' 08"	52' 00"	33' 04"
(Tatjana '00-'02, TMC Brazil '02-'02)								
Thekla	9259020	GC	2003	D	8,994	433' 09"	52' 01"	31' 08'
Victoria	9290074	GC	2004	D	10,500	468' 02"	59' 10"	33' 04"
Winona	9255622	GC	2003	D	10,000	433' 09"	52' 06"	32' 10"
Xenia	9217163	GC	2003	D	10,500	468' 02"	59' 10"	33' 04"

II-2   INTERSHIP NAVIGATION CO. LTD., LIMASSOL, CYPRUS *(intership-cyprus.com)*
      FOLLOWING VESSELS UNDER CHARTER TO FEDNAV LTD.

	IMO #							
Federal Danube	9271511	BC	2003	D	37,372	652' 11"	78' 05"	50' 02"
Federal Elbe	9230000	BC	2003	D	37,372	652' 11"	78' 05"	50' 02"
Federal Ems	9229984	BC	2002	D	37,372	652' 11"	78' 05"	50' 02"
Federal Leda	9229996	BC	2003	D	37,372	652' 11"	78' 05"	50' 02"
Federal Power	9190119	BC	2000	D	17,451	469' 02"	74' 10"	43' 08"
(Atlantic Power '00-'01, Seaboard Power '01-'07)								

II-3   INTREPID SHIPPING LLC., STAMFORD, CONNECTICUT, USA

	IMO #							
Intrepid Canada	9466740	TK	2011	D	16,421	476' 02"	76' 05"	41' 00"

Fleet Name / Vessel Name	IMO #	Vessel Type	Year Built	Engine Type	Cargo Cap. or Gross*	Overall Length	Breadth	Depth
IJ-1 **JO TANKERS BV, SPIJKENISSE, NETHERLANDS** *(jotankers.com)*								
Jo Spirit	9140841	TK	1998	D	6,248	352' 02"	52' 02"	30' 02"
IJ-2 **JUMBO SHIPPING CO. SA, ROTTERDAM, NETHERLANDS** *(jumboshipping.nl)*								
Daniella	8718873	HL	1989	D	7,600	322' 09"	60' 03"	37' 02"
(Stellaprima '89-'90)								
Fairlift	8806905	HL	1990	D	7,780	330' 08"	68' 10"	43' 08"
Fairload	9083134	HL	1995	D	5,198	314' 00"	60' 03"	37' 02"
Jumbo Spirit	9083122	HL	1995	D	5,198	314' 00"	60' 03"	37' 02"
Jumbo Vision	9153642	HL	2000	D	7,123	361' 03"	68' 05"	44' 03"
Stellanova	9085730	HL	1996	D	5,198	314' 00"	60' 03"	37' 02"
Stellaprima	8912326	HL	1991	D	7,780	330' 08"	68' 10"	43' 08"
IK-1 **KNUTSEN O.A.S. SHIPPING AS, HAUGESUND, NORWAY** *(knutsenoas.com)*								
Pascale Knutsen	9070905	TK	1993	D	14,910	464' 08"	75' 07"	38' 10"
Synnove Knutsen	9007207	TK	1992	D	17,071	464' 03"	75' 07"	38' 09"
Turid Knutsen	9039884	TK	1993	D	22,625	533' 03"	75' 06"	48' 07"
IK-2 **KOYO KAIUN CO. LTD., TOKYO, JAPAN** *(koyoline.com)*								
Federal Katsura	9293923	BC	2005	D	32,787	624' 08"	77' 05"	49' 10"
Federal Sakura	9288291	BC	2005	D	32,787	624' 08"	77' 05"	49' 10"
IK-3 **KOYO LINE LTD., TOKYO, JAPAN** *(koyotky.co.jp)*								
Maemi	9416044	TK	2008	D	19,998	481' 00"	77' 09"	42' 08"
IK-4 **KREY SCHIFFAHRTS GMBH & CO. KG, SIMONSWOLDE, GERMANY** *(krey-schiffahrt.de)*								
BBC Ontario	9312157	GC	2004	D	12,711	452' 10"	68' 11"	36' 01"
BBC Wisconsin	9283966	GC	2004	D	12,806	452' 09"	68' 11"	36' 01"
(Beluga Eternity '04-'10 , Beluga Windward '10-'11, Jette '10-'11)								
IL-1 **LAURANNE SHIPPING BV, GHENT, NETHERLANDS** *(lauranne-shipping.com)*								
LS Christine	9302009	TK	2007	D	8,400	411' 05"	59' 01"	27' 07"
LS Jacoba	9334428	TK	2006	D	15,602	485' 07"	70' 10"	37' 01"
IL-2 **LEHMANN REEDEREI, LÜBECK, GERMANY** *(hans-lehmann.de)*								
Edgar Lehmann	9396543	GC	2007	D	12,000	460' 04"	64' 07"	34' 05"
Hans Lehmann	9406702	GC	2007	D	12,000	460' 04"	64' 07"	34' 05"
IL-3 **LIAMARE SHIPPING BV, MAARTENSDIJK, NETHERLANDS** *(liamareshipping.nl)*								
Liamare	9166481	GC	1999	D	5,842	351' 03"	50' 02"	27' 03"
(Ameland '99-'07)								
IL-4 **LLOYD FONDS SINGAPORE PTE LTD., SINGAPORE, SINGAPORE** *(lloydfonds.de)*								
Ben	9311646	TK	2006	D	12,950	417' 04"	67' 00"	37' 09"
*(Songa Diamond '06-'03, **Brovig Bay** '03-'07, **Liquid Velvet** '07-'07)*								
Dale	9340398	TK	2007	D	13,032	421' 11"	66' 11"	37' 09"
(Pacificator '07-'07)								
Fen	9359600	TK	2006	D	12,950	417' 04"	67' 00"	37' 09"
*(Launched as Songa Onyx, **Brovig Ocean** '06-'07, **Liquid Blue** '07-'07)*								
Glen	9311634	TK	2005	D	12,950	417' 04"	67' 00"	37' 09"
*(Launched as Songa Pearl, **Brovig Fjord** '06-'07)*								
Moor	9359595	TK	2006	D	12,950	417' 04"	67' 00"	37' 09"
*(Brovig Sea '06-'06, Songa Saphire '06-'07, **Liquid Elegance** '07-'07)*								
Vale	9340350	TK	2007	D	13,032	421' 11"	66' 11"	37' 09"
IL-5 **LORENTZENS REDERI CO., OSLO, NORWAY**								
Songa Falcon	9482653	TK	2009	D	13,226	419' 07"	67' 00"	37' 09"
IM-1 **MAERSK LINE LTD., NORFOLK, VIRGINIA, UNITED STATES** *(maersklinelimited.com)*								
Maersk Illinois	9469778	GC	2011	D	19,000	485' 07"	76' 09"	44' 03"
IM-2 **MARIDA TANKERS INC., NORWALK, CONNETICUT, USA** *(marida.qfleet.com)*								
Marida Melissa	9438169	TK	2009	D	13,132	421' 11"	67' 00"	37' 09"
Marida Mimosa	9445667	TK	2008	D	13,226	419' 07"	67' 00"	37' 09"
Marida Mulberry	9474151	TK	2008	D	13,226	419' 07"	67' 00"	37' 09"

Fleet Name Vessel Name	IMO #	Vessel Type	Year Built	Engine Type	Cargo Cap. or Gross*	Overall Length	Breadth	Depth
IM-3	**MARSHIP BEREEDERUNGS GMBH & CO., HAREN MS, GERMANY** *(marship.de)*							
Thorco Arctic	9484209	BC	2009	D	8,500	433' 09"	52' 01"	31' 08"
(Beluga Notion '09-'09, BBC Newcastle '09-'11)								
IM-4	**MASSOEL MERIDIAN LTD., LIVERPOOL, UNITED KINGDOM** *(massoel.com)*							
Simano	9506409	GC	2008	D	7,300	370' 01"	56' 05"	29' 10"
IM-5	**MASTERMIND SHIPMANAGEMENT LTD., LIMASSOL, CYPRUS** *(mastermind-cyprus.com)*							
MSM Douro	9519028	GC	2012	D	6,500	357' 08"	49' 10"	25' 11"
(Dourodiep '12-'12)								
Onego Bora	9613604	GC	2011	D	7,658	383' 10"	64' 08"	27' 11"
(MSM Omodos '11-'11)								
IM-6	**MEGA CHEMICAL TANKERS LTD., SINGAPORE, SINGAPORE** *(mega-chemicals.ch)*							
MCT Alioth	9173094	TK	1999	D	19,996	489' 10"	77' 11"	41' 06"
(Alioth '99-'03)								
MCT Almak	9173109	TK	1999	D	19,996	489' 10"	77' 11"	41' 06"
(Almak '99-'03)								
MCT Altair	9173082	TK	1999	D	19,996	489' 10"	77' 11"	41' 06"
(Altair '99-'03)								
MCT Arcturus	9173111	TK	2000	D	19,996	489' 10"	77' 11"	41' 06"
(Arcturus '99-'03)								
MCT Monte Rosa	9298363	TK	2000	D	19,950	539' 02"	76' 01"	42' 00"
MCT Stockhorn	9298387	TK	2008	D	19,950	539' 02"	76' 01"	42' 00"
IM-7	**MINERALIEN SCHIFFAHRT SPEDITION, SCHNAITTENBACH, GERMANY** *(mega-chemicals.ch)*							
Cornelia	9216597	BC	2001	D	16,807	574' 02"	75' 09"	44' 09"
(Pine '01-'04)								
IN-1	**NAVARONE SA MARINE ENTERPRISES, LIMASSOL, CYPRUS**							
	FOLLOWING VESSELS UNDER CHARTER TO CANADIAN FOREST NAVIGATION LTD.							
Andean	9413925	BC	2009	D	30,770	606' 11"	77' 09"	47' 11"
Barnacle	9409742	BC	2009	D	30,807	606' 11"	77' 09"	47' 11"
Blacky	9393149	BC	2008	D	30,801	607' 04"	77' 09"	47' 11"
Bluebill	9263306	BC	2004	D	37,200	632' 10"	77' 09"	50' 10"
Brant	9393151	BC	2008	D	30,807	606' 11"	77' 09"	47' 11"
Chestnut	9477866	BC	2009	D	30,807	606' 11"	77' 09"	47' 11"
Greenwing	9230921	BC	2002	D	26,737	611' 08"	77' 09"	46' 07"
Labrador	9415222	BC	2010	D	30,899	606' 11"	77' 09"	47' 11"
Maccoa	9413913	BC	2009	D	30,930	606' 11"	77' 09"	47' 11"
Mandarin	9239812	BC	2003	D	26,747	611' 00"	77' 09"	46' 07"
Mottler	9477828	BC	2009	D	30,807	606' 11"	77' 09"	47' 11"
Ruddy	9459981	BC	2009	D	30,930	606' 11"	77' 09"	47' 11"
Shoveler	9459979	BC	2009	D	30,930	606' 11"	77' 09"	47' 11"
Torrent	9415210	BC	2010	D	30,930	606' 11"	77' 09"	47' 11"
Tufty	9393163	BC	2009	D	30,807	606' 11"	77' 09"	47' 11"
Tundra	9415208	BC	2009	D	30,930	606' 11"	77' 09"	47' 11"
IN-2	**NAVIG8 SHIPMANAGEMENT LTD., SINGAPORE, SINGAPORE** *(navig8group.com)*							
Morholmen	9553414	TK	2011	D	16,500	472' 05"	75' 06"	40' 08"
(CF Max '11-'11)								
Soley-1	9428073	TK	2009	D	20,000	491' 11"	75' 06"	42' 10"
(Messinia '09-'09)								
Soley-2	9428085	TK	2009	D	20,000	491' 11"	75' 06"	42' 10"
(Monfiero '09-'09)								
IN-3	**NAVIGATION MARITIME BULGARE LTD., VARNA, BULGARIA** *(www.navbul.com)*							
Bogdan	9132492	BC	1997	D	13,960	466' 04"	72' 10"	36' 07"
Kom	9132480	BC	1997	D	13,960	466' 04"	72' 10"	36' 07"
Lyulin	9498248	BC	2011	D	30,688	610' 03"	77' 09"	48' 01"
Osogovo	9498250	BC	2010	D	30,688	610' 03"	77' 11"	47' 11"
Perelik	9132507	BC	1998	D	13,960	466' 04"	72' 10"	36' 07"
Persenk	9132519	BC	1998	D	13,960	466' 04"	72' 10"	36' 07"

Fleet Name Vessel Name	IMO #	Vessel Type	Year Built	Engine Type	Cargo Cap. or Gross*	Overall Length	Breadth	Depth
Strandja	9564140	BC	2010	D	30,688	610' 03"	77' 11"	47' 11"
(Eastwind York '10-'10, Federal Yangtze '10-'10)								
Vitosha	9564138	BC	2010	D	30,688	610' 03"	77' 11"	47' 11"
IN-4 NESTE SHIPPING OY, ESPOO, FINLAND *(nesteoil.com)*								
Futura	9255282	TK	2004	D	25,084	556' 01"	77' 11"	48' 11"
IN-5 NICHOLAS G. MOUNDREAS SHIPPING SA, PIRAEUS, GREECE								
Spring	9416812	TK	2009	D	13,073	421' 11"	66' 11"	37' 09"
Winter	9416800	TK	2009	D	13,073	421' 11"	66' 11"	37' 09"
IN-6 NORDANA SHIPPING CO., COPENHAGEN, DENMARK *(nordana.com)*								
Aggersborg	9646455	HL	2012	D	12,645	454' 04"	68' 11"	36' 01"
IN-7 NORDIC TANKERS A/S, COPENHAGEN, DENMARK *(nordictankers.dk)*								
Harbour Clear	9230012	TK	2001	D	16,875	453' 01"	75' 06"	40' 02"
(Jo Chiara D '01-'04, Chiara '04-'06, Nora '06-'09)								
Harbour Cloud	9291066	TK	2004	D	16,875	453' 01"	75' 06"	40' 02"
(Fase D '04-'04, Fase '04-'09)								
Harbour Fashion	9473080	TK	2011	D	16,909	473' 02"	75' 06"	40' 08"
Harbour Feature	9473092	TK	2011	D	16,909	473' 02"	75' 06"	40' 08"
(Nordtank Lerner '11-'11)								
Harbour First	9473119	TK	2011	D	16,909	473' 02"	75' 06"	40' 08"
Harbour Kira	9337286	TK	2007	D	11,259	382' 03"	66' 07"	38' 05"
(Clipper Kira '07-'12)								
Harbour Leader	9286451	TK	2004	D	10,098	388' 04"	62' 04"	33' 02"
*(**Panam Trinity** '04-'06, Clipper Leader '06-'11)*								
Harbour Legend	9305403	TK	2004	D	10,098	388' 04"	62' 04"	33' 02"
(Clipper Legend '04-'11)								
Harbour Loyalty	9373929	TK	2007	D	10,098	388' 04"	62' 04"	33' 02"
(Clipper Loyalty '07-'11)								
Harbour Progress	9572745	TK	2010	D	19,122	530' 05"	75' 06"	40' 08"
Nordic Copenhagen	9300776	TK	2005	D	12,950	417' 04"	67' 00"	39' 09"
Nordic Oslo	9300788	TK	2005	D	12,950	417' 04"	67' 00"	39' 09"
(Sichem Oslo '05-'07)								
Nordic Stockholm	9328314	TK	2005	D	12,950	417' 04"	67' 00"	39' 09"

New Federal Satsuki makes her first trip to Toledo, Ohio. (Jim Hoffman)

Fleet Name Vessel Name	IMO #	Vessel Type	Year Built	Engine Type	Cargo Cap. or Gross*	Overall Length	Breadth	Depth
IO-1	**OCEAN CHALLENGE LTD., NICOSIA, CYPRUS**							
Bluewing	9230919	BC	2002	D	26,747	611' 00"	77' 09"	46' 07"
Cinnamon	9239800	BC	2002	D	26,747	611' 00"	77' 09"	46' 07"
IO-2	**OCEANEX INC., MONTREAL, QUEBEC, CANADA** *(oceanex.com)*							
Cabot {2}	7700051	RR	1979	D	7,132	564' 09"	73' 11"	45' 09"
Oceanex Avalon	9315044	CO	2005	D	14,747	481' 11"	85' 00"	45' 11"
Oceanex Sanderling	7603502	RR	1977	D	15,195	364' 01"	88' 05"	57' 07"

(Rauenfels '77-'80, Essen '80-'81, Kongsfjord '81-'83, Onno '83-'87, ASL Sanderling '87-'08)

IP-1	**OSM GROUP AS, KRISTIANSAND, NORWAY** *(www.osm.no)*							
Tromso	9435791	BC	2008	D	12,697	393' 08"	67' 00"	39' 00"

(Gemi '08-'08, M. Y. Arctic '08-'11)

IP-2	**PARAKOU SHIPPING LTD., HONG KONG, CHINA** *(parakougroup.com)*							
Emilie	9498236	BC	2010	D	29,800	610' 03"	77' 11"	47' 11"
Heloise	9498224	BC	2010	D	29,800	610' 03"	77' 11"	47' 11"
FOLLOWING VESSELS UNDER CHARTER TO CANADIAN FOREST NAVIGATION LTD.								
Eider	9285938	BC	2004	D	37,249	655' 10"	77' 09"	50' 02"
Gadwall	9358369	BC	2007	D	37,249	655' 10"	77' 09"	50' 02"
Garganey	9358383	BC	2007	D	37,249	655' 10"	77' 09"	50' 02"
Redhead	9285940	BC	2005	D	37,249	655' 10"	77' 09"	50' 02"
Whistler	9358371	BC	2007	D	37,249	655' 10"	77' 09"	50' 02"
Wigeon	9358395	BC	2007	D	37,249	655' 10"	77' 09"	50' 02"
IP-3	**PEROSEA SHIPPING CO. SA, PIRAEUS, GREECE**							
Sea Force	9322102	TK	2006	D	13,500	421' 11"	66' 11"	37' 09"
IP-4	**POLISH STEAMSHIP CO., SZCZECIN, POLAND** *(polsteam.com)*							
Drawsko	9393450	BC	2010	D	30,000	623' 04"	77' 11"	47' 11"
Ina	9521875	BC	2012	D	16,900	492' 00"	77' 05"	41' 00"
Irma	9180396	BC	2000	D	34,946	655' 10"	77' 05"	50' 02"
Iryda	9180384	BC	1999	D	34,946	655' 10"	77' 05"	50' 02"
Isa	9180358	BC	1999	D	34,946	655' 10"	77' 05"	50' 02"
Isadora	9180372	BC	1999	D	34,946	655' 10"	77' 05"	50' 02"
Isolda	9180360	BC	1999	D	34,946	655' 10"	77' 05"	50' 02"

Cargo of windmill parts on Vikingbank's deck. (Alain Gindroz)

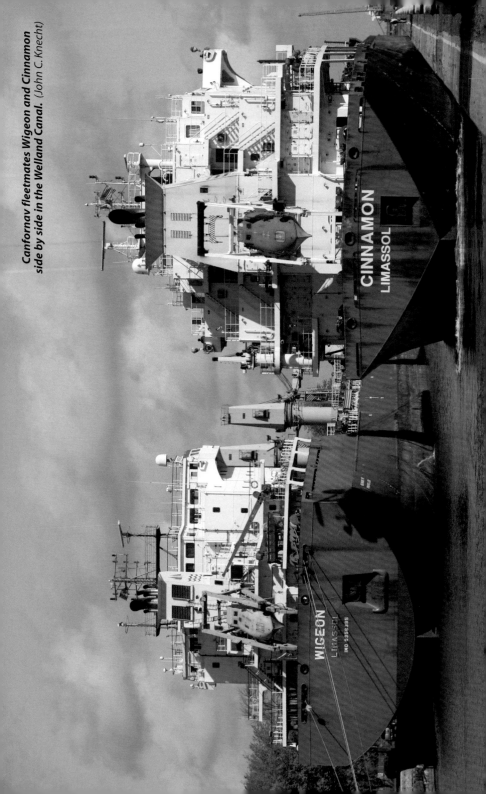

Canfornav fleetmates Wigeon and Cinnamon side by side in the Welland Canal. (John C. Knecht)

	Fleet Name Vessel Name	IMO #	Vessel Type	Year Built	Engine Type	Cargo Cap. or Gross*	Overall Length	Breadth	Depth
	Juno	9422378	BC	2011	D	30,000	623'04"	77'11"	47'11"
	Lubie	9441984	BC	2011	D	30,000	623'04"	77'11"	47'11"
	Mamry	9496264	BC	2012	D	30,000	623'04"	77'11"	47'11"
	Miedwie	9393448	BC	2010	D	30,000	623'04"	77'11"	47'11"
	Nogat	9154268	BC	1999	D	17,064	488'10"	75'06"	39'08"
	Orla	9154270	BC	1999	D	17,064	488'10"	75'06"	39'08"
	Pilica	9154282	BC	1999	D	17,064	488'10"	75'06"	39'08"
	Resko	9393462	BC	2010	D	30,000	623'04"	77'11"	47'11"
	Solina	9496252	BC	2012	D	30,000	623'04"	77'11"	47'11"
	Wicko	9393474	BC	2010	D	20,603	623'04"	77'11"	47'11"
	Ziemia Lodzka	8418746	BC	1988	D	26,264	591'02"	75'09"	45'07"

(Zimia Lodzka '88-'93, Lake Champlain '93-'03)

IP-5 **POT SCHEEPVAART BV, DELFZIJL, NETHERLANDS** *(pot-scheepvaart.nl)*
FOLLOWING VESSELS UNDER CHARTER TO WAGENBORG SHIPPING

	Kwintebank	9234288	GC	2002	D	8,664	433'10"	52'01"	31'08"
	Varnebank	9213739	GC	2000	D	8,664	433'10"	52'01"	31'08"
	Vikingbank	9604184	GC	2012	D	11,850	468'00"	52'01"	35'04"

IR-1 **REDERIET STENERSEN AS, BERGEN, NORWAY** *(stenersen.com)*

	Sten Aurora	9378723	TK	2008	D	16,613	472'07"	75'06"	40'08"
	Sten Suomi	9378723	TK	2008	D	16,611	472'11"	76'01"	40'08"

IR-2 **REEDEREI ECKHOFF & CO. GMBH, JORK, GERMANY** *(reederei-eckhoff.de)*

	BBC England	9258985	GC	2003	D	10,300	465'10"	59'10"	33'04"
	(Frida '03-'04)								
	Onego Ponza	9245263	GC	2002	D	9,900	455'07"	52'01"	35'07"

(Sider Ponza '02-'02, Sider Monique '02-'03, Sider Ponza '03-'09)

IR-3 **REEDEREI GERD GORKE GMBH & CO., HOLLERN-TWIELENFLETH, GERMANY** *(www.r-gg.de)*

	BBC Hawaii	9358010	TK	2006	D	12,706	452'11"	70'01"	30'01"

(Beluga Evaluation '06-'11, Nicola '11-'11)

IR-4 **REEDEREI KARL SCHLUTER GMBH & CO., RENDSBURG, GERMANY**
FOLLOWING VESSEL UNDER CHARTER TO FEDNAV LTD.

	Federal Mattawa	9315537	GC	2005	D	18,825	606'11"	77'09"	46'03"

IR-5 **REEDEREI NORD GMBH, HAMBURG, GERMANY** *(reederei-nord.com)*

	Nordisle	9457828	TK	2009	D	12,810	393'08"	66'11"	39'00")
	(Rio Daintree '09-'09)								
	Nordport	9404144	TK	2008	D	13,132	421'11"	67'00"	37'09")
	(E R Elbe '08-'08)								

IR-6 **RIGEL SCHIFFAHRTS GMBH, BREMEN, GERMANY** *(rigel-hb.com)*

	Amur Star	9480368	TK	2010	D	13,073	421'11"	66'11"	37'09"
	Colorado Star	9527609	TK	2010	D	13,073	421'11"	66'11"	37'09"
	Ganges Star	9496692	TK	2010	D	13,073	421'11"	66'11"	37'09"
	Isarstern	9105140	TK	1995	D	17,078	528'03"	75'06"	38'05"
	Kongo Star	9508823	TK	2010	D	13,073	421'11"	66'11"	37'09"
	Shannon Star	9503926	TK	2010	D	13,073	421'11"	66'11"	37'09"

IS-1 **SARGEANT MARINE INC., BOCA RATON, FLORIDA, USA** *(sargeant.net)*

	Asphalt Carrier	9293545	TK	2010	D	9,230	356'00"	61'00"	34'09"

IS-2 **SCANDINOR AS, BREVIK, NORWAY**

	Ternen	9341316	BC	2007	D	15,212	490'10"	72'03"	42'06"
	(Marida Boreas '07-'10)								

IS-3 **SCAN-TRANS SHIPPING, NAESTVED, DENMARK** *(www.scan-trans.com)*

	Oslo Bulk 6	9589968	BC	2011	D	8,053	355'00"	59'09"	29'06"
	(Xin Yang 83 '11-'11)								

IS-4 **SE SHIPPING, SINGAPORE, SINGAPORE** *(seshipping.com)*

	SE Potentia	9431472	BC	2009	D	12,840	454'05"	68'11"	36'01"
	(Brattingsborg '09-'09)								

Fleet Name Vessel Name	IMO #	Vessel Type	Year Built	Engine Type	Cargo Cap. or Gross*	Overall Length	Breadth	Depth
IS-5	**SEASTAR CHARTERING LTD., ATHENS, GREECE**							
FOLLOWING VESSELS UNDER CHARTER TO CANADIAN FOREST NAVIGATION CO. LTD.								
Apollon	9146821	BC	1996	D	30,855	606' 11"	77' 05"	48' 11"
(*Spring Laker* '96-'06)								
IS-6	**SERROMAH SHIPPING BV, ROTTERDAM, NETHERLANDS** (serromahshipping.com)							
Oriental Kerria	9294795	TK	2004	D	14,298	440' 02"	67' 04"	38' 01"
Oriental Protea	9330381	TK	2005	D	14,246	440' 02"	67' 03"	38' 01"
Shamrock Jupiter	9416082	TK	2009	D	19,998	481' 00"	77' 09"	42' 08"
IS-7	**SHANGHAI DIHENG SHIPPING CO., SHANGHAI, CHINA**							
Han Xin	9125889	BC	1996	D	7,713	352' 02"	62' 04"	34' 09"
(*Svenja* '96-'06, *Atlant Svenja* '06-'12)								
IS-8	**SHIH WEI NAVIGATION CO. LTD., TAIPEI, TAIWAN** (www.swnav.com.tw)							
Royal Pescadores	9151400	BC	1997	D	18,369	486' 01"	74' 10"	40' 00"
IS-9	**SIOMAR ENTERPRISES LTD., PIRAEUS, GREECE**							
Island Skipper	8312095	BC	1984	D	28,031	584' 08"	76' 02"	48' 05"
IS-10	**SLOMAN NEOTUN SHIFFAHRTS, BREMEN, GERMANY** (sloman-neptun.com)							
Sloman Dispatcher	9620657	HL	2012	D	12,634	453' 01"	68' 11"	36' 01"
Sloman Hera	9466714	TK	2012	D	16,500	476' 02"	76' 05"	41' 00"
IS-11	**SPLIETHOFF'S BEVRACHTINGSKANTOOR B.V., AMSTERDAM, NETHERLANDS** (spliethoff.com)							
FOLLOWING VESSELS UNDER CHARTER TO FEDNAV LTD.								
Apollogracht	9014896	HL	1991	D	12,200	423' 03"	62' 00"	38' 01"

Fleet Name / Vessel Name	IMO #	Vessel Type	Year Built	Engine Type	Cargo Cap. or Gross*	Overall Length	Breadth	Depth
Elandsgracht	9081332	HL	1995	D	15,593	452' 09"	74' 10"	42' 06"
Muntgracht	9571545	HL	2012	D	12,500	464' 11"	62' 00"	38' 03"

IS-12 STOLT PARCEL TANKERS INC., GREENWICH, CONNECTICUT, USA *(stolt-nielsen.com)*

Stolt Kite	8920555	TK	1992	D	4,735	314' 11"	49' 06"	26' 05

IS-13 SUNSHIP SCHIFFAHRTSKONTOR KG, EMDEN, GERMANY *(sunship.de)*

CL Hanse Gate	9283540	BC	2004	D	27,000	606' 11"	77' 09"	46' 03"
(Federal Matane '04-'11)								
Copenhagen	9457115	BC	2011	D	5,627	354' 11"	54' 06"	28' 03"
Lake Ontario	9283538	BC	2004	D	27,000	606' 11"	77' 09"	46' 03"
(Federal Manitou '04-'11)								

FOLLOWING VESSELS UNDER CHARTER TO FEDNAV LTD.

Federal Miramichi	9315549	BC	2004	D	27,000	606' 11"	77' 09"	46' 03"

IT-1 TARBIT TANKERS B.V., DORDRECHT, NETHERLANDS *(tarbittankers.nl)*

Stella Polaris	9187057	TK	1999	D	8,000	387' 02"	55' 09"	34' 05"

IT-2 TEAM SHIP MANAGEMENT GMBH & CO. KG, BREMERHAVEN, GERMANY *(teamship.de)*

OXL Lotus	9144471	HL	1996	D	5,147	331' 00"	62' 00"	31' 10"
*(Palawan '96-'96, **Scan Partner** '96-'02, **Palawan** '02-'08)*								
Team Spirit	9346421	HL	2006	D	11,145	424' 02"	62' 04"	38' 03"
(Normed Bremen '06-'11, Team Bremen '11-'12)								

IT-3 TRANSAL DENIZCILIK TICARET, ISTANBUL, TURKEY *(www.transal.com.tr)*

Ruby-T	9457878	TK	2010	D	21,224	541' 01"	75' 02"	42' 00"

Sichem Manila off Belle Isle, at Detroit. (Jeff Mast)

	Fleet Name Vessel Name	IMO #	Vessel Type	Year Built	Engine Type	Cargo Cap. or Gross*	Overall Length	Breadth	Depth
IT-4	**TRAVEL DYNAMICS INTERNATIONAL, NEW YORK, NEW YORK, USA** *(traveldynamicsinternational.com)*								
	Yorktown	8949472	PA	1988	D	97*	257' 00"	40' 00"	12' 05"
	(Yorktown Clipper '88-'06, Spirit of Yorktown '06-'11)								
IU-1	**UTKILEN AS, BERGEN, NORWAY** *(utkilen.no)*								
	Susana S	9406714	TK	2009	D	12,862	539' 02"	76' 01"	42' 00"
IV-1	**VIKEN SHIPPING AS, BERGEN, NORWAY** *(vikenshipping.com)*								
	FOLLOWING VESSELS UNDER CHARTER TO FEDNAV LTD.								
	Federal Polaris	8321929	BC	1985	D	29,643	599' 09"	76' 00"	48' 07"
IW-1	**W. BOCKSTIEGEL REEDEREI KG, EMDEN, GERMANY** *(reederei-bockstiegel.de)*								
	Atlantic Steamer	9210359	GC	2001	D	7,650	353' 06"	59' 09"	33' 02"
	(BBC Spain '01-'11)								
	Baltic Carrier	9505572	GC	2011	D	7,850	351' 00"	59' 01"	34' 05"
	BBC Alaska	9433262	GC	2008	D	12,840	454' 05"	68' 11"	36' 01"
	BBC Arizona	9501253	GC	2010	D	12,750	454' 05"	68' 11"	36' 01"
	(BBC Barbuda '10-'10)								
	BBC Campana	9291963	GC	2003	D	12,782	453' 00"	68' 11"	24' 07"
	BBC Colorado	9435117	GC	2004	D	12,750	454' 05"	68' 11"	36' 01"
	BBC Delaware	9357212	GC	2004	D	12,782	453' 00"	68' 11"	24' 07"
	BBC Louisiana	9435105	GC	2008	D	12,750	454' 05"	68' 11"	36' 01"
	BBC Maine	9357200	GC	2007	D	12,792	444' 05"	68' 11"	36' 01"
	BBC Oregon	9501265	GC	2010	D	12,750	454' 05"	68' 11"	36' 01"
	BBC Plata	9291975	GC	2005	D	12,750	454' 05"	68' 11"	36' 01"
	(Asian Voyager '05-'05)								
	Mareike B	9195248	GC	2002	D	3,486	283' 06"	42' 00"	23' 04"
	(BBC Portugal '02-'12)								
	BBC Vermont	9357236	GC	2008	D	12,000	453' 00"	68' 11"	36' 01"
	BBC Zarate	9337236	GC	2007	D	12,834	452' 09"	68' 11"	36' 01"
IW-2	**WAGENBORG SHIPPING BV, DELFZIJL, NETHERLANDS** *(wagenborg.com)*								
	Adriaticborg	9546497	GC	2011	D	17,294	469' 02"	70' 06"	43' 08"
	Africaborg	9365661	GC	2007	D	17,294	469' 02"	70' 06"	43' 08"
	(Africaborg '07-'08, Tianshan '08-'09)								

Greek-registered tanker Hellespont Centurion (this page) and an on-board view of her intricate deck piping (opposite page).

(Paul Beesely)

Fleet Name Vessel Name	IMO #	Vessel Type	Year Built	Engine Type	Cargo Cap. or Gross*	Overall Length	Breadth	Depth
Alamosborg	9466348	GC	2011	D	17,294	469' 02"	70' 06"	43' 08"
Amazoneborg	9365661	GC	2007	D	17,294	469' 02"	70' 06"	43' 08"
Americaborg	9365659	GC	2007	D	17,294	469' 02"	70' 06"	43' 08"
Amstelborg	9333527	GC	2006	D	17,294	469' 02"	70' 06"	43' 08"
Aragonborg	9546497	GC	2011	D	17,294	469' 02"	70' 06"	43' 08"
Arneborg	9333539	GC	2006	D	17,294	469' 02"	70' 06"	43' 08"
Arubaborg	9466295	GC	2010	D	17,294	469' 02"	70' 06"	43' 08"
Asiaborg	9333553	GC	2007	D	17,294	469' 02"	70' 06"	43' 08"
Atlanticborg	9466350	GC	2012	D	17,294	469' 02"	70' 06"	43' 08"
Australiaborg	9397171	GC	2007	D	17,294	469' 02"	70' 06"	43' 08"
Diezeborg	9225586	GC	2000	D	8,867	437' 08"	52' 00"	32' 02"
(Diezeborg '00-'01, MSC Marmara '01-'03)								
Dintelborg	9163685	GC	1999	D	8,867	437' 07"	52' 00"	32' 02"
(Dintelborg '00-'01, MSC Dardanelles '01-'04)								
Dongeborg	9163697	GC	1999	D	8,867	437' 08"	52' 00"	32' 02"
Drechtborg	9196163	GC	2000	D	8,867	437' 08"	52' 00"	32' 02"
(Drechtborg '00-'00, MSC Skaw '00-'02, Drechtborg '02-'03, Normed Rotterdam '03-'05)								
Ebroborg	9463451	GC	2010	D	10,750	452' 03"	52' 01"	36' 01"
Edenborg	9463449	GC	2010	D	10,750	452' 03"	52' 01"	36' 01"
Eeborg	9568328	GC	2012	D	12,000	474' 03"	52' 01"	36' 07"
Eemsborg	9225586	GC	2009	D	10,750	452' 03"	52' 01"	36' 01"
Elbeborg	9568249	GC	2011	D	12,000	474' 03"	52' 01"	36' 07"
Erieborg	9463437	GC	2009	D	10,750	452' 03"	52' 01"	36' 01"
Finnborg	9419321	GC	2011	D	14,603	507' 03"	56' 05"	37' 11"
Fivelborg	9419307	GC	2010	D	14,603	507' 03"	56' 05"	37' 11"
Flevoborg	9419292	GC	2010	D	14,603	507' 03"	56' 05"	37' 11"
Fraserborg	9419319	GC	2011	D	14,603	507' 03"	56' 05"	37' 11"
Fuldaborg	9559092	GC	2012	D	14,603	507' 03"	56' 05"	37' 11"
Kasteelborg	9155937	GC	1998	D	9,150	427' 01"	52' 01"	33' 06"
Keizersborg	9102904	GC	1996	D	9,150	427' 01"	52' 01"	33' 06"
Koningsborg	9155925	GC	1999	D	9,150	427' 01"	52' 01"	33' 06"
Kroonborg	9102899	GC	1995	D	9,085	428' 10"	52' 02"	33' 06"
Loireborg	9399404	GC	2008	D	7,350	401' 04"	47' 03"	26' 07"

(Alain Gindroz)

Fleet Name Vessel Name	IMO #	Vessel Type	Year Built	Engine Type	Cargo Cap. or Gross*	Overall Length	Breadth	Depth
Maineborg	9228980	GC	2001	D	9,141	441' 05"	54' 02"	32' 02"
Markborg	9142540	GC	1996	D	9,141	441' 05"	54' 02"	32' 02"
Medemborg	9142514	GC	1997	D	9,141	441' 05"	54' 02"	32' 02"
(Arion '97-'03)								
Merweborg	9142552	GC	1997	D	9,141	441' 05"	54' 02"	32' 02"
Metsaborg	9243801	GC	2002	D	9,141	441' 05"	54' 02"	32' 02"
Mississippiborg	9207508	GC	2000	D	9,141	441' 05"	54' 02"	32' 02"
Missouriborg	9228978	GC	2000	D	9,141	441' 05"	54' 02"	32' 02"
Moezelborg	9180839	GC	1999	D	9,141	441' 05"	54' 02"	32' 02"
Morraborg	9190274	GC	1999	D	9,141	441' 05"	54' 02"	32' 02"
Nassauborg	9248564	GC	2006	D	16,740	467' 03"	72' 06"	42' 00"
Vaasaborg	9196242	GC	1999	D	8,664	433' 10"	52' 01"	31' 08"
Vancouverborg	9213741	GC	2001	D	9,857	433' 10"	52' 01"	31' 08"
Vechtborg	9160334	GC	1998	D	8,664	433' 10"	52' 01"	31' 08"
Victoriaborg	9234276	GC	2001	D	9,857	433' 10"	52' 01"	31' 08"

Bulgarian-registered Vitosha readies for a pilot change on the Detroit River. (Alain Gindroz)

Fleet Name Vessel Name	IMO #	Vessel Type	Year Built	Engine Type	Cargo Cap. or Gross*	Overall Length	Breadth	Depth
Virginiaborg	9234290	GC	2001	D	9,857	433'10"	52'01"	31'08"
Vlieborg	9554781	GC	2012	D	11,850	468'00"	52'01"	35'04"
Vlistborg	9160346	GC	1999	D	8,664	433'10"	52'01"	31'08"
Voorneborg	9179373	GC	1999	D	8,664	433'10"	52'01"	31'08"

At press time, Wagenborg Shipping also had the following vessels under charter. Please consult their respective fleets for details: **Kwintebank, Marietje Deborah, Marietje Marsilla, Varnebank, Vikingbank.**

IY-1 YARDIMCI SHIPPING GROUP, ISTANBUL, TURKEY *(www.yardimci.gen.tr)*

CT Cork	9393060	TK	2008	D	10,303	383'10"	68'11"	31'02"
Elevit	9466609	TK	2012	D	17,000	472'07"	75'06"	40'08"

IY-2 YILMAR SHIPPING & TRADING LTD., ISTANBUL, TURKEY *(yilmar.com)*

YM Saturn	9362138	TK	2007	D	16,000	485'07"	70'10"	37'01"

GREAT LAKES GLOSSARY

AAA CLASS – Vessel design popular on the Great Lakes in the early 1950s. *Arthur M. Anderson* is one example.

AFT – Toward the back, or stern, of a ship.

AHEAD – Forward.

AMIDSHIPS – The middle point of a vessel, referring to either length or width.

ARTICULATED TUG/BARGE (ATB) – Tug-barge combination. The two vessels are mechanically linked in one axis but with the tug free to move, or articulate, on another axis. *Jacklyn M/Integrity* is one example.

BACKHAUL – The practice of carrying a revenue-producing cargo (rather than ballast) on a return trip from hauling a primary cargo.

BARGE – Vessel with no engine, either pushed or pulled by a tug.

BEAM – The width of a vessel measured at the widest point.

BILGE – Lowest part of a hold or compartment, generally where the rounded side of a ship curves from the keel to the vertical sides.

BOW – Front of a vessel.

BOW THRUSTER – Propeller mounted transversely in a vessel's bow under the water line to assist in moving sideways. A stern thruster may also be installed.

BRIDGE – The platform above the main deck from which a ship is steered/navigated. Also: PILOTHOUSE or WHEELHOUSE.

BULKHEAD – Wall or partition that separates rooms, holds or tanks within a ship's hull.

BULWARK – The part of the ship that extends fore and aft above the main deck to form a rail.

DATUM – Level of water in a given area, determined by an average over time.

DEADWEIGHT TONNAGE – The actual carrying capacity of a vessel, equal to the difference between the light displacement tonnage and the heavy displacement tonnage, expressed in long tons (2,240 pounds or 1,016.1 kilograms).

DISPLACEMENT TONNAGE – The actual weight of the vessel and everything aboard her, measured in long tons. The displacement is equal to the weight of the water displaced by the vessel. Displacement tonnage may be qualified as light, indicating the weight of the vessel without cargo, fuel and stores, or heavy, indicating the weight of the vessel loaded with cargo, fuel and stores.

DRAFT – The depth of water a ship needs to float. Also, the distance from keel to water line.

FIT OUT – The process of preparing a vessel for service after a period of inactivity.

FIVE-YEAR INSPECTION – U.S. Coast Guard survey, conducted in a drydock every five years, of a vessel's hull, machinery and other components.

FLATBACK – Lakes slang for a non-self-unloader.

FOOTER – Lakes slang for 1,000-foot vessel.

FORECASTLE – (FOHK s'l) Area at the forward part of the ship and beneath the main cabins, often used for crew's quarters or storage.

FOREPEAK – The space below the forecastle.

FORWARD – Toward the front, or bow, of a ship.

FREEBOARD – The distance from the water line to the main deck.

GROSS TONNAGE – The internal space of a vessel, measured in units of 100 cubic feet (2.83 cubic meters) = a gross ton.

HATCH – An opening in the deck through which cargo is lowered or raised. A hatch is closed by securing a hatch cover over it.

HULL – The body of a ship, not including its superstructure, masts or machinery.

IMO # – Unique number issued by International Maritime Organization, or IMO, to each ship for identification purposes.

INTEGRATED TUG/BARGE (ITB) – Tug-barge combination in which the tug is rigidly mated to the barge. *Presque Isle* is one example.

IRON DECKHAND – Mechanical device that runs on rails on a vessel's main deck and is used to remove and replace hatch covers.

JONES ACT – A U.S. cabotage law that mandates that cargoes moved between American ports be carried by U.S.-flagged, U.S.-built and U.S.-crewed vessels.

KEEL – A ship's steel backbone. It runs along the lowest part of the hull.

LAID UP or **LAY-UP** – Out of service.

MARITIME CLASS – Style of lake vessel built during World War II as part of the nation's war effort. *Mississagi* is one example.

NET REGISTERED TONNAGE – The internal capacity of a vessel available for carrying cargo. It does not include the space occupied by boilers, engines, shaft alleys, chain lockers or officers' and crew's quarters. Net registered tonnage is usually referred to as registered tonnage or net tonnage and is used to calculate taxes, tolls and port charges.

RIVER CLASS SELF-UNLOADER – Group of vessels built in the 1970s to service smaller ports and negotiate narrow rivers such as Cleveland's Cuyahoga. *Manitowoc* is one example.

SELF-UNLOADER – Vessel able to discharge its own cargo using a system of conveyor belts and a movable boom.

STEM – The extreme forward end of the bow.

STEMWINDER – Vessel with all cabins aft (also sternwinder).

STERN – The back of the ship.

STRAIGHT-DECKER – A non-self-unloading vessel. *Edward L. Ryerson* is one example.

TACONITE – Processed, pelletized iron ore. Easy to load and unload, this is the primary type of ore shipped on the Great Lakes and St. Lawrence Seaway. Also known as pellets.

TRACTOR TUG – Highly maneuverable tug propelled by either a Z-drive or cycloidal system rather than the traditional screw propeller.

TURKEY TRAIL – Route from North Channel (above Manitoulin Island) into the St. Marys River, named for the many courses which zigzag through the area's islands, shoals and ports, much like the trail that wild turkeys might take.

Marine Museums

A tug secures the Col. James M. Schoonmaker museum ship at her new berth at Toledo, Ohio, on Oct. 27, 2012. *(Matt Miner)*

COMING SOON!

THE NATIONAL MUSEUM OF THE GREAT LAKES, TOLEDO, OHIO

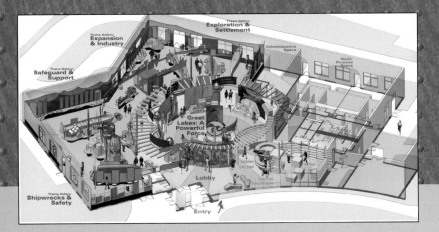

MUSEUMS AFLOAT

Museum Name Vessel Name	Vessel Type	Year Built	Engine Type	Cargo Cap. or Gross*	Overall Length	Breadth	Depth
MU-1 **BUFFALO AND ERIE COUNTY NAVAL & MILITARY PARK, BUFFALO, NY** *(buffalonavalpark.org)*							
Croaker	MU	1944	D	1,526*	311'07"	27'02"	33'09"
Former U. S. Navy Gato class submarine IXSS-246; open to the public at Buffalo, NY							
Little Rock	MU	1945	T	10,670*	610'01"	66'04"	25'00"
Former U. S. Navy Cleveland / Little Rock class guided missile cruiser; open to the public at Buffalo, NY							
The Sullivans	MU	1943	T	2,500*	376'06"	39'08"	22'08"
Former U. S. Navy Fletcher class destroyer; open to the public at Buffalo, NY (Launched as USS Putnam)							
MU-2 **CITY OF KEWAUNEE, KEWAUNEE, WI** *(cityofkewaunee.org)*							
Ludington	MU	1943	D	249*	115'00"	26'00"	13'08"
Built: Jakobson Shipyard, Oyster Bay, NY; former U.S. Army Corps of Engineers tug is open to the public as a marine museum at Kewaunee, WI (Major Wilbur F. Browder [LT-4] '43-'47)							
MU-3 **DOOR COUNTY MARITIME MUSEUM & LIGHTHOUSE PRESERVATION SOCIETY INC.,** **STURGEON BAY, WI** *(dcmm.org)*							
John Purves	TB/MU	1919	D	436*	150'00"	27'06"	16'08"
Built: Bethlehem Steel Co., Elizabeth, NJ; former Roen/Andrie Inc. tug has been refurbished as a museum display at Sturgeon Bay, WI (Butterfield '19-'42, LT-145 '42-'57)							
MU-4 **DULUTH ENTERTAINMENT CONVENTION CENTER, DULUTH, MN** *(decc.org/omnimax-irvin)*							
William A. Irvin	MU	1938	T	14,050	610'09"	60'00"	32'06"
Built: American Shipbuilding Co., Lorain, OH; former United States Steel Corp. bulk carrier last operated Dec. 16, 1978; open to the public at Duluth, MN							
MU-5 **ERIE MARITIME MUSEUM, ERIE, PA** *(flagshipniagara.org)*							
Niagara	MU/2B	1988	W	295*	198'00"	32'00"	10'06"
Reconstruction of Oliver Hazard Perry's U. S. Navy brigantine from the War of 1812							
MU-6 **FRIENDS OF THE NORISLE, MANITOWANING, ON** *(norisle.com)*							
Norisle	MU	1946	R	1,668*	215'09"	36'03"	16'00"
Built: Collingwood Shipyards, Collingwood, ON; former Ontario Northland Transportation Commission passenger vessel last operated in 1974; open to the public at Manitowaning, Manitoulin Island, ON							
MU-7 **GREAT LAKES NAVAL MEMORIAL & MUSEUM, MUSKEGON, MI** *(glnmm.org)*							
McLane	MU	1927	D	289*	125'00"	24'00"	12'06"
Built: American Brown Boveri Electric Co.,Camden, NJ; former U.S. Coast Guard Buck & A Quarter class medium endurance cutter; on display at Muskegon, MI (USCGC McLane [WSC / WMEC-146] '27-'70, Manatra II '70-'93)							
Silversides	MU	1941	D/V	1,526*	311'08"	27'03"	33'09"
Built: Mare Island Naval Yard, Vallejo, CA; former U.S. Navy Albacore (Gato) class submarine AGSS-236; open to the public at Muskegon, MI							

Long-awaited National Museum
of the Great Lakes opening soon at Toledo

More than two years after the Great Lakes Historical Society and the Toledo-Lucas County Port Authority announced plans to bring a maritime history museum from Vermilion, Ohio, to Toledo, the new National Museum of the Great Lakes is expected to open its doors this year, featuring more than 50 interactive exhibits as well as original artifacts in nearly 10,000 square feet of exhibit space. The largest exhibit will be the century-old lake freighter *Col. James M. Schoonmaker*, docked adjacent to the museum building. When complete, the complex will also include a new Maritime Park with several acres of landscaping as well as maritime artifacts and history.

Col. James M. Schoonmaker

The $10 million project has been funded extensively through the Ohio Cultural Facilities Commission with a grant worth over $6 million. Further funding has come from private and public sources, including a lease from the Port Authority for the building for $1 per year, and a capital campaign driven by the Great Lakes Historical Society.

MU-8 GREAT LAKES SCIENCE CENTER, CLEVELAND, OH (wgmather.nhlink.net)

William G. Mather {2}	MU	1925	T	13,950	618' 00"	62' 00"	32' 00"

Built: Great Lakes Engineering Works, Ecorse, MI; former Cleveland-Cliffs Steamship Co. bulk carrier last operated Dec. 21, 1980; open to the public at Cleveland, OH

MU-9 H. LEE WHITE MARINE MUSEUM, OSWEGO, NY (hleewhitemarinemuseum.com)

LT-5	MU	1943	D	305*	115' 00"	28' 00"	14' 00"

Built: Jakobson Shipyard, Oyster Bay, NY; former U.S. Army Corps of Engineers tug last operated in 1989; open to the public at Oswego, NY (Major Elisha K. Henson '43-'47, U.S. Army LT-5 '47-'47, Nash '47-'95)

MU-10 HMCS HAIDA NATIONAL HISTORICAL SITE, HAMILTON, ON (hmcshaida.ca)

Haida	MU	1943	T	2,744*	377' 00"	37' 06"	15' 02"

Former Royal Canadian Navy Tribal class destroyer G-63 / DDE-215; open to the public at Hamilton, ON

MU-11 ICEBREAKER MACKINAW MARITIME MUSEUM INC., MACKINAW CITY, MI (themackinaw.org)

Mackinaw [WAGB-83]	MU	1944	D	5,252*	290' 00"	74' 00"	29' 00"

Built: Toledo Shipbuilding Co., Toledo, OH; former U.S. Coast Guard icebreaker was decommissioned in 2006; open to the public at Mackinaw City, MI (Launched as USCGC Manitowoc [WAG-83])

MU-12 LAKE COUNTY HISTORICAL SOCIETY, TWO HARBORS, MN (lakecountyhistoricalsociety.org)

Edna G.	MU	1896	R	154*	102' 00"	23' 00"	14' 06"

Built: Cleveland Shipbuilding Co., Cleveland, OH; former Duluth, Missabe & Iron Range Railroad tug last operated in 1981; open to the public at Two Harbors, MN

MU-13 LE SAULT DE SAINTE MARIE HISTORIC SITES INC., SAULT STE. MARIE, MI (saulthistoricsites.com)

Valley Camp {2}	MU	1917	R	12,000	550' 00"	58' 00"	31' 00"

Built: American Shipbuilding Co., Lorain, OH; former Hanna Mining Co./Wilson Marine Transit Co./Republic Steel Corp. bulk carrier last operated in 1966; open to the public at Sault Ste. Marie, MI (Louis W. Hill '17-'55)

MU-14 MARINE MUSEUM OF THE GREAT LAKES AT KINGSTON, KINGSTON, ON (marmuseum.ca)

Alexander Henry	MU	1959	D	1,674*	210' 00"	44' 00"	17' 09"

Built: Port Arthur Shipbuilding Co., Port Arthur, ON; former Canadian Coast Guard icebreaker was retired in 1985; open to the public at Kingston, ON

MU-15 MICHIGAN MARITIME MUSEUM, SOUTH HAVEN, MI (michiganmaritimemuseum.org)

Friends Good Will	TV/ES	2004	D/W	54*	56' 05"	17' 00"	11' 03"

Built: Scarano Boatbuilding, Inc., Albany, NY

MU-16 MUSÉE MARITIME DU QUÉBEC, L' ISLET, QC (mmq.qc.ca)

Bras d'Or 400	MU	1968	D	250*	163' 11"	66' 00"	

Built: Marine Industries Limited, Sorel, QC; former Canadian Coast Guard anti-submarine warfare technology hydrofoil is on display at L'Islet, QC

Ernest Lapointe	MU	1941	R	1,179*	185' 00"	36' 00"	22' 06"

Built: Davie Shipbuilding Co., Lauzon, QC; former Canadian Coast Guard icebreaker; open to the public at L'Islet, QC

MU-17 MUSEUM SHIP COL. JAMES M. SCHOONMAKER, TOLEDO, OH (jmschoonmaker.org)

Col. James M. Schoonmaker	MU	1911	T	15,000	617' 00"	64' 00"	33' 01"

Built: Great Lakes Engineering Works, Ecorse, MI; former Shenango Furnace Co./Republic Steel Co./Cleveland-Cliffs Steamship Co. bulk carrier last operated in 1980; open to the public at Toledo, OH, under the auspices of the Great Lakes Historical Society (Col. James M. Schoonmaker 1911-'69, Willis B. Boyer '69-2011)

Tug Colonel tows the USS Edson past Port Huron, Mich., to a new home as a marine museum in Bay City, Mich. (Bob Powers)

MU-18 PORT HURON MUSEUM, PORT HURON, MI *(phmuseum.org)*

Huron	MU	1920	D	392*	96' 05"	24' 00"	10' 00"

Built: Charles L. Seabury Co., Morris Heights, NY; former U.S. Coast Guard lightship WLV-526 was retired Aug. 20, 1970; open to the public at Port Huron, MI (Lightship 103 – Relief [WAL-526] '20-'36)

MU-19 ROBERT AND SARA KLINGLER, MARINE CITY, MI

Bramble	MU	1944	DE	1,025*	180' 00"	37' 00"	17' 04"

Built: Zenith Dredge Co., Duluth, MN; former U.S. Coast Guard buoy tender/icebreaker was retired in 2003; expected to open as a marine museum at Port Huron, MI, in 2013 (USCGC Bramble [WLB-392] '1944-'2003)

MU-20 SAGINAW VALLEY NAVAL SHIP MUSEUM, BAY CITY, MI *(ussedson.org)*

Edson [DD-946]	MU	1958	D		418' 03"	45' 03"	

Built: Bath Iron Works, Bath, ME; Forrest Sherman-class destroyer was decommissioned in '88; from '89-'04 on display at the Intrepid Air and Sea Museum, New York City. Declared a U.S. National Historic Landmark in '90. Returned to U.S. Navy in '04; plans call for her to eventually become a marine museum at Bay City, MI

MU-21 SKYLINE INTERNATIONAL DEVELOPMENT INC., PORT McNICOLL, ON

Keewatin {2}	MU	1907	Q	3,856*	346' 00"	43' 08"	26' 06"

Built: Fairfield Shipbuilding and Engineering Co. Ltd., Govan, Scotland; former Canadian Pacific Railway Co. passenger vessel last operated Nov. 29, 1965; has served as a marine museum since 1967 in Douglas, MI; moved to Port McNicoll, ON, in 2012 to continue in a similar role

MU-22 S.S. CITY OF MILWAUKEE – NATIONAL HISTORIC LANDMARK, MANISTEE, MI *(carferry.com)*

Acacia	MU	1944	DE	1,025*	180' 00"	37' 00"	17' 04"

Built: Marine Iron and Shipbuilding Corp., Duluth, MN; former U.S. Coast Guard buoy tender/icebreaker was decommissioned in '06; (Launched as USCGC Thistle [WAGL-406])

City of Milwaukee	MU	1931	R	26 cars	360' 00"	56' 03"	21' 06"

Built: Manitowoc Shipbuilding Co., Manitowoc, WI; train ferry sailed for the Grand Trunk Railroad '31-'78 and the Ann Arbor Railroad '78-'81; open to the public at Manistee, MI

MU-23 S.S. COLUMBIA PROJECT, NEW YORK, NY *(sscolumbia.org)*

Columbia {2}	5077333	PA	1902	R	968*	216' 00"	60' 00"	13' 06"

Built: Detroit Dry Dock Co, Wyandotte, MI; former Detroit to Bob-Lo Island passenger steamer last operated Sept. 2, 1991; laid up at Ecorse, MI, awaiting funds for renovation and relocation to the East Coast

MU-24 S.S. METEOR WHALEBACK SHIP MUSEUM, SUPERIOR, WI *(superiorpublicmuseums.org)*

Meteor {2}	MU	1896	R	40,100	380' 00"	45' 00"	26' 00"

Built: American Steel Barge Co., Superior, WI; former ore carrier/auto carrier/tanker is the last vessel of whaleback design surviving on the Great Lakes; Cleveland Tankers vessel last operated in 1969; open to the public at Superior, WI (Frank Rockefeller 1896-'28, South Park '1928-'43)

MU-25 S.S. MILWAUKEE CLIPPER PRESERVATION INC., MUSKEGON, MI *(milwaukeeclipper.com)*

Milwaukee Clipper	MU	1904	Q	4,272	361' 00"	45' 00"	28' 00"

Built: American Shipbuilding Co., Cleveland, OH; rebuilt in '40 at Manitowoc Shipbuilding Co., Manitowoc, WI; former Wisconsin & Michigan Steamship Co. passenger/auto carrier last operated in 1970; undergoing restoration at Muskegon, MI (Juniata '04-'41)

MU-26 ST. MARYS RIVER MARINE CENTRE, SAULT STE. MARIE, ON *(norgoma.org)*

Norgoma	MU	1950	D	1,477*	188' 00"	37' 06"	22' 06"

Built: Collingwood Shipyards, Collingwood, ON; former Ontario Northland Transportation Commission passenger vessel last operated in 1974; open to the public at Sault Ste. Marie, ON

MU-27 USS COD SUBMARINE MEMORIAL, CLEVELAND, OH *(usscod.org)*

Cod	MU	1943	D/V	1,525*	311' 08"	27' 02"	33' 09"

Built: Electric Boat Co., Groton, CT; former U.S. Navy Albacore (Gato) class submarine IXSS-224 open to the public at Cleveland, OH

MU-28 USS LST 393 PRESERVATION ASSOCIATION, MUSKEGON, MI *(lst393.org)*

LST-393	MU	1942	D	2,100	328' 00"	50' 00"	25' 00"

Built: Newport News Shipbuilding and Dry Dock Co., Newport News, VA; former U.S. Navy/Wisconsin & Michigan Steamship Co. vessel last operated July 31, 1973; open to the public at Muskegon, MI (USS LST-393 '42-'47, Highway 16 '47-'99)

MU-29 WISCONSIN MARITIME MUSEUM, MANITOWOC, WI *(wisconsinmaritime.org)*

Cobia	MU	1944	D/V	1,500*	311' 09"	27' 03"	33' 09"

Built: Electric Boat Co., Groton, CT; former U. S. Navy Gato class submarine AGSS-245 is open to the public at Manitowoc, WI

MUSEUMS ASHORE

Information can change without notice. Call ahead to verify location and hours.

ANTIQUE BOAT MUSEUM, 750 MARY ST., CLAYTON, NY – (315) 686-4104: A large collection of freshwater boats and engines. Annual show is the first weekend of August. Seasonal. (*abm.org*)

ASHTABULA MARINE & U.S. COAST GUARD MEMORIAL MUSEUM, 1071 WALNUT BLVD., ASHTABULA, OH – (440) 964-6847: Housed in the 1898-built former lighthouse keeper's residence, the museum includes models, paintings, artifacts, photos, the world's only working scale model of a Hullett ore unloading machine and the pilothouse from the steamer *Thomas Walters*. Seasonal. (*ashtabulamarinemuseum.org*)

CANAL PARK MARINE MUSEUM, ALONGSIDE THE SHIP CANAL, DULUTH, MN – (218) 727-2497: Museum provides displays, historic artifacts and programs that explain the roles of Duluth and Superior in Great Lakes shipping as well as the job of the U.S. Army Corps of Engineers in maintaining the nation's waterways. Many excellent models and other artifacts are on display. Open all year. (*lsmma.com*)

DOOR COUNTY MARITIME MUSEUM & LIGHTHOUSE PRESERVATION SOCIETY INC., 120 N. MADISON AVE., STURGEON BAY, WI – (920) 743-5958: Many excellent models help portray the role shipbuilding has played in the Door Peninsula. Open all year. (*dcmm.org*)

DOSSIN GREAT LAKES MUSEUM, 100 THE STRAND, BELLE ISLE, DETROIT, MI – (313) 852-4051: Models, interpretive displays, the smoking room from the 1912 passenger steamer *City of Detroit III*, an anchor from the *Edmund Fitzgerald* and the pilothouse from the steamer *William Clay Ford* are on display. Reopening in May 2013. (*detroithistorical.org/main/dossin*)

ELGIN MILITARY MUSEUM, ST. THOMAS, ON – (519) 633-7641. The museum has obtained *HMCS Ojibwa*, a Cold War Oberon-class submarine, and will open it to the public at Port Burwell, Ont., in 2014, the 100th anniversary of the Canadian Submarine Service. (*projectojibwa.ca*)

ERIE MARITIME MUSEUM, 150 E. FRONT ST., ERIE, PA – (814) 452-2744. Displays depict the Battle of Lake Erie and more. Check ahead to see if the U.S. brig *Niagara* is in port. Open all year. (*eriemaritimemuseum.org*)

Retired Canadian submarine HMCS Ojibwa en route via floating drydock to her new role as a museum. (Ron Walsh)

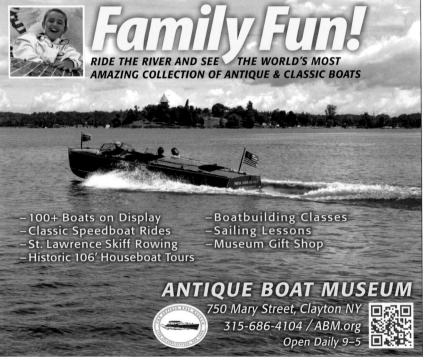

FAIRPORT HARBOR MUSEUM, 129 SECOND ST., FAIRPORT, OH – (440) 354-4825: Located in the Fairport Lighthouse, displays include the pilothouse from the *Frontenac* and the mainmast of the first *USS Michigan*. Seasonal. *(www.ncweb.com/org/fhlh)*

GREAT LAKES HISTORICAL SOCIETY – (800) 893-1485: The Great Lakes Historical Society has closed at its longtime Vermilion, Ohio, location and is in the process of moving its operation to Toledo, Ohio, where it will oversee the creation of a new national maritime museum of the Great Lakes, scheduled to open this year. Among the exhibits is the historic Great Lakes freighter *Col. James M. Schoonmaker*. *(inlandseas.org)*

GREAT LAKES SHIPWRECK MUSEUM, WHITEFISH POINT, MI – (906) 635-1742 or (800)-635-1742: Museum includes lighthouse and shipwreck artifacts, a shipwreck video theater, the restored lighthouse keeper's quarters and an *Edmund Fitzgerald* display that includes the ship's bell. Seasonal. *(shipwreckmuseum.com)*

LE SAULT DE SAINTE MARIE HISTORIC SITES, INC., 501 E. WATER ST., SAULT STE. MARIE, MI – (906) 632-3658: The 1917-built steamer *Valley Camp* is the centerpiece of this museum. The ship's three cargo holds house artifacts, models, aquariums, photos and other memorabilia, as well as a tribute to the *Edmund Fitzgerald* that includes the ill-fated vessel's lifeboats. Seasonal. *(thevalleycamp.com*

LOWER LAKES MARINE HISTORICAL SOCIETY, 66 ERIE ST., BUFFALO, NY – (716) 849-0914: Exhibits explore local maritime history. Open all year, Thursday and Sunday only. *(llmhs.org)*

MARITIME MUSEUM OF SANDUSKY, 125 MEIGS ST., SANDUSKY, OHIO – (419) 624-0274: Exhibits explore local maritime history. Open all year. *(sanduskymaritime.org)*

MARQUETTE MARITIME MUSEUM, EAST RIDGE & LAKESHORE BLVD., MARQUETTE, MI – (906) 226-2006: Museum re-creates the offices of the first commercial fishing and passenger freight companies. Displays also include charts, photos, models and maritime artifacts. Seasonal. *(mqtmaritimemuseum.com)*

MICHIGAN MARITIME MUSEUM, 260 DYCKMAN AVE., SOUTH HAVEN, MI – (269) 637-8078: Exhibits dedicated to the U.S. Lifesaving Service and Coast Guard. Displays tell the story of different kinds of boats and their uses on the lakes. The tall ship *Friends Good Will* operates during the summer. Open all year. *(michiganmaritimemuseum.org)*

OWEN SOUND MARINE & RAIL MUSEUM, 1155 FIRST AVE. WEST, OWEN SOUND, ON – (519) 371-3333: Museum depicts the history of each industry. Seasonal. *(marinerail.com)*

Museum Ship Stack Markings

Museum Ship
City of Milwaukee
Manistee, MI

Museum Ship Col.
James M. Schoonmaker
Toledo, OH

Museum Ship
Keewatin
Port McNicoll, ON

Museum Ship
Alexander Henry
Kingston, ON

Museum Ship
HMCS Haida
Hamilton, ON

Museum Ships
USS Little Rock
USS The Sullivans
Buffalo, N.Y.

Museum Ship
Meteor
Superior, WI

Museum Ship
Milwaukee Clipper
Muskegon, MI

Museum Ships
Norgoma (Sault Ste. Marie, ON)
Norisle (Manitowaning, ON)

Museum Ship
Valley Camp
Sault Ste. Marie, MI

Museum Ship
William A. Irvin
Duluth, MN

Museum Ship
William G. Mather
Cleveland, OH

Museum Ship
USCG Mackinaw
Mackinaw City, MI

Museum Tug
John Purves
Sturgeon Bay, WI

Museum Tug
Edna G
Two Harbors, MN

PORT COLBORNE HISTORICAL AND MARINE MUSEUM, 280 KING ST., PORT COLBORNE, ON – (905) 834-7604: Wheelhouse from the steam tug *Yvonne Dupre Jr.*, an anchor from the *Raleigh* and a lifeboat from the steamer *Hochelaga* are among the museum's displays. Seasonal.

U.S. ARMY CORPS OF ENGINEERS MUSEUM, SOO LOCKS VISITOR CENTER, SAULT STE. MARIE, MI – (906) 632-7020: Exhibits include a working model of the Soo Locks, historic photos and a 25-minute film. Free; open May-November. Check at the Visitor Center information desk for a list of vessels expected at the locks.

WELLAND CANAL VISITOR CENTRE, AT LOCK 3, THOROLD, ON – (905) 984-8880: Museum traces the development of the Welland Canal. Museum and adjacent gift shop open year 'round. Observation deck open during the navigation season. Check at the information desk for vessels expected at Lock 3.

WISCONSIN MARITIME MUSEUM, 75 MARITIME DRIVE, MANITOWOC, WI – (866) 724-2356: Displays explore the history of area shipbuilding and also honor submariners and submarines built in Manitowoc. One of the massive engines of the Straits of Mackinac trainferry *Chief Wawatam* is impressively on display. The World War II sub *Cobia* is adjacent to the museum and open for tours. Open all year. (wisconsinmaritime.org)

(Bill Bird)

The relocation of the 1907-vintage former Canadian Pacific Railroad passenger steamer Keewatin from her longtime home at Douglas, Mich., to Port McNicoll, Ont., attracted a lot of interest in the summer of 2012. She will continue as a museum ship and be the centerpiece of a waterfront redevelopment project at Port McNicoll.

Above, Keewatin welcomed at Port McNicoll, Ont. Below, tug Wendy Anne and Keewatin stopping off at Mackinaw City, Mich. (Bob Campbell)

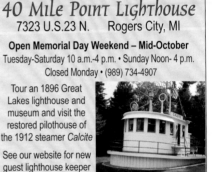

Great Lakes lighthouses attract attention

Visiting lighthouses has become more popular than ever, and the Great Lakes region has plenty from which to choose. A few highlights include:

• **Marblehead:** The oldest continuously operating lighthouse on the Great Lakes is at Marblehead, Ohio.

• **Whitefish Point:** Light, which stands guard over the entrance to Whitefish Bay, is the oldest active such structure on Lake Superior.

• **Split Rock:** The highest and most dramatic light on the lakes is on Lake Superior, north of Two Harbors, Minn.

• **DeTour Reef Light:** Beautifully restored, this light is only accessible by boat. The resident keeper programs have proved very popular.

Mackinac Straits' Round Island Light was seen in the movie "Once Upon a Time." (Matt Yocum)

.• **Old Mackinaw Point:** Located next to the Mackinac Bridge in Mackinaw City, Mich., the park surrounding the lighthouse is a great place to view the bridge and watch the boats.

• **Grand Haven:** Built in 1905, this set of bright red range lights marks the entrance to the Grand River at Grand Haven, Mich. An elevated catwalk connects the two lights.

• **Fort Gratiot Light:** Newly opened to the public, Michigan's oldest lighthouse, located at Port Huron, Mich., offers a spectacular view of lower Lake Huron from its tower.

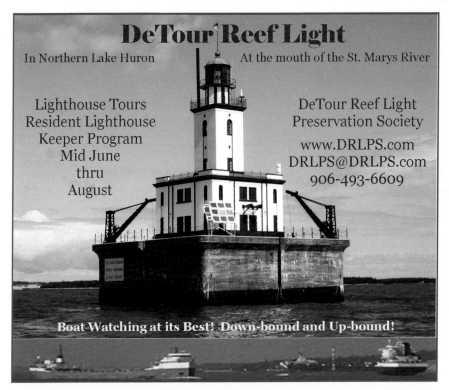

The Welland Canal

Lock up the perfect fun day out!

The **Welland Canals** were built to circumvent the mighty Niagara Falls. Marvel as lake and ocean freighters are raised and lowered in the locks on their journey between Lake Erie and Lake Ontario.

Welland Canals Centre at Lock 3
1932 Welland Canals Parkway,
St. Catharines, ON L2R 7K6
t 905-984-8880 ext. 226
toll free 1-800-305-5134
e museuminfo@stcatharines.ca
w www.stcatharines.ca

THOROLD

Lock 7 Viewing Complex
50 Chapel Street South,
Thorold, ON L2V 2C6
t 905-680-9477
toll free 1-888-680-9477
e thoroldtourism@bellnet.ca
w www.thoroldtourism.ca

Call daily for ship schedules (April - December)

Motorcoach/Group Friendly!
Ship Viewing Platform - Always FREE!

Stacks
and
Flags

CSL Niagara in the Welland Canal.
(Roger LeLievre)

Abaco Marine Towing
Clayton, NY

Algoma Central Corp.
St. Catharines, ON

Algoma Central Corp.
St. Catharines, ON

American Marine Constructors
Benton Harbor, MI

American Steamship Co.
Williamsville, NY

Andrie Inc.
Muskegon, MI

Andrie Inc.
Muskegon, MI

ArcelorMittal Mines Canada
Port Cartier, QC

Arnold Transit Co.
Mackinac Island, MI

Basic Marine Inc.
Escanaba, MI

Bay City Boat Lines
Bay City, MI

Beaver Island Boat Co.
Charlevoix, MI

Blue Heron Co.
Tobermory, ON

Buffalo Dept. of Public Works
Buffalo, N.Y.

Busch Marine Inc.
Carrollton, MI

Calumet River Fleeting
Chicago, IL

Canada Steamship Lines
Montreal, QC

Canada Steamship Lines
Montreal, QC

Canadian Coast Guard
Ottawa, ON

Central Marine Logistics Inc. Operator for ArcelorMittal
Griffith, IN

Chicago Fire Dept.
Chicago, IL

Cleveland Fire Dept.
Cleveland, OH

Croisières AML Inc.
Québec, QC

Dean Construction Co.
Belle River, ON

Detroit City Fire Dept.
Detroit, MI

Diamond Jack's River Tours
Detroit, MI

Duc D'Orleans Cruise Boat
Corunna, ON

Durocher Marine
Cheboygan, MI

Eastern Upper Peninsula Transportation Authority
Sault Ste. Marie, MI

Edward E. Gillen Co.
Milwaukee, WI

Equipments Verreault Inc.
Les Méchins, QC

Erie Sand & Gravel
Erie, PA

Essroc Canada Inc. Algoma Central – Mgr
North York, ON

Fincanteri Marine Group
Sturgeon, Bay, WI

Fraser Shipyards Inc.
Superior, WI

Gaelic Tugboat Co.
Detroit, MI

Gallagher Marine Construction Co. Inc.
Escanaba, MI

Gananoque Boat Line
Gananoque, ON

Geo. Gradel Co.
Toledo, OH

Goodtime Cruise Line
Cleveland, OH

Grand Portage / Isle Royale Trans. Line
Superior, WI

Gravel & Lake Services
Thunder Bay, ON

Great Lakes Dock & Materials
Muskegon, MI

Great Lakes Fleet Inc. Key Lakes Inc.– Mgr.
Duluth, MN

Great Lakes & International Towing & Salvage
Burlington, ON

Great Lakes Maritime Academy
Traverse City, MI

Great Lakes Towing Co.
Cleveland, OH

Groupe C.T.M.A.
Cap-Aux-Meules, QC

Groupe Desgagnés Inc.
Québec, QC

Groupe Desgagnés Inc.
Québec, QC

Groupe Desgagnés Inc.
Québec, QC

Hamilton Port Authority
Hamilton, ON

Heritage Marine
Two Harbors, MN

Hornbeck Offshore Services
Covington, LA

Horne Transportation
Wolfe Island, ON

Inland Lakes Management
Alpena, MI

Interlake Steamship Co.
Lakes Shipping Co.
Richfield, OH

J.W. Westcott Co.
Detroit, MI

Kindra Lake Towing
Chicago, IL

The King Company
Holland, MI

Lafarge Canada Inc.
Montreal, QC

Lafarge North America Inc.
Southfield, MI

Lake Erie Island Cruises
Sandusky, OH

Lake Michigan Carferry
Service Inc.
Ludington, MI

Le Groupe Ocean Inc.
Québec, QC

Lower Lakes Towing
Lower Lakes Transportation
Port Dover, ON / Williamsville, NY

Luedtke Engineering
Frankfort, MI

MCM Marine Inc.
Sault Ste. Marie, MI

MacDonald Marine Ltd.
Goderich, ON

Madeline Island
Ferry Line Inc.
LaPointe, WI

Malcolm Marine
St. Clair, MI

Manitou Island Transit
Leland, MI

Marine Tech LLC
Duluth, MN

Mariposa Cruise Line
Toronto, ON

McAsphalt Marine
Transportation
Scarborough, ON

McKeil Marine Ltd.
Hamilton, ON

McKeil Marine Ltd.
Hamilton, ON

McNally Construction
Hamilton, ON

Midwest Maritime Corp.
Milwaukee, WI

Miller Boat Line
Put-in-Bay, OH

Ministry of Transportation
Downsview, ON

Montreal Port Authority
Montreal, QC

Muskoka Steamship
& Historical Society
Gravenhurst, ON

M/V Zeus LC
Chesapeake City, MD

Nadro Marine Services
Port Dover, ON

New York State Marine
Highway Transportation
Troy, NY

Owen Sound
Transportation Co. Ltd.
Owen Sound, ON

Pere Marquette Shipping
Ludington, MI

Port City Steamship
Port City Tug Inc.
Muskegon, MI

Provmar Fuels Inc.
Hamilton, ON

Purvis Marine Ltd.
Sault Ste. Marie, ON

Relais Nordik Inc.
Rimouski, QC

Roen Salvage Co.
Sturgeon Bay, WI

Ryba Marine Construction
Cheboygan, MI

Selvick Marine Towing Corp.
Sturgeon Bay, WI

Shoreline Sightseeing Co.
Chicago, IL

Société des Traversiers Du Québec
Québec, QC

Soo Locks BoatTours
Sault Ste. Marie, MI

St. Lawrence Cruise Lines Inc.
Kingston, ON

St. Lawrence Seaway Development Corp.
Massena, NY

St. Lawrence Seaway Management Corp.
Cornwall, ON

St. Marys Cement Inc.
Toronto, ON

T.F. Warren Group
Brantford, ON

Thousand Islands & Seaway Cruises
Brockville, ON

Thunder Bay Tug Services Ltd.
Thunder Bay, ON

Thunder Bay Tug Services Ltd.
Thunder Bay, ON

Toronto Parks & Recreation Department
Toronto, ON

Transport Nanuk Inc. Spliethoff's (Owner)
Montreal, QC

United States Army Corps of Engineers
Chicago, IL

United States Coast Guard 9th Coast Guard District
Cleveland, OH

Upper Lakes Towing Co.
Escanaba, MI

Warner Petroleum Corp.
Clare, MI

Zincs Marine Towing
Westlake, OH

SALTWATER FLEETS ON THE SEAWAY

Aksay Denizcilik Ve Tickaret
Istanbul, Turkey

Amalthia Marine Inc.
Athens, Greece

Ardmore Shipping Ltd.
Cork, Ireland

Atlantska Plovidba
Dubrovnik, Croatia

Bergesen Worldwide Ltd.
Oslo, Norway

Bernhard Schulte Group
Hamburg, Germany

BigLift Shipping
Amsterdam, Netherlands

Blystad Tankers Inc.
Oslo, Norway

Briese Schiffahrts GMBH & Co. KG
Leer, Germany

Brostrom AB
Goteburg, Sweden

Canadian Forest Navigation Co. Ltd.
Montreal, Canada

Chemfleet Shipping
Istanbul, Turkey

Chemikalien Seetransport
Hamburg, Germany

Chemnav Inc.
Athens, Greece

Clipper Group AS
Copenhagen, Denmark

Coastal Shipping Ltd. (Div. Woodward Group)
Goose Bay, NL, Canada

Danser Van Gent
Delfzul, Netherlands

De Poli Tankers BV
Spijkenisse, Netherlands

Eitzen Chemical ASA
Oslo, Norway

Empire Chemical Tankers
Piraeus, Greece

Energy Shipping SPA
Genoa, Italy

Enzian Shipping AG
Berne, Switzerland

Fairfield Chemical Carriers
Wilton, CT, USA

Fednav International Ltd.
Montreal, Canada

Fednav International Ltd.
Montreal, Canada

Finbeta
Savona, Italy

Flinter Shipping
Barendrecht, Netherlands

Franco Compania Naviera SA
Athens, Greece

Freese Reederei Group
Stade, Germany

Freese Shipping
Stade, Germany

Giuseppe Messina S.R.L.
Genoa, Italy

Hapag Lloyd GMBH
Hamburg, Germany

Hansa Heavy Lift GMBH
Bremen, Germany

Harren & Partner Schiffahrts GMBH
Bremen, Germany

Hartman Seatrade
Urk, Netherlands

Hellespont Ship Management
Hamburg, Germany

Herning Shipping AS
Herning, Denmark

Intersee Schiffahrts-Gesellschaft MbH & Co.
Haren-Ems, Germany

Intership Navigation Co.
Limassol, Cyprus

Jo Tankers
Spijkenisse, Netherlands

Jumbo Shipping Co. SA
Rotterdam, Netherlands

Knutsen O.A.S. Shipping
Haugesund, Norway

Knutsen O.A.S. Shipping
Haugesund, Norway

Krey Schiffahrts GMBH & Co.
Simonswolde, Germany

Lauranne Shipping BV
Ghent, Netherlands

Lehmann Reederei
Lübeck, Germany

Liamare Shipping BV
Maartensdijk, Netherlands

Lloyd Fonds Singapore
Singapore, Singapore

Marbulk Shipping Inc. CSL International – Mgr.
Montreal, Canada

Marida Tankers Inc.
Norwalk, CT, USA

Mastermind Shipmanagement Ltd.
Limassol, Cyprus

Mega Chemical Tankers Ltd.
Singapore, Singapore

Navigation Maritime Bulgare Ltd.
Varna, Bulgaria

Neste Shipping OY
Espoo, Finland

Nicholas G. Moundreas Shipping
Piraeus, Greece

Nordana Shipping Co.
Copenhagen, Denmark

Nordic Tankers A/S
Copenhagen, Denmark

Novorossiysk Shipping
Novorossiysk, Russia

Oceanex Inc.
Montreal, QC, Canada

OSM Group AS
Kristiansand, Norway

Parakou Shipping Ltd.
Hong Kong, China

Perosea Shipping Co. SA
Piraeus, Greece

Polish Steamship Co.
Szczecin, Poland

Pot Scheepvaart BV
Delfzijl, Netherlands

Rederiet Stenersen AS
Bergen, Norway

Reederei Eckhoff and Co. GMBH
Jork, Germany

Reederei Nord GMBH
Hamburg, Germany

Rigel Schiffahrts GMBH
Bremen, Germany

Sargeant Marine Inc.
Boca Raton, FL, USA

Scan-Trans Shipping
Naestved, Denmark

Scandinor AS
Brevik, Norway

SE Shipping
Singapore, Singapore

Shih Wei Navigation
Taipei, Taiwan

Sloman Neotun Shiffahrts
Bremen, Germany

Stolt Parcel Tankers
Greenwich, CT, USA

Tarbit Tankers B.V.
Dordrecht, Netherlands

Team Ship Management
Bremerhaven, Germany

Transal Denizcilik Tickaret
Istanbul, Turkey

Travel Dynamics International
New York, NY, USA

Utkilen AS
Bergen, Norway

W. Bockstiegel Reederei KG
Emden, Germany

Wagenborg Shipping
Delfzijl, Netherlands

Yardimci Shipping Group
Istanbul, Turkey

Yilmar Shipping & Trading Ltd.
Istanbul, Turkey

FLAGS OF REGISTRY

Bahamas	Barbados	Belgium
Bermuda	Bulgaria	Canada
Croatia	Cyprus	Denmark
Egypt	Finland	France
Germany	Greece	Hong Kong
Iceland	India	Israel
Italy	Japan	Liberia
Lithuania	Malta	Monaco
Netherlands	Norway	Panama
Philippines	Poland	Russia
Singapore	Spain	St.Vincent and The Grenadines
Sweden	Switzerland	Taiwan
Turkey	Ukraine	United States
Vanuatu	Yugoslavia	

FLEET HOUSEFLAGS

Algoma Central Corp.
St. Catherines, ON

American Steamship Co.
Williamsville, NY

Andrie Inc.
Muskegon, MI

Canada Steamship Lines Inc.
Montreal, QC

Canadian Coast Guard
Ottawa, ON

Canadian Forest Navigation Co. Ltd.
Montreal, QC

Fednav Ltd.
Montreal, QC

Flinter Shipping
Darendrecht, Netherlands

Gaelic Tugboat Co.
Detroit, MI

Great Lakes Fleet Inc. Key Lakes Inc. - Mgr.
Duluth, MN

Great Lakes Maritime Academy
Traverse City, MI

Great Lakes Towing Co.
Cleveland, OH

Groupe Desgagnés Inc.
Québec, QC

Inland Lakes Management Inc.
Alpena, MI

Interlake Steamship Co Lakes Shipping Co.
Richfield, OH

J.W. Westcott Co.
Detroit, MI

LaFarge Canada Inc.
Montreal, QC

Lake Michigan Carferry Service Inc.
Ludington, MI

Le Groupe Ocean Inc.
Québec, QC

Lower Lakes Towing Ltd. Lower Lakes Transportation Co.
Port Dover, ON / Williamsville, NY

McAsphalt Marine Transportation Ltd.
Scarborough, ON

McKeil Marine Ltd.
Hamilton, ON

Owen Sound Transportation Co. Ltd.
Owen Sound, ON

Pere Marquette Shipping Co.
Ludington, MI

Polish Steamship Co.
Szczecin, Poland

Purvis Marine Ltd.
Sault Ste. Marie, ON

St.Lawrence Seaway Development Corp.

St.Lawrence Seaway Management Corp.

U.S. Army Corps of Engineers
Cincinnatti, OH

U.S. Coast Guard
Cleveland, OH

Wagenborg Shipping
Delfzijl, Netherlands

Other Flags of Note

Dangerous Cargo On Board

Pilot On Board

Diver Down

DONT GIVE UP THE SHIP

Extra Tonnage

- **Ports**
- **Cargoes**
- **Locks**
- **Canals**

H. Lee White unloading at Indiana Harbor, Ind. (Roger LeLievre)

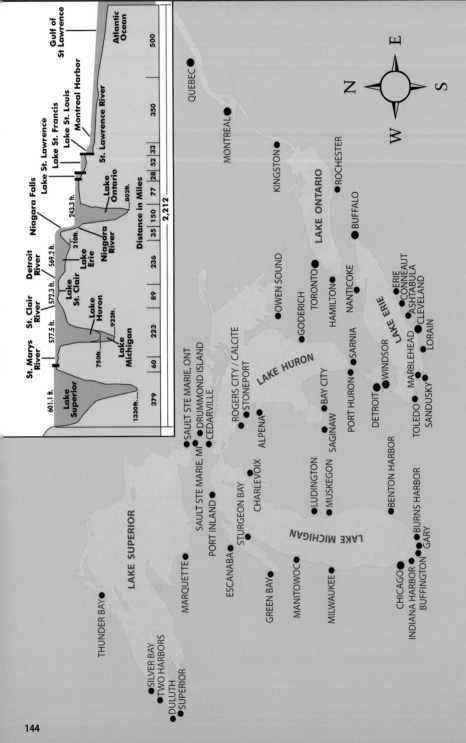

PORTS / *Loading & Unloading*

Taconite ore is loaded for delivery to lower lakes steel mills at Duluth, Two Harbors, and Silver Bay, Minn, as well as Superior, Wis. and Escanaba, Mich. Limestone-loading ports are Port Inland, Cedarville, Drummond Island, Calcite, Rogers City and Stoneport, Mich., and Marblehead, Ohio. Coal ports are Superior, Wis., S. Chicago, Ill., and the Ohio ports of Toledo, Sandusky, Ashtabula and Conneaut. Petroleum is loaded aboard vessels at Sarnia, Ont., and E. Chicago, Ind. Grain export ports include Duluth, Minn., Milwaukee and Superior, Wis.; and the Ontario ports of Thunder Bay, Sarnia and Owen Sound.

The primary U.S. iron ore and limestone receiving ports are Cleveland and Chicago, as well as Gary, Burns Harbor and Indiana Harbor, Ind., Detroit and Toledo, as well as Lorain, Ashtabula and Conneaut, Ohio. Nanticoke, Hamilton, and Sault Ste. Marie, Ont., are major ore-receiving ports in Canada. Coal is carried by self-unloaders to power plants in the U.S. and Canada. Most grain loaded on the lakes is destined for export via the St. Lawrence Seaway. Cement from Alpena and Charlevoix, Mich., is delivered to terminals from Lake Superior to Lake Ontario. Tankers bring petroleum products to cities as diverse in size as Cleveland, as well as Cheboygan, Detroit, Escanaba and Muskegon, Mich. Self-unloaders carry limestone, coal, road salt and sand to cities throughout the region.

American Courage and Great Lakes Trader at Silver Bay, Minn. (Chris Mazzella)

AVERAGE RUNNING TIMES

Times listed are for downbound passages. Reverse for upbound times. Times vary with speed / weather / traffic.

LAKE SUPERIOR
Duluth/Superior – Soo Locks .... 24 hrs
Marquette or Thunder Bay – Soo Locks .... 12 hrs

ST. MARYS RIVER
Soo Locks – DeTour, Mich. .... 6 hrs
DeTour – Port Huron .... 19 hrs

LAKE HURON
DeTour – Mackinac Bridge .... 2 hrs
DeTour – Port Huron .... 19 hrs
Harbor Beach – Port Huron .... 4 hrs

LAKE MICHIGAN
Gray's Reef Light – Gary, Ind. .... 22 hrs

LAKE ERIE
Detroit River Light – Toledo .... 1.75 hrs
Detroit River Light – Southeast Shoal .... 3 hrs
Southeast Shoal – Long Point .... 9 hrs
Long Point – CIP 15 (Welland Canal) .... 7 hrs
Detroit River Light – Port Colborne piers
(Welland Canal) .... 19 hrs

LAKE ONTARIO
Welland Canal (Port Weller) – Hamilton .... 2 hrs
Welland Canal (Port Weller) – Cape Vincent, N.Y.
(call-in points at Newcastle, mid-lake and
Sodus Point) .... 12 hrs

AGRICULTURAL PRODUCTS – Wheat, grain, soybeans, canola, flax and oats are shipped on the Great Lakes. Some is used domestically, but most is shipped to international markets overseas.

BUNKER C – A special grade of heavy fuel oil, also known as No. 6 fuel.

CEMENT CLINKER – A material, made by heating ground limestone and clay, that is ground up to a fine powder to produce cement.

CLINKER – The incombustible residue that remains after the combustion of coal.

COAL – Both eastern (high sulfur, used in industry) and western (low sulfur, burned at power plants) coal are shipped aboard Great Lakes vessels.

COKE – A byproduct of blended coals baked in ovens until mostly pure carbon is left. Coke is used to generate the high heat necessary to make steel in blast furnaces.

COKE BREEZE – Byproduct of coke production.

DOLOMITE – Rock similar to limestone but somewhat harder and heavier.

FLUXSTONE – Taconite pellets premixed with limestone, so no limestone needs to be added to the mix in a blast furnace.

IRON FINES – Fines (ore less than 6mm in diameter) are created as a result of mining, crushing and processing the larger pieces of ore. See **SINTER**.

LIMESTONE – Common sedimentary rock consisting mostly of calcium carbonate used as a building stone and in the manufacture of lime, carbon dioxide and cement.

MILL SCALE – Byproduct of the shaping of iron and steel.

PETROLEUM COKE – Petroleum coke (petcoke) is the ultimate bottom end of oil refining – the parts of crude oil that will not vaporize in the refining process. It is mostly used as fuel (sometimes blended with coal) in power plants. **BUG DUST** is extremely fine coal (or coke) dust.

PIG IRON – Crude iron that is the direct product of the blast furnace and is refined to produce steel, wrought iron or ingot iron.

POTASH – A compound used for fertilizer.

SALT – Most salt shipped on the Great Lakes is used on roads and highways during the winter to melt ice.

SINTER – Broken taconite pellets, a.k.a. taconite pellet chips and fines. Small, but still useful in the blast furnace.

SLAG – Byproduct of the steelmaking process is used in the production of concrete and as seal coat cover, a base for paving, septic drain fields and railroad ballast.

TACONITE – A low-grade iron ore, containing about 27 percent iron and 51 percent silica, found as a hard rock formation in the Lake Superior region. It is pelletized for shipment to steel mills.

TRAP ROCK – Rock, usually ground fairly fine, for use as foundations and roads or walkways. It is mined near Bruce Mines, Ont., and loaded there.

Great Lakes ships most efficient

In terms of energy efficiency and greenhouse gas emissions, a study by transportation consultants Research and Traffic Group found that:

- The Great Lakes-Seaway fleet is nearly seven times more fuel-efficient than trucks and 1.14 times more fuel-efficient than rail.

- Rail and trucks would emit 19 percent and 533 percent more greenhouse gas emissions respectively if these modes carried the same cargo the same distance as the Great Lakes-Seaway fleet.

- It would take three million train trips to carry the total cargo transported by the Great Lakes-Seaway fleet in 2010, as much as double the existing traffic on some rail lines in Canada and mean at least a 50 percent increase in traffic on some of the busiest U.S. lines.

- It would take 7.1 million truck trips to carry the total cargo transported by the Great Lakes-Seaway fleet in 2010. That would increase existing truck traffic by between 35-100 percent depending on the highway.

- If Great Lakes-Seaway marine shipping cargo shifted to trucks, it would lead to $4.6 billion in additional highway maintenance costs over a 60-year period.

Mesabi Miner unloads coal at St. Clair, Mich. (Peter Groh)

Vessels transiting the St. Clair River, Lake St. Clair and the Detroit River are under the jurisdiction of Sarnia Traffic, and must radio their positions at predetermined locations. Call-in points (bold type on map) are not the same for upbound and downbound traffic. Average running times between call-in points are below. *

UPBOUND	Buoys 1&2	Black River	Stag Isl.	Salt Dock	X-32	Crib Light	Grassy Isl.
Detroit River Lt.	8:10	7:50	7:20	6:00	4:20	4:00	1:35
Grassy Island	6:45	6:25	5:55	4:35	2:55	2:35	
St. Clair Crib	4:10	3:50	3:20	2:00	0:25		
Light X-32	3:50	3:30	3:00	1:35			
Salt Dock	2:10	1:50	1:20				
Stag Isl. Upper	0:50	0:35					
Black River	0:20						

DOWNBOUND	Det. River	Grassy Isl.	Belle Isl.	Crib Light	Light 23	Salt Dock	Black River	7&8
30 min. above buoys 11 & 12	9:05	7:35	6:25	5:10	3:55	3:10	1:20	0:40
Buoys 7 & 8	8:15	6:55	5:45	4:30	3:15	2:30	0:40	
Black River	7:45	6:15	5:05	3:50	2:35	1:50		
Salt Dock	5:55	4:25	3:15	2:00	0:45			
Light 23	5:10	3:40	2:30	1:10				
St. Clair Crib	3:55	2:25	1:10					
USCG Belle Isle	2:40	1:10						
Grassy Isl.	1:30							

* Times can change if vessels stop for fuel or are delayed by other traffic.

Map labels:

BUOYS 11 & 12 → DOWNBOUND ONLY

BUOYS 7 & 8 → DOWNBOUND ONLY

BUOYS 1 & 2 → UPBOUND ONLY

LAKE HURON

BLACK RIVER →

PORT HURON

SARNIA

IMPERIAL FUEL DOCK ←

STAG ISLAND UPPER → UPBOUND ONLY

SHELL FUEL DOCK ←

ST. CLAIR

ST. CLAIR EDISON POWER PLANT RECOR POINT →

MARINE CITY

SALT DOCK ←

ALGONAC

HARSENS ISLAND

LIGHT 23 ← DOWNBOUND ONLY

X(RAY) 32 ← UPBOUND ONLY

ST. CLAIR CRIB LIGHT →

LAKE ST. CLAIR

USCG BELLE ISLE DOWNBOUND ONLY

J.W. WESTCOTT MAILBOAT →

DETROIT

WINDSOR

MISTERSKY FUEL →

STERLING FUEL

ROUGE RIVER →

GRASSY ISLAND →

FIGHTING ISLAND ←

GROSSE ILE →

LIVINGSTONE CHANNEL →

AMHERSTBURG CHANNEL ←

DETROIT RIVER LIGHT →

N

W — E

S

POINT PELEE

PELEE PASSAGE

MONROE

LAKE ERIE

PELEE ISLAND

SOUTHEAST SHOAL

TOLEDO

147

The St. Marys River flows out of the southeast corner of Lake Superior in a southeasterly direction to Lake Huron. Vessels transiting the St. Marys River system are under the jurisdiction of Soo Traffic, part of the U.S. Coast Guard at Sault Ste. Marie, Mich., and must radio their positions on VHF Ch. 12 (156.600 MHz) at predetermined locations. Vessels in the vicinity of the Soo Locks fall under the jurisdiction of the lockmaster, who must be contacted on VHF Ch. 14 (156.700 MHz) for lock assignments.

Call-in points (bold type on map) are not the same for upbound and downbound traffic. Approximate running times between call-in points are at left; times may vary due to other traffic and weather. Because of their size, 1,000-footers take more time to transit than smaller vessels.

Arrival times at the Soo Locks are available at the Information Center located in the locks park. Upbound vessels must make a pre-call to Soo Traffic one hour before entering the river at DeTour, and downbound traffic is required to make a one-hour pre-call above Ile Parisienne.

** Upbound traffic passes Neebish Island on the east side. Downbound traffic passes the island to the west, through the Rock Cut, a channel dynamited out of solid rock in the early 1900s.

CANADA

WEST PIER
GROS CAP *UPBOUND ONLY*
SAULT STE. MARIE, ON
EAST PIER
MISSION POINT
SOO LOCKS
BIG POINT
SAULT STE MARIE, MI

U.S.A.

ILE PARISIENNE *DOWNBOUND ONLY*

WHITEFISH BAY

LAKE GEORGE
SUGAR ISLAND
NINE MILE POINT
LAKE NICOLET
BARBEAU
ROCK CUT
NEEBISH ISLAND**
STRIBLING POINT
JOHNSON POINT
WINTER POINT
MUNUSCONG LAKE
MUD LAKE
JUNCTION BUOY
ST. JOSEPH ISLAND
LIME ISLAND
RABER
DETOUR VILLAGE →
DE TOUR REEF LIGHT →

DRUMMOND ISLAND

LAKE HURON

UPBOUND

	J'ct. Buoy	Nine Mile	Miss. Point	Clear Locks	Gros Cap
DeTour	1:35	3:35	4:20	5:50	7:25
Junction Buoy		1:50	2:45	4:15	5:50
Nine Mile Point			0:55	2:25	4:00
Mission Point*				1:30	3:05
Clear of Locks					1:35

DOWNBOUND

	Gros Cap	Big Point	Clear Locks	Nine Mile	J'ct Buoy	DeTour
Ile Parisienne	0:45	1:55	3:25	4:20	6:20	8:00
Gros Cap		1:10	2:40	3:35	5:35	7:15
Big Point*			1:30	2:25	4:25	6:05
Clear of Locks				0:55	2:55	4:35
Nine Mile Point					2:00	3:40
Junction Buoy						1:40

* Lockmaster only

148

The Soo Locks at Sault Ste. Marie, Mich., overcome a 21-foot difference in water levels between Lake Superior and lakes Huron, Michigan and Erie.

Under the jurisdiction of the U.S. Army Corps of Engineers, the locks operate on gravity, as do all locks in the St. Lawrence Seaway system. No pumps are used to empty or fill the lock chambers; valves are opened, and water is allowed to seek its own level. All traffic passes through the locks toll-free.

Traffic is dispatched by radio to the appropriate lock according to size, other vessels in the locks area and the time the captain first calls in to the lockmaster. All vessels longer than 730 feet and/or wider than 76 feet are restricted by size to the Poe, or second, lock. A vessel is under engine and thruster control at all times, with crews ready to drop mooring lines over bollards on the lock wall to stop its movement.

As soon as the vessel is in position, engines are stopped and mooring lines made fast. If the vessel is being lowered, valves at the lower end of the lock chamber are opened to allow the water inside to flow out. If the vessel is being raised, valves at the upper end of the chamber are opened to allow water to enter. When the water reaches the desired level, the valves are closed, the protective boom is raised, the gates are opened, and the vessel leaves the lock.

The first canal on the American side was built from 1853-55. That canal was destroyed in 1888 by workers making way for newer, bigger locks.

MacArthur Lock

Named after World War II Gen. Douglas MacArthur, the MacArthur Lock is 800 feet long (243.8 meters) between inner gates, 80 feet wide (24.4 meters) and 31 feet deep (9.4 meters) over the sills. The lock was built in 1942-43 and opened to traffic on July 11, 1943. Vessel size is limited to 730 feet long (222.5 meters) by 76 feet wide (23 meters).

Poe Lock

The Poe Lock is 1,200 feet long (365.8 meters), 110 feet wide (33.5 meters) and has a depth over the sills of 32 feet (9.8 meters). Named after Col. Orlando M. Poe, it was built in the years 1961-68. The lock's vessel size limit is 1,100 feet long (335.3 meters) by 105 feet wide (32 meters).

Davis and Sabin locks

Dating from the first two decades of the 20th century, these two locks are no longer used. Work began in 2009 to replace them with one new Poe-sized lock, at an estimated cost of more than $500 million, however the project remains stalled due to lack of funding.

Canadian Lock

The Canadian Lock at Sault Ste. Marie, Ont., has its origin in a canal constructed from 1887-95. The present lock, operated by Parks Canada, is used by pleasure craft, tugs and tour boats.

Shippers feel impact of low water levels

Historic low water levels on the Great Lakes and their connecting channels are impacting all vessels, commercial and recreational. Measurements taken this past January show Lake Huron and Lake Michigan have reached their lowest ebb since record keeping began in 1918, and the lakes could set additional records over the next few months, according to the U.S. Army Corps of Engineers. In January 2013, the lakes were 29 inches below their long-term average and had declined 17 inches since January 2012. The rest of the Great Lakes are also several inches below normal. That means lake vessels are carrying 1,200-1,500 fewer tons per trip than they did a year ago, and have to make extra trips – at extra expense – to make up the difference. One more inch of draft can increase a ship's load anywhere from 50 tons to 270 tons depending on its size. Many smaller ports are now off-limits due to shallow water.

Shippers are taxed to support a harbor maintenance fund, but only about half of the revenue is spent on dredging, with the remainder diverted to the treasury for other purposes. Legislation to change that policy is pending before Congress, and securing the release of those funds is a priority for the Cleveland-based Lake Carriers' Association.

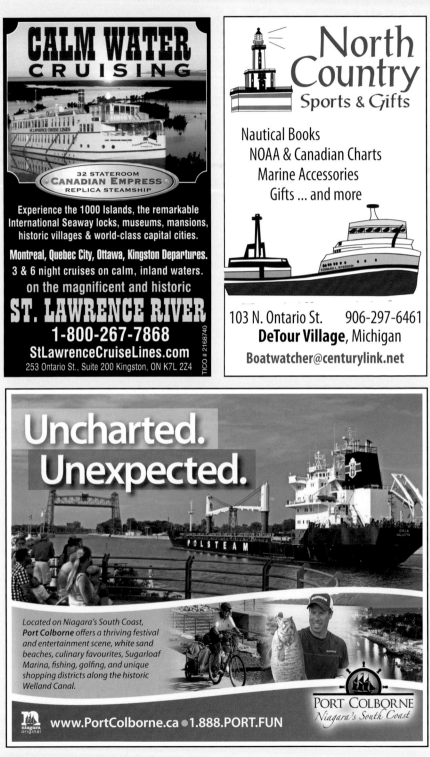

LOCKS & CANALS / *Welland Canal*

The 28-mile (44 km) Welland Canal is the fourth version of a waterway link between Lake Ontario and Lake Erie, first built in 1829. The present canal was completed in 1932, deepened in the 1950s as part of the Seaway project, and further straightened in 1973. Today its eight locks, all Canadian, lift ships 326 feet (100 meters) over the Niagara Escarpment.

Each of the seven Welland Canal locks has an average lift of 46.5 feet (14.2 meters). All locks (except Lock 8) are 859 feet (261.8 meters) long, 80 feet (24.4 meters) wide and 30 feet (9.1 meters) deep. Lock 8 measures 1,380 feet (420.6 m) long.

The largest vessel that may transit the canal is 740 feet (225.5 meters) long, 78 feet (23.8 meters) wide and 26 feet, 6 inches (8.08 meters) in draft. Locks 1, 2 and 3 are at Port Weller and St. Catharines, Ont., on the Lake Ontario end of the waterway. At Lock 3, the Welland Canal Viewing Center and Museum houses an information desk (which posts a list of vessels expected at the lock), a gift shop and restaurant.

At Thorold, Locks 4, 5 and 6, twinned to help speed passage of vessels, are controlled with an elaborate interlocking system for safety. These locks (positioned end to end, they resemble a short flight of stairs) have an aggregate lift of 139.5 feet (42.5 meters). Just south of Locks 4, 5 and 6 is Lock 7. Lock 8, seven miles (11.2 km) upstream at Port Colborne, completes the process, making the final adjustment to Lake Erie's level.

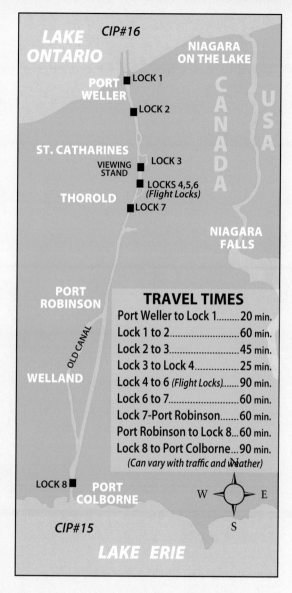

TRAVEL TIMES

Port Weller to Lock 1	20 min.
Lock 1 to 2	60 min.
Lock 2 to 3	45 min.
Lock 3 to Lock 4	25 min.
Lock 4 to 6 *(Flight Locks)*	90 min.
Lock 6 to 7	60 min.
Lock 7-Port Robinson	60 min.
Port Robinson to Lock 8	60 min.
Lock 8 to Port Colborne	90 min.

(Can vary with traffic and weather)

In 1973, a new channel was constructed to replace the section of the old canal that bisected the city of Welland. The Welland bypass eliminated long delays for navigation, road and rail traffic. Two tunnels allow auto and train traffic to pass beneath the canal.

The average passage time for the canal is 8-11 hours, with the majority of the time spent transiting Locks 4-7. All vessel traffic though the Welland Canal is regulated by a control center, Seaway Welland, which also remotely operates the locks and the traffic bridges over the canal. Vessels passing through the Welland Canal and St. Lawrence Seaway must carry a qualified pilot at all times.

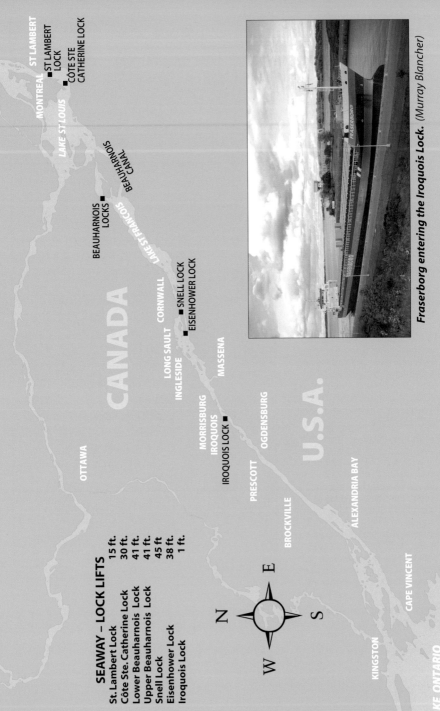

Fraserborg entering the Iroquois Lock. (Murray Blancher)

SEAWAY – LOCK LIFTS

Lock	Lift
St. Lambert Lock	15 ft.
Côte Ste. Catherine Lock	30 ft.
Lower Beauharnois Lock	41 ft.
Upper Beauharnois Lock	41 ft.
Snell Lock	45 ft
Eisenhower Lock	38 ft.
Iroquois Lock	1 ft.

MONTREAL

ST LAMBERT

ST LAMBERT LOCK

CÔTE STE CATHERINE LOCK

LAKE ST LOUIS

BEAUHARNOIS CANAL

BEAUHARNOIS LOCKS

LAKE ST FRANÇOIS

CANADA

CORNWALL

SNELL LOCK

EISENHOWER LOCK

LONG SAULT

INGLESIDE

MASSENA

OTTAWA

MORRISBURG

IROQUOIS

IROQUOIS LOCK

OGDENSBURG

U.S.A.

PRESCOTT

BROCKVILLE

ALEXANDRIA BAY

CAPE VINCENT

KINGSTON

LAKE ONTARIO

N E S W

The St. Lawrence Seaway is a waterway extending some 2,038 miles (3,701.4 km) from the Atlantic Ocean to the head of the Great Lakes at Duluth, Minn., including Montreal harbor and the Welland Canal. More specifically, it is a system of locks and canals (U.S. and Canadian), built between 1954 and 1958 at a cost of $474 million and opened in 1959, that allows vessels to pass from Montreal to the Welland Canal at the western end of Lake Ontario. For the Montreal-Lake Ontario section, the average transit time is 24 hours upbound and 22 hours downbound. The difference is mainly due to the current in the St. Lawrence River. The vessel size limit within this system is 740 feet (225.6 meters) long, 78 feet (23.8 meters) wide and 26 feet (7.9 meters) draft. It takes 8-10 days for a ship to go from Lake Superior to the Atlantic Ocean.

LOCK DIMENSIONS

Length	766' (233.5 meters)
Width	80' (24 meters
Depth	30' (9.1 meters)

Closest to the ocean is the St. Lambert Lock, which lifts ships some 15 feet (4.6 meters) from Montreal harbor to the level of the Laprairie Basin, through which the channel sweeps in a great arc 8.5 miles (13.7 km) long to the second lock. The Côte Ste. Catherine Lock, like the other six St. Lawrence Seaway locks, is built to the dimensions shown in the table above. The Côte Ste. Catherine lifts ships from the level of the Laprairie Basin 30 feet (9.1 meters) to the level of Lake Saint-Louis, bypassing the Lachine Rapids. Beyond it, the channel runs 7.5 miles (12.1 km) before reaching Lake Saint-Louis.

The Lower Beauharnois Lock, bypassing the Beauharnois Power House, lifts ships 41 feet (12.5 meters) and sends them through a short canal to the Upper Beauharnois Lock, where they are lifted 41 feet (12.5 meters) to reach the Beauharnois Canal. After a 13-mile (20.9 km) trip in the canal and a 30-mile (48.3 km) passage through Lake Saint Francis, vessels reach the U.S. border and the Snell Lock, which has a lift of 45 feet (13.7 meters) and empties into the 10-mile (16.1 km) Wiley-Dondero Canal.

After passing through the Wiley-Dondero, ships are raised another 38 feet (11.6 meters) by the Dwight D. Eisenhower Lock, after which they enter Lake St. Lawrence, the pool upon which nearby power-generating stations draw for their turbines located a mile to the north.

At the western end of Lake St. Lawrence, the Iroquois Lock allows ships to bypass the Iroquois Control Dam. The lift here is only about 1 foot (0.3 meters). Once in the waters west of Iroquois, the channel meanders through the Thousand Islands to Lake Ontario and beyond.

Flintersun departs the St. Lambert Lock. (Paul Beesley)

Philip R. Clarke loading at Duluth, Minn., as the 2012 shipping season draws to a close. (Peter Groh)

FOLLOWING THE FLEET

With an inexpensive VHF scanner, boatwatchers can tune to ship-to-ship and ship-to-shore traffic using the following frequency guide.

Calling/distress only	**Ch. 16 – 156.800 MHz**	Calling/distress only
Commercial vessels only	**Ch. 06 – 156.300 MHz**	Working channel
Commercial vessels only	**Ch. 08 – 156.400 MHz**	Working channel
DeTour Reef – Lake St. Clair Light	**Ch. 11 – 156.550 MHz**	Sarnia Traffic - Sect. 1
Long Point Light – Lake St. Clair Light	**Ch. 12 – 156.600 MHz**	Sarnia Traffic - Sect. 2
Montreal – Mid-Lake St. Francis	**Ch. 14 – 156.700 MHz**	Seaway Beauharnois – Sect. 1
Mid-Lake St. Francis – Bradford Island	**Ch. 12 – 156.600 MHz**	Seaway Eisenhower – Sect. 2
Bradford Island – Crossover Island	**Ch. 11 – 156.550 MHz**	Seaway Iroquois – Sect. 3
Crossover Island-Cape Vincent	**Ch. 13 – 156.650 MHz**	Seaway Clayton – Sect. 4
		St. Lawrence River portion
Cape Vincent – Mid-Lake Ontario	**Ch. 12 – 156.600 MHz**	Seaway Sodus – Sect. 4
		Lake Ontario portion
Seaway Pilot Office – Cape Vincent	**Ch. 14 – 156.700 MHz**	Pilotage Traffic
Mid-Lake Ontario – Welland Canal	**Ch. 11 – 156.550 MHz**	Seaway Newcastle – Sect. 5
Welland Canal	**Ch. 14 – 156.700 MHz**	Seaway Welland – Sect. 6
Welland Canal to Long Point Light	**Ch. 11 – 156.550 MHz**	Seaway Long Point – Sect. 7
Montreal Traffic	**Ch. 10 – 156.500 MHz**	Vessel traffic
Soo Traffic	**Ch. 12 – 156.600 MHz**	Vessel control, Sault Ste. Marie,
Lockmaster, Soo Locks	**Ch. 14 – 156.700 MHz**	Soo Lockmaster (WUE-21)
Coast Guard traffic	**Ch. 21 – 157.050 MHz**	United States Coast Guard
Coast Guard traffic	**Ch. 22 – 157.100 MHz**	United States Coast Guard
U.S. mailboat, Detroit, MI	**Ch. 10 – 156.500 MHz**	Mailboat *J. W. Westcott II*

These prerecorded messages help track vessel arrivals and departures.

Boatwatcher's Hotline	**(218) 722-6489**	Superior, Duluth, Two Harbors,
		Taconite Harbor and Silver Bay
CSX Coal Docks/Torco Dock	**(419) 697-2304**	Toledo, Ohio, vessel information
Eisenhower Lock	**(315) 769-2422**	Eisenhower Lock vessel traffic
Michigan Limestone docks	**(989) 734-2117**	Calcite, Mich., vessel information
Michigan Limestone docks	**(906) 484-2201**	Press 1 – Cedarville passages
Presque Isle Corp.	**(989) 595-6611**	Stoneport vessel information ext. 7
Seaway Vessel Locator	**(450) 672-4115**	
Soo Traffic	**(906) 635-3224**	Previous day – St. Marys River
Soo Traffic – Hotline	**(906) 253-9290**	Soo Locks traffic information
Superior Midwest Energy	**(715) 395-3559**	Superior, Wis., vessel information
Thunder Bay Port Authority	**(807) 345-1256**	Thunder Bay, Ont., vessel info
Great Lakes Fleet	**(800) 328-3760**	Ext. 4389 – GLF vessel movements
Vantage Point, Boatnerd HQ	**(810) 985-9057**	St. Clair River traffic
Welland Canal tape	**(905) 688-6462**	Welland Canal traffic

MEANINGS OF BOAT WHISTLES

1 SHORT: I intend to leave you on my port side (answered by same if agreed upon).

2 SHORT: I intend to leave you on my starboard side (answered by same if agreed upon). (Passing arrangements may be agreed upon by radio. If so, no whistle signal is required.)

1 PROLONGED: Vessel leaving dock.

3 SHORT: Operating astern propulsion.

1 PROLONGED, SOUNDED AT INTERVALS OF NOT MORE THAN 2 MINUTES: Vessel moving in restricted visibility.

1 SHORT, 1 PROLONGED, 1 SHORT: Vessel at anchor in restricted visibility (optional). May be accompanied by the ringing of a bell on the forward part of the ship and a gong on the aft end.

3 PROLONGED & 2 SHORT: Salute (formal).

1 PROLONGED & 2 SHORT: Salute (commonly used).

3 PROLONGED & 1 SHORT: International Shipmasters' Association member salute.

5 OR MORE SHORT BLASTS SOUNDED RAPIDLY: Danger.

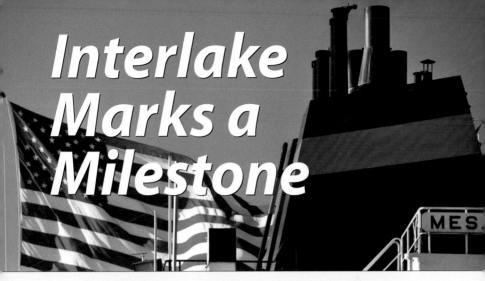

Interlake Marks a Milestone

Company celebrates 100th birthday, but roots on the lakes go back even further

The Interlake Steamship Co. is officially marking its 100th birthday in 2013, but the fleet's origins go back even further, to the waning years of the Civil War.

Colonel James Pickands, a Union veteran, dreamed about making a fortune in the north and thus, following the conclusion of the hostilities, made his way to Marquette and in 1867 founded James Pickands and Co., dealers in hardware and mining supplies. In his first year in Marquette, he became a close friend with mining agent Jay C. Morse. Also, he became acquainted with Samuel Mather, founder of Cleveland Cliffs and half-brother of William G. Mather, its chief operating officer.

In 1883, the threesome purchased control of the new vessel *V.H. Ketcham* (some resources spell it *Ketchum*), then the largest ship on the upper lakes at the time of its build, and their interest in shipping began. By 1883, Pickands had sold his hardware store, Mather had sold his interest in Cleveland Cliffs, and the two formed Pickands Mather and Co. with Morse as their iron ore country agent. By the turn of the century, Pickands Mather owned a number of ships and managed several fleets.

Early Interlake steamer Augustus B. Wolvin.

In 1901, major changes occurred in Great Lakes shipping, and Pickands Mather relinquished management of two substantial fleets. Determined to retain Pickands Mather's prominent position in Great Lakes commerce, Harry Coulby directed the formation of two more fleets and construction of new vessels. The year 1906 saw the acquisition of seven ships from the various A.B. Wolvin-managed fleets of Acme, Standard and Provident companies. Lackawanna Steamship was created as part of a venture

Continued on Page 159

Compare V.H. Ketcham (left) to the William J. De Lancey to see how much the fleet's ships have grown in size. (Tom Manse Collection)

WILLIAM J. DE LANCEY

THE
INTERLAKE
STEAMSHIP CO.

begun by Mather and others in helping develop the Bethlehem Steel Co. assets. Lackawanna ordered eight ships for delivery in 1907-'08 and all were made part of the fleet managed by Pickands Mather. Seven of these ships made it to the merger of 1913, while the eighth, *Cyprus*, was lost on its second trip on Lake Superior in 1907. The seven survivors were *Hemlock, Calumet, Odanah, Adriatic, Elbe, Crete* and *Verona*. When Pickands Mather combined its separate fleets to form The Interlake Steamship Co. in 1913, the new fleet numbered 39 ships, the second largest U.S. fleet, which included *Augustus B. Wolvin, James C. Wallace, Ward Ames* (later *C.H. McCullough Jr.*), *James H. Hoyt* (later *Bricoldoc*), *D.G. Kerr* (later *Harry R. Jones*), *James H. Reed* and *H.P. Bope* (later *E.A.S. Clarke*).

In 1916, Interlake built the *Henry G. Dalton*. Between 1923 and the Depression, several other new ships were added. They included *Charles M. Schwab* in 1923, *Samuel Mather* (iv) and *Colonel James Pickands* in 1926 and, in 1927, *Harry Coulby, Robert Hobson* and *William McLaughlan*. The *Coulby*

Odanah of 1907.
(Tom Manse Collection)

was larger than any other contemporary lake freighter at 631 x 65 feet and, as the first to carry more than 16,000 tons, broke many cargo records in her early days.

Over the years, Interlake continued fleet modernization and expansion. Some of the older ships were sold off as their usage decreased. For example, in 1926, 10 were sold to the newly-formed N.M. Paterson Co. of Fort William, Ont., and most ended their days with the familiar "doc" (Dominion of Canada) ending to their names. In 1940, the *William B. Davock* sank in a summer storm in Lake Michigan. In 1943, the U.S. Maritime Administration (MARAD) formulated an equal tonnage trade program with several firms in which new ships would be constructed for usage for the duration of the war effort, while following the war, the companies would relinquish or trade in superannuated ships that had equivalent tonnage to the new ones acquired. As a result, Pickands Mather acquired three new ships – *Frank Purnell, E. G. Grace* and *Frank Armstrong* – in exchange for seven old ones that were surrendered in 1945 for scrapping. These were *Cetus, Corvus, Cygnus* and *Taurus* (from the original Gilchrist fleet) and *Pegasus, Saturn* and *Vega* (from the Cleveland Steamship fleet aquisition).

Following the war, more changes occurred. Some of the newer ships were updated and repowered, while others were sold to various concerns for other uses. In 1952 and 1953, two new ships – *Elton*

Continued on Page 161

Record-breaker Harry Coulby loading ore at a Lake Superior port. *(Tom Manse Collection)*

Above: Robert Hobson at Ford's Rouge River plant in 1973. Below: Samuel Mather upbound on the St. Marys River in the summer of 1972. (Both: Roger LeLievre)

Hoyt II and *J.L. Mauthe* – joined the fleet, which together with the end of hostilities in South Korea, caused a full-scale purge of older vessels shortly thereafter. *John Sherwin* (ii) was built in 1958, and *Herbert C. Jackson* entered service in 1959. In1967, a trial charter with the defunct Shenango Furnace Co. resulted in their flagship, *Shenango II*, staying in the P-M fleet as *Charles M. Beeghly*. In 1972, the *Beeghly* received an additional 96-foot midbody section. A similar lengthening of the *Sherwin* followed. In 1975, *Herbert C. Jackson* was the first of three Interlake straight deckers converted to a self-unloader.

When the motor vessel *James R. Barker* entered service in 1976, she was not only four feet longer than the largest existing lake freighter, but also the first 1,000-foot class ship built entirely on the Great Lakes. Interlake's fleet expansion included delivery of three more 1,000-footers between 1976 and 1981 - *James R. Barker, Mesabi Miner* and *Paul R. Tregurtha* (originally named *William J. De Lancey*). Each represented an initial construction investment of more than $60 million. Together they added 194,600 gross tons to Interlake's total trip capacity.

The coming out of the *De Lancey* in 1981 – and still the largest vessel on the lakes – was the beginning of the end for the old fleet, as steel prices had dropped during a severe downturn in the economy and the need for a large fleet diminished rapidly. As a result, the company soon sold off almost all of its older fleet and upgraded newer ships such as the *Beeghly, Sherwin, Hoyt* and *Jackson*, making them longer and, in some cases, converting them to self-unloaders. Even the 1943-vintage ships were laid up, with the *E.G. Grace* being the first of the World War II Maritime Class to meet the scrappers' torch in 1984.

Following several Pickands Mather & Co., corporate changes, The Interlake Steamship Co. became a privately held concern in 1987 under the direction of James R. Barker, Chairman of the Board, and Paul R. Tregurtha, vice chairman of the board. In April 1989, the three remaining boats of the Rouge Steel (Ford) fleet – *William Clay Ford* (ii), *Benson Ford* (iii) *Henry Ford II* were purchased and organized as Lakes Shipping Co., Inc. under Interlake management. *William Clay Ford* was renamed *Lee A. Tregurtha* and *Benson Ford* became *Kaye E. Barker,* while the vintage *Henry Ford II* was first renamed *Samuel Mather* (vii), but never operated, remaining idle until being scrapped in 1994.

Continued on Page 162

Two vessels were named Elton Hoyt II. Both survive today, the one inset as Michipicoten, the one below as St. Marys Challenger. *(Tom Manse Collection)*

Launch of Herbert C. Jackson at Detroit, Feb. 19, 1959.

In 1997, the idle steamer *J.L. Mauthe* was converted to the self-unloading barge *Pathfinder* (iii), which began operation in 1998. While this work was progressing, Interlake started construction of a new 7,200-horsepower, twin Z-drive tug, *Dorothy Ann*. Today, the two form a technologically advanced, integrated tug-barge unit that increases the fleet's versatility. In 2000, Interlake became the first U.S.-flagged Great Lakes shipping company to receive ISO and ISM certification. Interlake Leasing III, a subsidiary of Interlake Steamship, secured the bareboat charter of the 1,000-foot *Stewart J. Cort* – the Great Lakes' first 1,000-footer – in 2005.

Interlake began a steam-powered vessel modernization program in 2006 by repowering the *Lee A. Tregurtha* with a highly automated Bergen diesel engine power plant. The modernization program continued with the 2008 repowering of *Charles M. Beeghly* with a similar power plant to that of the *Tregurtha*. In 2010, Interlake re-engined *Paul R. Tregurtha*, with the ship's original, 30-year-old Pielstick engines replaced with modern, reduced emissions MAK diesels. Following this project, Interlake received the Midwest Clean Diesel Initiative Leadership Award, which recognized Interlake "for demonstrating outstanding leadership by making significant measurable improvements in air quality through the development and implementation of clean diesel actions."

At a 2011 ceremony at Duluth, Minn., *Charles M. Beeghly* was renamed *Hon. James L. Oberstar*, honoring the 30-plus years of service that the former Minnesota congressman had given to the United States and the Great Lakes region. Continuing its modernization program, Interlake converted *Kaye E. Barker* from steam to diesel in 2012 with installation of an identical power plant to that of the *Oberstar*. Today, Interlake remains a major force in Great Lakes commerce and is committed to providing the best customer service on the Great Lakes through innovation, teamwork and integrity, something the company has been accomplishing for over a century.

Sources: John M. Kenn, Skip Meier, Interlake Steamship Co.

Built in 1926, Colonel James Pickands served the fleet her entire career before being scrapped in 1974. *(Roger LeLievre)*

John Sherwin, Frank Armstrong and Charles M. Beeghly at Ashtabula, Ohio – year unknown. (Tom Manse Collection)

Lee A. Tregurtha and the tug North Dakota. (Glenn Blaszkiewicz)

Thousand-footer Paul R. Tregurtha in Rock Cut ice. (Roger LeLievre)

Mesabi Miner meets Stewart J. Cort. (Roger LeLievre)

Remembering 1913's Great Storm

It's been termed the "Great Storm of 1913" for a reason. Never before, and never since has such unprecedented weather struck the Great Lakes region, wreaking havoc ashore and afloat. Ships that left port on November 7, 1913, had little warning of what was in store the next few days – blizzard conditions, hurricane-force winds and waves over 35 feet high. The tempest, the result of the convergence of two major storm fronts and fueled by the still relatively warm waters of the Great Lakes, took an especially harsh toll on the vessels caught on Lake Huron. When the weather finally moderated, the grim results were revealed in the numbers of sunken or stranded ships and lost lives. Vessels sunk, and the number of victims on each, were:

Lake Huron
> **Argus**: crew of 28
> **James Carruthers**: 22
> **Hydrus**: 25
> **John A. McGean**: 28
> **Charles S. Price**: 28
> **Regina**: 20
> **Isaac M. Scott**: 28
> **Wexford**: 20

Lake Superior
> **Leafield**: 18
> **Henry B. Smith**: 25

Lake Michigan
> **Plymouth** (barge): 7

Lake Erie
> **Lightship LV 82**: 6

The 529-foot *James Carruthers* was nearly a brand-new boat, christened just a few months before. When the storm abated, a hull was spotted floating upside down in southern Lake Huron. Divers eventually confirmed the vessel as the coal-laden *Charles S. Price*, turned turtle in the storm. One of the crew members – assistant engineer Milton Smith – left the ship before it departed on its last voyage after he had a premonition of disaster. Smith was later called upon to identify the bodies, some of which were wearing life preservers from another ship, the *Regina*, only adding to the mystery. All in all, nearly 250 sailors lost their lives in the Great Storm.

From top, the ill-fated Charles S. Price, Wexford and John A. McGean, lost with all hands on Lake Huron.
(All photos: Tom Manse Collection)

Continued on Page 169

McKenzie photo, courtesy Dick Wicklund

Argus (above) sank on Lake Huron with all 28 of her crew. Regina (left) and James Carruthers (below), the newest boat in the Canadian fleet, were also lost with all hands on the stormy lake.

THE LONDON EVENING FREE PRESS

BIGGEST STEAMER ON THE LAKES IS LOST

WRECKAGE OF THE JAMES CARRUTHERS WASHED ASHORE AT GODERICH

MORE BODIES OF VICTIMS OF BIG STORM FOUND ALONG LAKE HURON

Thirty Steamers Are Lost or Ashore As Result of Storm; The Death List On the Lakes Now Totals Over Two Hundred

IT'S BRIGHTER THAN ANY SUNRISE

LONDON MEN WERE Wreckage Floating Along Shore

Top, Henry B. Smith, shown in a postcard view at Ashtabula, Ohio. Hydrus is at right, and Isaac M. Scott is below. All met their fate on Lake Huron. *(Photos, Tom Manse Collection)*

L.C. Waldo (below), which stranded on Lake Superior. The inset shows her ashore, photographed by members of the U.S. Lifesaving Service, who bravely removed the crew.

THE GREAT STORM OF 1913

In a storm that struck Lake Huron on November 9, 1913, ten lake freighters were lost. Seven of them vanished, ranging from the 30-year-old, 270-foot "Wexford" to the 550-foot "James Carruthers", launched six months earlier at Collingwood. The bulk of the wreckage was cast up on the shore of Huron County, where recovery and identification of the crews' bodies were directed by a Lake Carriers' Association committee based at Goderich. The storm, which ravaged the Great Lakes region for three days, destroyed a total of 19 vessels and resulted in the stranding of 19 others, with a loss of 244 lives.

Erected by the Archaeological and Historic Sites Board,
Department of Public Records and Archives of Ontario

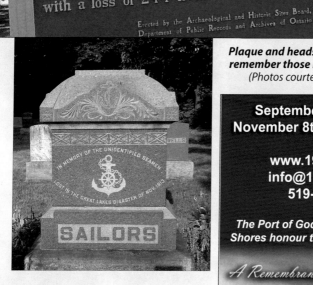

Plaque and headstone in Goderich, Ont., remember those lost in the Great Storm.
(Photos courtesy David MacAdam)

IN MEMORY OF THE UNIDENTIFIED SEAMEN
LOST IN THE GREAT LAKES DISASTER OF NOV. 1913
WELLS
SAILORS

In addition to the vessels lost, many more were driven ashore. Among them, steamers like the *L.C. Waldo* and *William Nottingham* (Lake Superior); *Matthew Andrews, H.M. Hanna Jr.* and *D.O. Mills* (Lake Huron), and others were refloated and continued to ply the Great Lakes for many years.

There will be ceremonies marking the 100th anniversary of the Great Storm of 1913 throughout this year. The Port of Goderich, Ont., where the bodies of many of those who were lost washed ashore, will honor the lost souls and ships with events this fall, making sure they are not forgotten.

Sewell Avery in the MacArthur Lock, with Lake Manitoba at right. The hull of the Avery now serves as a dock at Sault Ste. Marie, Ont. (Tom Manse Collection)

Upper Lakes Shipping's Frank A. Sherman in 1978. (Roger LeLievre)

Historic Gallery

Lake Winnipeg in the Welland Canal.
(Al Sagon-King)

Ford Motor Co.'s John Dykstra pushes past Henry Ford II on Lake St. Clair. *(Paul C. LaMarre Jr.)*

Thomas F. Cole of the U.S. Steel fleet in 1971. *(Roger LeLievre)*

N.M. Paterson & Sons' grain carrier Paterson in 1977. *(Roger LeLievre)*

Maunaloa passes the lookout station at Mission Point at Sault Ste. Marie in 1908. The man with the megaphone relayed messages to the captain and also reported the passage to the ship's owners. The inset shows the view from the tower, looking downriver. Many vessel fans gather at this location today for the excellent angle it presents for pictures. (Detroit Publishing Co., courtesy Matt Miner)

Bayswater Shipping
Brockville, Ont.

Canadian Oil Co.
Toronto, Ont.

Chesapeake & Ohio Railway Co.
Detroit, Mich.

Labrador Steamship Co. (Interlake)
Montreal, Quebec

Law Quarries Shipping, Ltd.
Port Colborne, Ont.

Midland Steamship Line
Cleveland, Ohio

Minneapolis, St. Paul & Buffalo Steamship Co. (Soo Line) – Late 1890s
Buffalo, N.Y.

Mohawk Navigation Co.
St. Catharines, Ont.

Nicholson-Universal Steamship Co.
Detroit, Mich.

Paisley Steamship Co.
Cleveland, Ohio

Powell Transports
Winnipeg, Man.

Providence Shipping Co.
Nassau, Bahamas

Captain John Roen (Boland & Cornelius)
Buffalo, N.Y.

Schneider Transportation Co.
Fairport, Ohio

Texaco Canada Ltd.
Montreal, Que.

Franquelin, of the Quebec & Ontario fleet. *(Tom Manse Collection)*

Detroit & Cleveland Navigation Co. passenger ship Eastern States last ran in 1950 and was scrapped in 1957. *(Tom Manse Collection)*

Sandsucker C.W. Cadwell ashore east of Leamington, Ont., after a 1929 storm. (Tom Manse Collection)

Hall Corp. tanker Cape Transport in the 1960s. (Tom Manse Collection)

National Steel Corp.'s George M. Humphrey in 1978.
She would be sold for scrap in 1986. (Paul C. LaMarre Jr.)

Dutch vessel Prins Willem III arrives at
Detroit in 1948. (Tom Manse Collection)

Mohawk Navigation Co.'s Golden Hind in 1971. (Roger LeLievre)

GOLDEN HIND

Sulfuric acid tanker Norman P. Clement was deliberately sunk October 23, 1968, after suffering damage in a shipyard explosion. (Tom Manse Collection)

NORMAN P. CLEMENT

News ❧ Photos ❧ Information

BoatNerd.com

Great Lakes & Seaway Shipping On-Line Inc.

Duluth Shipping News

www.duluthshippingnews.com

Starting Our 18th Year Providing the Shipping News in the Port of Duluth/Superior

Arrivals/departures *www.duluthboats.com*

Watch Our Live Video, 24/7 on the Duluth Aerial Lift Bridge
www.duluthshippingnews.com/dsntv

Clocks • Shower Curtains • Mugs
Sweatshirts and More
www.Cafepress/duluth

knewhams@duluthshippingnews.com

Know Your 2013 SHIPS

T-shirts – All Sizes
BoatNerd & KYS Caps

Stack & Flag Poster – $8.95

'KYS' back issues available for 1978-'79 and 1982-2012 – $8.50

Marine Publishing Co., 317 S. Division St., Ann Arbor, MI 48104

TOLL FREE: **855-KYS-SHIP (855-597-7447)** FAX: **734-661-7295**

order @ KnowYourShips.com

BECOME A FAN

DATE	NAME	LOCATION / DETAILS

INDEX TO ADVERTISERS

Lake Huron's White Shoal
Light at dusk. (Roger LeLievre)

MORE PICTURES ON LINE

Every year, *Know Your Ships* **gets** over 1,000 photos from readers who hope to see their images included in the next edition. Obviously there isn't room for them all. So we've created a gallery of some of these photos on our Web site. Please stop by and enjoy these additional submissions. To view, go to our home page, and click on the **GALLERIES** link. While you're there, enoy some of our KYS video clips as well, and take a look at some of the photos from past editions.

knowyourships.com

Memorable Experiences for 60 Years!

S.S. BADGER
LAKE MICHIGAN CARFERRY

★ 60th Anniversary ★

800-841-4243 | www.ssbadger.com